A SECOND CHANCE

Amnesty for the First Offender

A SECOND CHANCE

Amnesty for the First Offender

AARON NUSSBAUM

HAWTHORN BOOKS, INC.
Publishers / NEW YORK

To Helen,
in grateful appreciation

Contents

Foreword

George Bernard Shaw wrote, "There is nothing as irrevocable as death and a prison sentence."

"The record" is always with the ex-convict causing him to be in constant fear of losing his job if his record becomes known to his employer.

District Attorney Aaron Nussbaum has put his finger on a real sociological problem—the rehabilitation of first offenders to a new direction for their future as rehabilitated members of society. This proposal could absolve the first offenders of the lifelong stigma of their criminal record and will serve as a powerful incentive toward their self-rehabilitation. They could do this all the more easily if they were given a second chance by wiping the slate clean after they have satisfied the authorities that they intend to lead useful and honorable lives.

This plan of a second chance starts from the premise that justice has been served by punishment already handed out to them. And there is no punishment in this world like the punishment of detention.

But justice is not served by "over-punishment," by stigmatizing the offender and making it difficult, if not impossible, for him to gain his self-respect and good standing in the community. The great Justice Cardozo said it in 1928: "I will not shut the door on hope behind me."

The rule of law would help turn the tide of public opinion for the ultimate forgiveness of the first offender. We have a good example of what law can do in the recent experience of the South. The South was able to change a social pattern of some 150 years standing and it did it all within 20 years—because of law.

Law doesn't change the hearts of men but it changes their practices.

The amnesty—the second chance is tied to a completion of a probationary period following the termination of the sentence. This second chance would not only give individuals an opportunity for self-rehabilitation, but would add considerably to the reduction of recidivism and thus to the well-being of our country.

HARRY GOLDEN

Preface

It should come as no surprise that this proposal of a second chance should spring directly from the ranks of the tough-minded guild of criminal prosecutors—for one could not labor long in the revolving-door vicinage of criminal justice without perceiving at once that in the mold of the first offender lies our supreme challenge for reclamation at the very cradle of criminality.

The full-blown blueprint of total forgiveness for the first offender after punishment is done, here presented, had its modest beginnings out of a frustrated undertaking of mine as a young lawyer, some twenty-five years ago, to obtain the restoration of voting rights for a convicted ex-offender, long after his dues had been paid in the hard coin of punishment. Here was a supplicant who had fulfilled every requirement of "good moral character" many times over, entitling him to resume his place in society once again—a devoted family man who desperately needed this simple token of citizenship, if only to keep the skeleton of his past record mercifully hidden from two adoring legally adopted children who just couldn't understand why their dad had failed to avail himself of the freeman's right to vote. The bureaucratic roadblocks placed in this man's path consumed all of five long years and gradually sparked a probing interest on my part into the hollowness of our vaunted concepts of rehabilitation and reform.

I soon discovered that the lifelong second punishment facing every convicted ex-offender had always been a neglected element in the critical scales of penal treatment and recidivism; that the first offender had rarely, if ever, been singled out for special correctional concern in the unique and intrinsic challenge it offered for behavioral modification and experimentation in social engineering; and that, most startling of all, no less than fifty million Americans are now permanently stigmatized with criminal records as first offenders in our volatile democratic society.

Startling as the figures seem, the statistical studies and mathematical projections presented in *A Second Chance* represent reasonably reliable estimates in a completely virgin and uncharted field of criminal statistical exploration.

Up to now, the very concept of the first offender as an entity of particular correctional concern has hardly received the attention it has long deserved. Also, the total number of "criminals" in our society—that is, persons stigmatized with a criminal record—has always remained a missing and elusive quantity.

One must recognize, therefore, that the sheer attempt to project these figures necessarily involves a treacherous excursion into the already troubled and turbulent waters of criminal statistical science. In that context, I hasten to say that the mathematical estimates here presented are all mine, and I assume sole responsibility for their accuracy and validity.

In this connection, I acknowledge my deep appreciation and gratitude to the late J. Edgar Hoover, director of the Federal Bureau of Investigation; Dr. Thorsten Sellin, renowned criminal statistician; and the esteemed Sol Rubin, counsel to the National Council on Crime and Delinquency, for their eminently constructive and time-consuming analyses and evaluations of the statistical aspects of *A Second Chance*.

To my son, Robert, a doctoral candidate in the behavioral science of clinical psychology, goes full credit for originating the seminal idea of the experimental amnesty project presented in the closing chapter of *A Second Chance*.

A special word now about Dean Roscoe Pound's classical introduction to the book, written almost fifteen years ago. Just as time and events conspired against its publication at an earlier date, so now does the unique urgency of *A Second Chance* give to Dean Pound's words an even greater significance than ever before. I share with the reader the genuinely warm sentiments accompanying the introduction: "I can see the work you are doing is deserving every encouragement. Anything I can contribute toward it I should be glad to do so." Needless to say, I am profoundly in the debt of this legendary master of the law —whose influence, in Ralph Nader's eulogium, "has permeated the whole of American jurisprudence"—for all that he contributed in making *A Second Chance* a living reality for fifty million Americans and their families.

In my collection of illustrative cases, all names are masked wherever possible to shield the identity of the persons concerned against unnecessary notoriety. In the few exceptional instances where the identity of some had to be openly divulged, it will be readily seen that these individuals had themselves thrown their criminal records into the public domain or, in balance, proved of such impelling stature or example that the overall cause of amnesty would best be served by frank and open disclosure.

The blow-by-blow account of the infighting in the legislative arena is previewed here as a primer of pitfalls to ward by all who would join hands on the flagship of forgiveness in amnesty's journeys ahead. The Model Amnesty Bill set out in the appendix is the identical measure that had been introduced in the Congress of the United States on June 28, 1967, by former Representative Leonard Farbstein, limited to federal first offenders. As a model, of course, it is readily adaptable to all the states of the union.

Beyond words to express, I acknowledge my profound appreciation and gratitude to all who rallied to amnesty's call in its infancy. As recounted here, chief in the vanguard were Paul W. Tappan, former chairman of the United States Parole Board; Chief Judge Albert Conway of the New York Court of Appeals; Dean Emeritus Roscoe Pound of the Harvard Law School; Judge Samuel S. Leibowitz; Aryeh Neier, executive director of the

American Civil Liberties Union; Paul O'Dwyer, veteran battler in freedom's cause; and Edward S. Silver, former district attorney of Kings County and president of the National District Attorneys Association.

I also salute Patricia Lewis for her unwavering faith in *A Second Chance* all these many years; Jim Neyland, senior editor, who picked up the vibes; and H. R. N., among many others, for his constructive contributions in making this book possible.

Introduction

When Huckleberry Finn's father stumbled over a barrel, he got up, turned around, and kicked it. To hit back is an instinctive human response when anything goes wrong. Hurt must be met by hurt. We say instinctively, "Somebody must pay for this."

In the legal order, in the regime of administration of justice, punishment is the first and only instrument of maintaining the general security. And when, later, men begin to think about a rational basis of legal institutions, they argue that punishment has an intrinsic value. It is required to satisfy the public that a balance of right and wrong has been restored. The root idea is not one of remedy. Punishment originally is not thought of as remedy. It is held the inevitable consequence of wrong.

Later we come to an idea of just equivalence. The punishment is a necessary consequence. But it must fit the crime. There is to be a measured infliction upon the wrongdoer—an infliction to the measure of his wrongdoing. Such an idea is still behind the familiar system of degrees of crime. But that system does not proceed on any theory of purpose of penal treatment. It still thinks of an inevitable consequence, not of a purposefully employed expedient to reach a socially desired result.

In the eighteenth century men began to get humanitarian ideas as to punishment; and as this was given a metaphysical form, it lent itself to the idea of mathematical equivalence of degree and kind of punishment to crime. As said above, punishment then and later is held to be an inevitable consequence, not a purposefully imposed legal institution.

But today we think otherwise. We ask, Why punishment? What is its social purpose?—not what is its logically established place in the general scheme of things. What social end are we seeking to achieve through a penal regime, and how do we expect to achieve it? Those are the questions we put to the lawmaker of today. It is not a quest of logical consistency but one of conscious human purposes that impels us to make laws and set up legal institutions.

What, then, is the end or purpose of punishment or, if we are not thinking simply of meeting hurt with hurt, of penal treatment? Indeed, when we cease thinking of punishment as an inevitable consequence, may it not be there is more than one end? Perhaps we may say there is one end having two sides. At any rate, I submit we seek today: (1) deterrence (a) to deter the offender, making him realize he cannot afford to do again what he has done, and (b) to deter others, showing them they cannot afford to imitate in like cases what the offender has done; and (2) rehabilitation of the offender, assuming not merely that he will not repeat his offense but that he will hereafter be a useful member of the community, not a burden upon it—so that he may make of himself a happy asset to society, not a discouraged potential liability.

So today we have come to two root ideas instead of the one idea of the beginning. Instead of punishment as an end in itself, we think of penal treatment adjusted to the offender as well as to the offended and directed to the two purposes, deterrence and rehabilitation.

The social interest in the general security calls for deterrence. Repetition by the wrongdoer and imitation by others must be precluded so far as they can be by a system of penal treatment. But what creates assurance that the wrongdoer will not repeat —that his misconduct will not became habitual? Punishment of itself does not suffice for this. We now seek to bring it about by rehabilitation—by restoring him, after penal treatment has performed its purpose of deterrence, to a normal, healthy place in society.✗

One of the vexing problems confronting those who seek to keep the administration of justice abreast of its social purpose in the changing social and economic conditions of today is to get rid of ideas that have become deep rooted in legal history and have not merely been outgrown for purposes of today but have become simply mischievous in their effects in action.

The law of evidence was long vexed by one of these outworn ideas of the beginnings of the administration of justice—the idea of fixed measures of value of different modes of proof. It was considered that an issue must be proved by evidence corresponding to its gravity—this issue by writing, that by oath or ordeal, that by a fixed number of witnesses of specified rank, and so on. This witness's testimony had that value, that witness's testimony had such and such value. Witnesses might have actually seen and heard what happened, but because of the class in which their testimony was put it had no legal value. An individual may have lost his legal personality or his legal personality may have been impaired, so that he could not be a witness. Even after much of this had become obsolete and forgotten, there remained testimonial incapacities of the convict.

Later, when we came to see that it was unwise to refuse to hear those who had heard and seen and knew, we laid down that what had gone to admissibility was no longer to bar admission as evidence but was to be heard as bearing on the credibility of the witness, even if it had no bearing on the truthfulness of his tale. Hence a former conviction for taking part in a riot might be shown against one who saw an automobile accident a generation later. In fact the former conviction may have no bearing at all on credibility. But if it had any, its usefulness would be more than outweighed by the harm done to a now respected and useful member of the community by forcing him to recite in public the forgotten and now irrelevant incident.

The doctrine of evidence of prior conviction, merely as such as going to credibility of the witness, is one of those remnants in legal procedure that still confront those who are seeking to make the law conform to reason under the conditions of today.

Weighed in terms of the cardinal purposes of deterrence and rehabilitation, the evidence of prior charge or conviction has no place in a modern trial as it is used. It defeats both purposes: the one because it hangs over the first offender who is struggling to regain his place in society, impairing his resistance to temptation by hanging continual dread of humiliation over him; and the other because he can never be assured that he is rehabilitated in public estimation however well conducted he continues to be.

Indeed the idea of going into an item of past misconduct of a witness having no relevance whatever to the issue on trial is a leftover from crude beginnings of a law of evidence. It is not merely useless for any real purpose of today but, I repeat, it is mischievous in its effect upon a cardinal purpose of the administration of remedial justice today.

When Lord Coke wrote his Third Institute, expounding the criminal law as it had come down to England of the age of adventurous exploration and colonization and individual free self-assertion from the relationally organized society of the Plantagenets, he exclaimed, "Blessed be the amending hand!"

The criminal law of his time sadly needed making over. The criminal law both in England and America has been made over twice since Coke's day. But the amending hand is still needed.

ROSCOE POUND
Dean Emeritus
Law School of Harvard University
Cambridge, Mass.

PART I

The Second Punishment

"There is nothing more tragic in life than the utter impossibility of changing what you have done."

John Galsworthy
Justice, Act II

1
The Hidden Life Sentence

If the bitter fruit of crime is punishment, the bitter seed within punishment is the lifelong criminalization of every convicted offender.

He who thinks that he has paid his debt to society with the expiation of punishment under the penal codes finds out all too soon that his is a debt that will never be repaid in the coin of this realm.

Whatever the sentence may be—whether it be the length of only a day, a year, or the "maximum" of five or even twenty years or more, it is as nothing compared to the hidden lifetime sentence that is the consequence of every conviction. For long after the ordeal of the prescribed punishment has passed into oblivion, the lasting and irreversible stain of the criminal record will shadow the offender wherever he goes.

As A. M. Kirkpatrick, president of the International Prisoners Aid Association, so succinctly put it, "They return to the community and then, all too often, their second punishment begins."

Most vulnerable of all to the whiplash of the second punishment, of course, are the legions of marked men daily streaming

3

from our prisons and jails throughout the land. And, despite the heady nomenclature of prison reform, the stigma of a prison commitment is as disastrous to the inmates of the so-called reformatories as it is to the seasoned graduates of the maximum security prisons.

Even the forbearing grant of a prison-free discharge, or probation, or a suspended sentence, or a mere monetary fine is, in each case, only an illusory second chance in the galaxy of the second punishment. For these too, in their own subtle way, exact their crushing toll in an interminable handicap against all convicted offenders.

No matter how genuine a reformation the ex-offender may have achieved, or how earnest his quest for rehabilitation and reform, he will remain a prisoner of his criminal record throughout his days.

In society's roll call of the condemned, even a petty offense is ofttimes as virulent in the aftermath of punishment as are the more serious transgressions of criminality. Legion are the lost opportunities in private and public employment and in the licensed occupations or professions, impaled on some innocuous disorderly conduct or gambling charge, or some juvenile indiscretion resurrected from the dim past of yesteryear.

The picayune penalty of a twenty-dollar fine meted out to student demonstrators of Harvard University for criminal trespass in the unlawful occupation of its Administration Building in 1969 was but the veneer of a lifetime hidden punishment that will trail these youths for the rest of their lives.

The impasse of a criminal record is an acrid pill swallowed in mute resentment by millions upon millions of ex-offenders.

The very real case of the harassed salesman who, in his rapid climb to success, dared not accept promotion to the job of crew supervisor for fear that the routine fingerprinting by a bonding company would uncover the skeleton of a criminal record . . .

The trusted public accountant earning twenty thousand dollars a year as controller of millions of dollars of corporate funds—yet permanently beyond reach of the coveted licensure as a certified public accountant only because of a single criminal misdeed redressed many years ago . . .

The rehabilitated youthful offender mercifully cleared of the stigma of a "criminal" record through the paternalistic interdiction of the juvenile laws—yet disqualified for a barber's license for lack of "good moral character" . . .

The tormented public official holding a key sensitive position of fiduciary trust—dreading the golden opportunity for civil service advancement, which could only revive the ghost of an old petty larceny conviction of which even his own family was unaware . . .

The blind job prospector whose all-but-forgotten virginal brush with the law proved a more formidable disqualification for employment than his total sightlessness . . .

The corporate tycoon of the food industry constrained to abandon a scheduled public offering of his company stock lest he have to make public disclosure in the required registration statement to the Securities Exchange Commission of a larceny sentence some forty-five years in the past . . .

The cab driver fully passing muster of a police department medallion to operate a taxi yet barred from voluntary service as an auxiliary policeman because of a misdemeanor of twelve years vintage . . .

The distraught night-watchman for a complex of industrial buildings in the heart of a major metropolitan area who was ruled ineligible for an occupational gun permit because of a robbery rap he acquired as an adolescent some thirty years back—although he had been pardoned for that crime and had ultimately emerged as a decorated radio crewman for the United States Air Force, regularly entrusted with special mission flights involving the personal safety of both General Eisenhower and Secretary of the Army Patterson . . .

The twenty-eight-year-old Newark resident, a member of the

super-IQ Mensa organization, who had attained federal security clearance to a sensitive position as an electronics technician—yet whose name was stricken from the voting lists because of a three-year suspended sentence for auto theft meted out to him while he was still in his early teens . . .

The ex-felon father of two children, ages ten and twelve, summarily disqualified as their guardian in favor of a maternal aunt—simply because twenty-three years earlier, while in his teens, he had gone through the wringer of a burglary arrest—to which he had pleaded guilty—for the first and last time . . .

The Louisiana school bus driver fired from his job of ten-year tenure because the state constitution forbade the hiring of convicted persons regardless of the passage of time—which in this case happened to be a quarter of a century . . .

The physician ultimately restored to medical practice after having surrendered his license because of a conviction for criminal abortion—now, for ten long years, futilely pounding on every hospital door for rights as a visiting or staff member . . .

These are some of the random cases epitomizing our uncompromising war against the criminal first offender.

Drummed out of the mainstream of normal life, inextricably trapped by the phalanx of economic sanctions and social barriers lined up against him in a closed society, permanently detoured along marginal paths of subemployment, doomed to chronic unemployment, relegated to the lowest strata of exploitative labor—consigned to jobs and stipends that often debase his native skills and talents and interests—the stigmatized offender hangs on in the unequal, despairing struggle for existence against all odds.

The myriad parries and thrusts of public and private inquisitiveness, the telltale fingerprints, the ubiquitous questionnaire, the proliferating security clearances, the endless personality quizzes in "good moral character" tests, the bonding requirements, the background lie-detector probes—all these restrict and confound the ex-offender at the very threshold of each new start.

It is indeed a heart-breaking dilemma. If he admits the truth of his past transgression, the ex-offender's opportunities for employment or licensure are systematically red-penciled into the morgue of the untouchables; even worse, if he conceals the record and manages to inveigle a job or license, he risks all the potentials of his future to the fears of exposure and ruin. And if he picks up stakes, scurrying at long last into the seeming sanctuary of another state or country, the omnipotent second punishment will continue to shadow him.

Everywhere it will be the same badgering question, the same apologia, the same rejection slip pursuing him in practically every job application, every civil service opportunity, every application for admission to college, every petition for a professional license, for a whole lifetime. As criminologist Harry Best put it in his *Crime and Criminal Law,* "He must spend his days in torture for fear of its discovery."

In one of its landmark opinions, the United States Supreme Court allowed, "Of course the record of a conviction for a serious crime is often a lifelong handicap. There are a dozen ways in which even a person [who] has reformed, never offended again, and constantly endeavored to lead an upright life may be prejudiced thereby. The stain on his reputation may at any time threaten his social standing or affect his job opportunities."

Nor is this all of society's second punishment.

The convicted felon is automatically excluded from the higher professions, such as the law, medicine, engineering, teaching, architecture, and certified public accountancy.

In most of the states, he is deprived of the right to vote and to hold public office. He is barred from jury service. And in some few states, he is even legally incapacitated to testify as a witness in a court of law, or to serve as an executor or administrator of a decedent's estate, or to function as a lawful guardian on behalf of his own child.

Under the restrictive federal law, he is permanently barred

from serving as an officer or director of any labor organization; in most states, he is effectively blacklisted from police or correctional work of any kind.

To top it off, the combined federal, state, and local governments in the United States now record the fingerprints of over twelve million public jobholders—one out of every six workers in the land.

If economically dependent upon an automobile for his livelihood, the ex-offender is not only ruled off the road by mandatory revocation or suspension of his right to drive, but even after the ban is eventually lifted he must run the gauntlet of an outright refusal of insurance coverage or, at best, helplessly submit to reclassification into the assigned risk pool of up-rated premiums—all because the overarching criminal record would tend to prejudice a jury into a civil verdict against the ex-offender.

Regardless of a man's discordant quest for rehabilitation, his eligibility for personal life insurance is often placed in jeopardy, outright in some cases, deferred in others, for as long as ten years following the completion of sentence.

And the ex-offender is severely restricted from entering an increasing variety of licensed vocations. In California, typical of all the states, approximately sixty major occupations require a state license, for which a conviction for a felony or any offense involving moral turpitude can result in perpetual disqualification. The ban holds even if the offense be totally unrelated to the regulated activity, as is illustrated in the denial of a taxi license to a Maryland youth convicted merely for distributing socialist literature at a college campus. In the scope of "good moral character," a felonious criminal record—regardless of its nature—would instantly disqualify from licensure a seller of hearing aids in the state of Michigan, an operator of a dry-cleaning plant in California, a midwife in Connecticut, a poultry technician in Pennsylvania, a forester in Oklahoma, a cosmetologist in Arizona, a solicitor or canvasser in New Jersey, a second-hand goods dealer in New York.

In New York State, an estimated one-third of all unskilled jobs are off limits to ex-felons by the edict of a single agency alone. The Alcoholic Beverage Control Law prohibits the employment of ex-offenders in any capacity in premises licensed by the ABC Board—whether as a salesclerk behind a supermarket counter selling packaged beer, as a waiter, cook, or dishwasher in a restaurant where liquor is served, or as a doorman or bootblack in a bottle country club. "I was always astounded," declared William Vanden Heuvel, chairman of the New York City Board of Corrections at hearings held in May, 1972, by the Commission on Human Rights, "that ex-prisoners who could stand at a bar and get drunk could not, by law, be employed as sweepers or busboys in the same tavern."

In New York City, not unlike other large metropolitan centers throughout the country, a long string of diverse occupations and specialties—well over a hundred in number—are at the unfettered mercy of the licensing authorities.

"As a result," declared the President's Crime Commission Task Force report on *Corrections* in 1967, "convicted persons are generally subject to numerous disabilities and disqualifications which have little relation to the crime committed, the person committing it or, consequently, the protection of society. They are often harsh out of all proportion to the crime committed. And by cutting the offender off from society, including, perhaps, his chosen occupation, they may impede efforts at rehabilitation."

Once lost, forfeited civil rights are only grudgingly and sparingly returned, most often on a piecemeal and limited basis only. So tight are the binds and so many are the roadblocks of bureaucratic controls that few of the ex-offenders even bother to apply for the restoration of their voting or licensing rights.

And even in the rarity of an executive pardon, or the limited expungement of a criminal record now available in a handful of the states, the stigma of the arrest record nevertheless remains no less potent in the riptides of the second punishment.

Totally oblivious to the basic imperatives of correctional need, the administrative mandarins consistently turn their back on the ex-offender in systematic cop-out to a fail-safe expediency.

Occasionally, an aroused court would flex its judicial muscles against the autocratic action of some official commissar, but by and large, regardless of merit or empathy, the judges are legally helpless against the almost untouchable exercise of discretion. And though the courts are flooded with petitions for relief from the aggrieved victims of the second punishment, the cases of purely arbitrary actions being rectified are few and far between.

The stigmatic record can lie dormant for years, but then suddenly re-erupt at any given time.

It can unexpectedly bob into view in such unlikely settings as an application for a G.I. mortgage loan, an enlistment in the army, a petition for naturalization, a request for a visa, a bid for jury service, a fishing or gun permit—to name but a few.

The criminal record persistently flares up in the limitless minefields of litigation in courts and administrative agencies alike, where the oath of a witness may be mercilessly shattered, a contract lawsuit all but wrecked, a stockholder's action or legacy contest permanently derailed, a criminal prosecution against the plainly guilty aborted, an innocent man unjustly convicted, all with the cross-examiner's single, devastating stock question: "Were you ever convicted of a crime?"

In the endless paroxysms of the second punishment, potential armies of youthful ex-felons are literally blackballed out of the armed services on the "moral grounds" of their criminal record, even while the Pentagon and harried draft boards keep scraping the barrels of dwindling manpower to keep the Yanks coming.

In innocent passage through hundreds of cities and townships, the ex-offender is besieged by road signs reading: "Warning: Criminal Registration"—often forcing the carrier of the criminal record to improvise a detour from a planned vacation site or fixed business itinerary rather than submit to a degrading and humbling registration as a common criminal over and over again.

To take a random few, the city of Miami, Florida, requires that registration be accomplished within twenty-four hours after establishing residence; Fort Lauderdale, twelve hours. In such favorite resorts as Hialeah, Atlantic City, or St. Paul, to name some others in the roadmap of the second punishment, the ex-offender must sign in with the police immediately upon entering the city lines.

The stigmatic record can strike against the ex-offender at the least opportune time. Over one thousand formerly convicted Wall Street personnel—including some staid partners and principals of leading stock firms—found themselves suddenly caught short in the wake of New York's rigid catchall statute mandating the fingerprinting of all handlers of securities. It is a matter of gossipy conjecture how many others had strategically retreated into the sanctuary of other jobs rather than risk the embarrassment and humiliation of palm-print denouement.

Quite unexpectedly, the recent publication of an unauthorized scandal-mongering biography of IBM's illustrious founder, Thomas John Watson, unearthed the all-but-forgotten one-year prison sentence that had been meted out to him more than a half century ago.

Fresh in memory to any reader of the daily press is the recent embattlement of ex-Beatle John Lennon, whose four-year-old criminal conviction in England for possession of marijuana suddenly loomed against him after he had filed an alien's application for permanent residence in the United States as a person ostensibly of good moral character.

What offer would the underworld's Meyer Lansky have not gladly made to hush the notoriety of his criminal record, so that he could partake of the Law of Return which opens the Israeli door of welcome to every Diaspora Jew except those with "a criminal past likely to endanger the public weal"?

The muckrakings of the second punishment are particularly prolific in the political arena. One recalls the public admission by a major Democratic contender for the office of president of the United States, in full view of a nationwide television audience, that he had indeed stumbled into a juvenile rap for an automobile joyride in his early years.

The distinguished nominee of the Kennedy administration for director of the Export-Import Bank had to run through a fiery gauntlet of public hearings for Senate confirmation, openly admitting that he had been arrested fourteen years earlier for having used a car without the owner's timely consent.

A congressional committee investigating the Bernard Goldfine–Sherman Adams shenanigans during the Eisenhower administration had a field day of cross-examination against the beleaguered industrialist by asking him, in the full glare of televised publicity, whether it was not true that he had been indicted on a bankruptcy charge some forty-nine years ago.

Though the impeccable Attorney General Elliot L. Richardson had successfully hurdled exhaustive Senate confirmation hearings into his fitness to serve as the nation's topmost legal officer, as well as his capacity to serve as secretary of defense and as secretary of housing, education and welfare, the malicious exhumation of a thirty-five-year-old drunken driving conviction when he was barely eighteen years of age was suddenly injected into the supercharged atmosphere of his tug-of-war with the Nixon administration over the firing of Special Watergate Prosecutor Archibald Cox.

The public has witnessed the mortification of an honored Boston philanthropist who was innocently caught in the cross fire between a newspaper publisher and an outspoken federal judge —after the latter had publicly charged that the paper's corporate stock was now owned "by a man convicted of crime in this court." Forced to publicly unveil the "criminal" stockholder, the publisher responded that it was all but a tempest in a teapot, that the individual in question had been merely convicted of an innocuous bootlegging charge of more than forty years vintage, and besides, his financial interest in the newspaper amounted to less than one-half of 1 percent.

Only international fame as America's double gold medal winner of the 100-meter dash, and member of the winning 400-meter team at the 1964 Olympic games in Tokyo, flushed out the shocking news that track star Bob Hayes had been under a probationary sentence for a criminal conviction five years before.

The ubiquitous record can crop up routinely in confidential credit investigations, summarily ending the cherished fulfillment of a potential business venture or the opportunity for a loan or credit.

In the Orwellian nightmare that looms within the next decade, the credit dossier of every American will be fed into the unyielding memory of a computerized national network which, in its encompassing sphere of cognition, will be suffused with such vital economic indicators as arrest and conviction records wherever obtainable.

Professor Arthur R. Miller of the University of Michigan Law School, in testimony given on February 23, 1971, warned the watchdog Subcommittee on Constitutional Rights of the gathering clouds of the "dossier dictatorship," pointing to the chilling statistic that the Associated Credit Bureaus of America now maintain files on approximately one out of every two persons in the nation. The Retail Credit Company of Atlanta, catering largely to insurance companies, now has forty-five million files in its inventory. The TRW Credit Data, based in Anaheim, California, has a hoard of thirty-two million names, to which it is adding an estimated fifty thousand files every week. In a four-day symposium at Dickinson College on "The Invasion of Privacy in Our Computerized Society," Ralph Nader bluntly charged that anyone posing as a prospective employer and willing to pay a five-dollar or ten-dollar fee could pry into the selected data of the seventy-two million computerized Americans in the files of the country's two largest credit rating bureaus, the Retail Credit Company and the Credit Data Corporation.

The official files of fingerprint records are no less foreboding. The New York State Identification and Intelligence System alone has a current file on over two million people tagged with criminal records.

In New York, typical of most states, fingerprinting is required for any person arrested for a felony or misdemeanor. Fingerprints may also be taken for any offense where the police officer is unable to ascertain an arrestee's identity, or reasonably suspects that the identification given by such person is not accurate.

Once taken, one copy of such fingerprints must be forwarded to the central archives of the state identification and intelligence system. A second copy is simultaneously transmitted to the master identification division of the Federal Bureau of Investigation.

The FBI's burgeoning files are not only routinely disseminated to all official agencies of the federal government, the states, and the cities of the nation, but are in the grab bag of information to banks, insurance companies, railroads, defense contractors, and subcontractors alike, under security clearances steadily operational throughout every hamlet in the land. And, given the fingerprint-obsessed, military-industrial complex sprawling everywhere, accounting for one of every ten jobholders in our economy, the constricting net against the ex-offender draws tighter and tighter each year.

In most of the states, the criminal files are deemed public records, freely open to public inspection. In about twenty-five states, any private person or organization may purchase copies and transcripts on payment of a minor fee. In New York City, a 1971 grand jury investigation of a flourishing police racket (involving the handout of illegal gratuities by potential employers and detective agencies for easier access to criminal records) urgently recommended that such records be made readily available upon payment of an appropriate fee, to conform with the practice of the upstate cities of Buffalo and Rochester.

As an example of what is in the offing in this gargantuan threat to the privacy of every ex-offender, Ralph Nader's irrepressible Raiders—this time tilting lances with the potential evils of computerized snoopery—dredged up the dreadful faux pas of an unemployed man who had been kept out of a job for four agonizing years only because some data-happy programmer had carelessly fed the computer with the fallacious report that the subject had been dishonorably discharged from the army.

"A file may show that an individual was arrested," noted Supreme Court Justice William O. Douglas, "but will it show the arrest was unconstitutional because it was solely for purposes of investigation? Or that the charges were dropped? Or that a jury acquitted him?"

Tragically, it is not only the convicted offender, but his family as well who must carry the burden of the second punishment.

Bernard Shaw once quipped of his alcoholic father: "If you cannot get rid of the family skeleton, make it dance." This was a workable formula for an alcoholic, perhaps, but the family skeleton of a criminal record is hardly as viable.

All too often, the dread scandal of a long-forgotten past would be suddenly breathed back into life onto the obituary pages of the daily press, automatically triggered into resurrection by the demise of some public figure in the world of business or politics.

"Society talks about the debt being paid," said the late Judge Jonah Goldstein of New York, "but then hounds a person for the rest of his life. Time and time again, I will pick up a newspaper and then read that so-and-so was a criminal twenty-five years ago. There is no way of living it down regardless of the extent of his rehabilitation."

When the surviving relatives of the late Moses L. Annenberg, founder of the family fortune, proudly announced the gift of one million dollars to medical science in honor of the eighty-sixth birthday of their mother, one man's criminal record was thrust into prominence. Walter H. Annenberg, the renowned Philadelphia publisher, ambassador to Great Britain, declared, "We want to pay a tribute to our mother that will last forever." Turning to Moses L. Annenberg in its front page story, the *New York Times* added: "His purchase in 1922 of the Daily Racing Form opened a new phase of his career, which was to lead him to earning what was believed to be one of the largest incomes in the United States. In 1939, he, his son and several aides were indicted for income tax evasion and engaging in various aspects in gambling. He pleaded not guilty but served a brief term in jail in 1942. He was released for reasons of health and died soon thereafter leaving his entire property in trust to his widow and eight children and appointing his son trustee."

Of what news shattering significance was the postmortem tidbit that the late Rex Ingram (the unforgettable "De Lawd" of *Green Pastures*) had once been convicted of a long-forgotten crime, especially when this had always been a securely closed chapter in the lifetime of one of the most revered characters of the American stage?

In the obituary for America's authentic war hero Audie Murphy, who had won more medals for gallantry in action than any other person in United States military history—including the Medal of Honor, the Distinguished Service Cross, the Legion of Merit, the Silver Star, the Bronze Star with Oakleaf Cluster, the Purple Heart, and four medals from allied foreign governments —was it really necessary to dredge up his forgotten criminal record? Did the people's right to know, in this instance, actually advance the cause of deterrence one iota?

What would the gifted O. Henry have given to eradicate the record of his federal conviction during his lifetime of literary kingship? What would his revering circle of friends not have done to clear his name from the sullying drag of his prison record—even to the day when, his ninety-one-year-old widow still alive, the Texas Heritage Foundation petitioned for a pardon in his behalf only to receive the staggering response that the president of the United States was powerless to grant a posthumous forgiveness?

What would Oscar Wilde have given for the supreme unction of societal forgiveness on the heels of his two-year prison sentence for homosexuality? "Society, as we have constituted it, will have no place for me, has none to offer," he sadly lamented in *De Profundis*. "But Nature, whose sweet rains fall on unjust and just alike, will have clefts in the rocks where I may hide, and secret valleys in whose silence I may weep undisturbed."

Within the decade of the volatile 1960s, tens of thousands of youths were driven by motives of conscience into the jaws of arrest or conviction because they would neither submit to a racist society nor play a role in what they deemed to be an unconscionable and illegal war.

In many states, countless persons have suffered a crushing sentence for such innately victimless crimes as mutually consenting fornication or homosexuality. Many carriers of the second punishment have been convicted through the years for purely private "pornographic" indulgences now no longer taboo.

Numerous criminal offenders have been stigmatized by unconstitutional statutes, or under laws no longer fashionable in the contemporary mores of public policy—of which the prohibition amendment, the liberalized abortion standards, the radically changed obscenity criteria, and the new look at pot-smoking are classic examples.

The second punishment implicates the unintentional transgressor no less than the calculating wrongdoer. Considering the bottomless fertility of our lawmaking factories and the recurring unpredictability of judicial constructions, it is not uncommon that a criminal record can be spawned out of sheer ignorance or honest mistake, without the slightest evil or criminal intent whatever.

"Mistaken notions about one's legal right are not sufficient to bar prosecution for crime," declared our highest court in the celebrated bigamy case of *Williams* v. *North Carolina,* 325 US 238.

It is a tantalizing question—which can only be answered by a court's decision—whether the maverick Daniel Ellsberg was guilty of the crime of larceny in the theft of the "top-secret" Pentagon papers, or, in the opposite scale of value judgments, whether he truly deserved the people's Purple Heart for his act of civil disobedience in vindication of the people's right to know the truth.

The tangle with First Amendment rights is a thorny one indeed. "Any one who acts on it is taking a chance," declared Arthur Schlesinger, Jr. "Only the aftermath can prove him right or wrong in deciding that government has violated its part of the contract."

When dissenting opinions on momentous questions of right and wrong, of life and death, abound in every facet of the judicial process—when the Supreme Court itself splits five to four as to whether a contumacious flag-burning accompanied by profane and incendiary invective is protected as an absolute right of free speech, or when the high court narrowly upholds Maryland's verdict outlawing *I Am Curious (Yellow)* by a deadlocked decision of four to four even though forty states had already approved the film—then it is all too plain to see that one can literally stumble into a criminal record by pure chance.

The vulgar difference between allowable and criminal obscenity may well hang on the dice-throw of a jury's verdict, or on the changing criteria in the flux of judicial precedents. Publisher Ralph Ginzburg found himself under a three-year prison sentence not for publishing or selling obscene material, but for "pandering" by salacious advertising, "for distributing printed matter about sex," lamented Justice Hugo Black in classic dissent, "which neither Ginzburg nor anyone else could possibly have known to be criminal."

Never in their wildest dreams did Abbie Hoffman and Jerry Rubin anticipate that, in doing their thing in the streets of Chicago during the 1968 Democratic National Convention, they would be enmeshing themselves in the net of a federal conspiracy indictment for crossing state lines to incite a riot.

The unresolved issue in the hopelessly deadlocked prosecution of antiwar activists, the Reverend Philip F. Berrigan and Sister Elizabeth McAlister—charged with conspiracy to kidnap Presidential Assistant Henry A. Kissinger—was whether (in the government's view) the pair should be convicted as "ecclesiastical gangsters," or rather (as viewed by the defense) the accused should be awarded the Nobel Peace Prize for their truly Christian self-sacrifice at the altar of pacifism.

When Bayard Rustin, the honored civil rights leader, was recently arrested for carrying a sword cane in self-protection, little did he realize that his possession of this contraband weapon had just been made illegal by an unpublicized law enacted, without his or anyone else's awareness, only a short time before.

It took four years of tumultuous litigation, right on to the closely split decision of the United States Supreme Court, to determine that the First Amendment right of free speech permitted an anti-Vietnam protester to flaunt the words "Fuck the Draft" on his jacket while sauntering through the corridors of the Los Angeles Municipal Court.

Adding grist to the mill of the second punishment are the hundred-odd independent and semiautonomous federal commissions, boards, and agencies sprawling alongside a spate of state and local administrative agencies of every description—what the *Wall Street Journal* called the "headless fourth branch" of government—all grinding out a loaded thicket of sporadic rules and regulations, enough to send a man to a stretch in prison just for turning his back against their sanctions.

With characteristic totality and thoroughness, the lifelong sequelae of the second punishment is even visited upon all those who are merely arrested or indicted, without conviction. The sullying record of an arrest, though it results in an outright acquittal or even dismissal without trial, remains an ever-festering source of social and economic repression for tens of millions. Robert F. Kennedy, while attorney general of the United States, took pains to note that "a policeman, by making an arrest in a small community, may ruin the life of the person charged. The mark is on the man's record, the word has gone out and even if he is completely cleared, it can be too late."

The ambitious proposal of a college-degree police force may be disdainfully dismissed as a pipe dream impossible of fulfillment, but the specter of 523,000 law officers in the nation capable of arresting any one of us on flimsy suspicion, or for disorderly conduct or "resisting an officer," or for exaggerated "harassment" or "obstruction of governmental administration" charges growing out of a traffic argument or a civil rights encounter with the police is of vital concern to the millions who have gone through the wringer of a permanently maiming arrest record, even though exonerated of the empty charge.

Mass arrests for civil disobedience, antiwar protests, racial confrontations, possession of marijuana, narcotic and drug "loitering," are increasingly commonplace everywhere, permeating the campuses, the military forces, and the mainstreets of every city in the nation. Tens of thousands of families of all kinds, in the inner ghettos and the affluent suburbs, including dozens of governors and United States senators and congressmen, have paid their dues in the nonexclusive club of the second punishment.

Symptomatic of the escalation of illegal arrests throughout the country is that in 1970, in New York City alone, 95,000 of the 129,000 misdemeanor cases were dismissed without so much as a trial. District Attorney Frank S. Hogan of New York County publicly charged that 89 percent of all narcotic loitering arrests, sampled in a quarterly test survey, were unwarranted and unlawful.

It took a jury but fifty minutes to exonerate Clay Shaw of the indictment of conspiracy to kill President John F. Kennedy, concocted against him by District Attorney James Garrison, but the defamation of his good name and reputation wrought by the arrest record can never be repaired.

Though an arrest may be patently illegal or a judgment of conviction wiped out on appeal, the irreversible arrest record branded into the personality of the arrestee will continue to pursue the innocent for a whole lifetime. Despite the fact that serious charges of criminal trespass had been dropped against some four hundred students out of the one thousand arrested in the 1968 riots at Columbia University, the arrest record will remain as a permanent monument to the unprosecuted crimes. Though the Brooklyn College student activists may have had their indictments for arson and riot quashed to spare them from the stigma of a criminal record, their arrest records will nevertheless cast their own long shadows in an unending punishment.

Writing in the *Yale Law Review* in November, 1960, Justice Douglas charged that vagrancy and loitering statutes across the nation are freely employed to bag hundreds of thousands into lawless arrests each year, based on mere suspicion.

To stem the tide of indiscriminate arrests, for the first time, the Supreme Court finally ruled in 1971 that it would no longer tolerate warrantless felony arrests without a convincing showing by police of "exigent circumstances" to justify the arrest without a warrant. In the meantime, however, countless millions of presumably innocent persons remain permanently saddled with arrest records.

Of the 12,00 May Day Vietnam demonstrators hauled in by the capital police in preventive detention, only a mere handful were ever convicted. Poignantly, scores of those arrested had defiantly refused to submit to fingerprint processing. "They object," stated the public defender, "because their fingerprints will be sent to the FBI for dissemination to 15,000 employers and employment agencies, and a dossier will be begun on them. These are people illegally arrested."

Similarly, untold numbers of youths have gone through the wringer of a "loitering" conviction under a Cincinnati ordinance —a sample of loitering statutes everywhere—which made it a criminal offense for three or more people to congregate on city sidewalks "in a manner annoying to persons passing by," until finally—on June 1, 1971, by a five-to-four ruling—the United States Supreme Court struck it down for lack of specificity as to what conduct is "annoying."

It is small solace indeed for the tainted multitudes of the second punishment that the National Commission on Marijuana and Drug Abuse has now finally recommended that the private possession and use of marijuana no longer be criminalized by penal sanctions of any kind.

In a broad study of the employment policies of employment agencies in the New York City area, the New York Civil Liberties Union has found that 75 percent of all those sampled would not make a referral of any job applicant with an arrest record, whether convicted or not.

In still another survey by a team of social researchers, the National Council on Crime and Delinquency reported that sixty-six out of seventy-five employers flatly averred that they would not consider hiring anyone arrested for even a minor crime such as assault, even if they had been acquitted.

The appalling fact is that 40 percent of all male children now living in the United States will be arrested for some criminal offense during their lifetime. This is the authoritative estimate of the President's Commission on Law Enforcement, in its February, 1967, report to the American people entitled *The Challenge of Crime in a Free Society.*

In a parallel study for the National Crime Commission, the Institute of Defense Analysis—a respected think-tank research organization restricted to matters affecting the national security— declared that its arrest-rate projections indicated that six out of every ten boys now growing up in American cities will be arrested sometime in their lives; for urban Negro boys, the figure will be nine out of ten.

The short-changing of our youth in the matter of rehabilitation is unquestionably the cruelest weapon in the arsenal of the second punishment.

Though we have embraced the saintly postulate that our youth should not be onerously scarred with the lifelong taint of a criminal record—gracing our law with safeguards "in the progress of philanthropic and humanitarian purpose," as the courts have put it, "for the protection of young children from the consequence of the acts which were believed to be destructive of a chance for reform and a better life thereafter"—the bottom truth is that our paternalistic efforts have been all but emasculated in the proving test of actuality.

Juvenile or not, the arrest record has proven to be as baneful an entry in the youth's dossier as any "criminal" record might have been. And the vaunted confidentiality of the ostensibly classified record, in all literalness, has been more faithfully honored in the breach.

"This claim of secrecy is more rhetoric than reality," acknowledged the United States Supreme Court in its precedential *Gault* decision. "Disclosure of court records is discretionary with the judge in most jurisdictions. Statutory restrictions almost invariably apply only to the court records, and even as to those the evidence is that many courts routinely furnish information to the FBI and the military, and on request to government agencies and even to private employers."

Systematically, a bid for a job or license, membership in a labor organization or for apprenticeship training, even a scholarship grant, can founder on the rocky shoals of the single omnibus question, "Have you ever been arrested, taken into custody, held for investigation or questioning, or charged by an enforcement authority?"

Typical of every hiring agency in the corporate structure of the nation, the William J. Burns International Detective Agency, Inc., requires all applicants for jobs with their client companies to fill out a standard employee card profile containing the following information: "Have you ever been complained of, indicted for or convicted of any violation of the law or ordinance? If so, give details."

With gymnastic ambivalence, the newly liberalized regulations of the United States Civil Service Commission no longer require that arrests be shown on applications for government employment —yet, incongruously, the commission's new form 941, issued February, 1968, and entitled "Employment of the Rehabilitated Offender in the Federal Service," flatly stipulates that "circumstances surrounding an arrest may be evaluated when determining an applicant's suitability for employment."

True to the pattern of most statutes, Pennsylvania specifically authorizes any person or institution "having a legitimate interest" to inspect the juvenile records. Youths seeking employment with city, state, and federal agencies are routinely required to sign waivers of the secrecy provisions of the youthful offender laws, reducing their intended beneficence to a paper protection only.

Characteristically, every person seeking enlistment in the army is asked (*DA form 3286, Part II*) if he has ever been arrested, cited, charged, or held by federal, state, county, city, or other law enforcement authorities, or by juvenile court or probation officials for any violation of law.

The air force "Statement of Law Violations" form sternly requires every recruitee to acknowledge in writing: "I certify that the Recruiter has instructed me that the concealment of any police, court or juvenile court records pertaining to me can result in a dishonorable discharge from the United States Air Force."

So relentless is the institutionalized persecution of the adolescent offender that a number of the country's universities and colleges systematically pry into the criminal and delinquent history of all candidates for admission. New York's Cornell University, for example, bluntly asks, "Have you ever been placed on probation or parole, or had any other penalty, scholastic or disciplinary, imposed?" New York University's standard questionnaire for admission focuses its inquiry on whether the student applicant has ever been arrested and, if so, asks him to spell out the details.

Thus the madness of our method has even penetrated our halls of learning, striking at our youth with the lash of the second punishment in the very first test of society's good faith toward them, at the very inception of their budding rehabilitation.

The perceptive jurist Musmanno, in one of his outspoken opinions in a 1954 case, declared: "A most disturbing fallacy abides in the notion that a Juvenile Court record does its owner no harm. . . . In point of fact it will be a witness against him in the court of business and commerce, it will be a bar sinister to him in the court of society where the penalties inflicted for deviation from conventional codes can be as ruinous as those imposed in any criminal court, it will be a sword of Damocles hanging over his head in public life."

The recoil of the second punishment has even desecrated the inner sanctum of the temples of justice, where it has taken a terrible toll in every court in the land. The convicted offender dare not take the witness stand to defend himself against an unjust accusation of crime, or even in the defense or prosecution of any meritorious personal claim. However rehabilitated or reformed he may be and no matter how ancient the record, without even rational distinction between the singleton misfeasor and the incorrigible repeater, the odium of untrustworthiness hovers over him in every court of law, and he must forever answer for his criminal record.

A businessman contemplating suit to enforce a just contract claim is routinely forced to settle out of court on badly compromised terms rather than submit himself to the pillory of his criminal record under cross-examination. An heir in a legacy contest would gladly rush into a bargained settlement rather than give up the ghost of his criminal past. The victim of an automobile accident might well go unrecompensed for serious injuries simply because he or his sole eyewitness would not ride the obstacle course of a criminal record.

The archives are full of innocent men unjustly trapped into a conviction because they would not risk taking the witness stand in their own defense.

Conversely, guilty men have gone free, time and time again, because the people's only available witnesses could not disprove a false alibi or a phony claim of self-defense, or bolster a shaky identification, or corroborate a lawful search, principally because —as ex-offenders themselves—these key witnesses could not survive an assault upon their own credibility in the glaring spotlight of their self-damning criminal records.

Conspicuous by their enforced absence from the witness box is the muted eyewitness to a homicide or a robbery, or the court-shy witness for the people in a racketeering or drug trafficking prosecution, who systematically boycott the courtroom rather than involve themselves in the inevitable exposure of their criminal past.

As Professor Borchard of Yale has noted in his classic work, *Convicting the Innocent:* "Many prisoners often refuse to take the witness stand in order to avoid questions by the prosecutor concerning their previous record."

"The defendant is presented with the Hobson's choice of sitting mute in the face of adverse testimony, or of taking the stand and permitting the prosecutor to present his prior convictions," declared Richard L. Braun, the executive assistant, Criminal Division, United States Department of Justice. "It is impossible to say how many innocent defendants have thereby been coerced into pleading guilty, but I am convinced, on the basis of personal experience and discussion with other attorneys, that the number is significant."

Not even a pardon or the expungement or nullification of a

criminal conviction under existing mores have neutralized the accusing finger of eternal guilt against the ex-offender in the perennial hotbox of the witness stand.

Indeed, we have advanced little beyond the anachronisms of a discredited past when even firstling felons were deemed so inherently untrustworthy as to be legally incompetent to testify as witnesses altogether, irrespective of such alien considerations as reformation or rehabilitation in the interests of justice.

Of this long-festering cancer in the judicial process, the topmost authority on the law of evidence, Professor John Henry Wigmore, bluntly stated: "With the prospect of such an examination as a possibility, the public is certain to dread the witness box. From time to time those whose knowledge would have been valuable will seek to evade disclosing it; the ascertainment of the truth will be hampered and perhaps prevented. That such a feeling exists today, in a greater or lesser degree, can hardly be doubted."

The grim harvest we have reaped is that prospective key witnesses, in wholesale numbers, have been literally driven from the halls of justice, in headlong flight from the hostile atmosphere of the courtroom, thus depriving countless litigants in civil and criminal proceedings alike of the only critical evidence available in the overall quest for truth.

If, as the criminologist Sutherland has posited in his *Principles of Criminology,* "the most serious consequence of punishment is the loss of self-respect," then we have cast a long shadow of shame and disrepute across whole multitudes of our people. If, in the hierarchy of our democratic values, the right of privacy means above all else—in Brandeis's dictum—"the right to be let alone, the most comprehensive of rights and the right most valued by civilized man," then we have mindlessly surrendered the very quintessence of our democratic heritage to the leprous scourge of the second punishment.

If a statistical profile were ever attempted as to the actual number of ex-offenders there are in our population, the resulting figures would literally shock the nation into incredulity.

"A substantial portion of the population is affected by the law in this area," recently reported the President's Crime Commission Task Force on Corrections. "Approximately 1.3 million people are at any one time subject to correctional authority; untold millions have criminal records." The question is, really, how many?

The late Professor Kinsey, surely no novice in the sophisticated techniques of behavioral countdowns, was amazed at the lack of existing data on the number of "criminals" in our population. There simply are no available figures, and the bookshelves of criminology and sociological research are void in this area of vital national statistics.

Thorsten Sellin, University of Pittsburgh sociologist, one of the country's ace criminal statisticians, has long decried the fact that "nowhere in the United States today is it possible to find a well-integrated and reasonably adequate system of criminal statistics, either on the local, federal, or national basis, in spite of the fact that we have long been deeply concerned with the serious character of our crime problem."

Symptomatic of the great need, it was not until 1972 that the Law Enforcement Assistance Administration committed nearly twelve million dollars to finance a comprehensive data systems program in a crash effort to develop a reliable body of statistics on criminal justice in all fifty states—a century-late acknowledgment that "we need better information in such vital areas as the incidence of crime, the effect of corrections or recidivism and the nature and scope of criminal justice operations and expenditures."

The undeniable truth is that there has been hardly a smidgen of interest or concern as to how long a person, once convicted, remains a "criminal" in the value judgments of our society.

We have taken for granted that the lifetime second punishment—like the eternal planets, the stars, the earth, and the heavens—is one immutable fixture of existence, and that, in Gertrude Steinian logic, a criminal is a criminal is a criminal.

Saddest of all, we have paid scant attention to the first offender as such, as a particular target for rehabilitation and reform in the echelon of criminality.

The question then is, How many first offenders are there in our midst? How many of these "criminals" are there, in our multiplying criminalized society, carrying the crushing burden of the lifetime second punishment?

As near as can be projected from the available crime figures contained in the annual Uniform Crime Reports of the Federal Bureau of Investigation, approximately 4.5 million persons are arrested each year for crimes and offenses ranging the whole spectrum from homicide to disorderly conduct—traffic offenses, drunkenness, and vagrancy arrests excluded.

Of those prosecuted, approximately 62 percent are found guilty, totaling 2.5 million persons convicted each and every year.

Catalogued in this awesome gallery of criminality are first offenders as well as chronic repeaters.

Assuming an overall recidivist rate of 25 percent to cover all types of crimes and offenders, the estimated annual total of first offenders would be approximately 1.8 million.

Thus, projected over the period of a single generation, there will accumulate a total of approximately fifty million first offenders branded with a criminal record circa 2000 A.D., implicating at least one out of every five persons in this nation.

Even were these figures to be discounted fourfold or drastically cut by such variables as the fluctuant crime patterns within a given generation, or the recidivist rate, or changes in life expectancy, the mammoth multimillions remaining would still rock our national welfare and future well-being to the deepest foundations.

Incredible as these figures are, they do not yet begin to pour out the full miasmic thrust of a police record upon all those directly affected by the second punishment. For in addition to all those who are convicted and sentenced, they do not take into account all those who are merely arrested and then acquitted or discharged, yet who carry their own special badge of opprobrium against career, livelihood, and self-esteem. Nor do they reflect the sizeable list of persons convicted by court martial—1.3 million by the army alone between 1941 and 1968—or administratively drummed out of the service with less than an honorable discharge.

"We can find no error in the computation," affirms Sol Rubin, counsel to the National Council on Crime and Delinquency, in his classic work *Crime and Juvenile Delinquency*. "Perhaps the F.B.I. data are incorrect, enlarged somewhat. But even based on a generation of twenty years, and lopping off some millions, the number of persons with a criminal record still would reach tens of millions—gigantic in its implications."

If, then, this be the full measure of the second punishment permeating this land, we have concocted for a sizeable part of our population a patentable prescription for riot, rebellion, and radicalization against the existing order, under the banner of any cause. If this be the extent of the participatory democracy we have promised to all those permanently crippled with the life sentence of a criminal record, then we have entrapped ourselves into a suicidal delusion that fifty million first offenders can be forever wrong.

2
Rehabilitation, Anyone?

When our prisons are surfeited with turnstile repeaters who as first offenders had firmly resolved never to return to prison again, when 40 percent of all parolees, desperately thirsting for the final dispensation of freedom, find themselves once again reincarcerated for new criminal acts, when the crime rate shrieks out the grim statistic that over 80 percent of all serious crime is recidivistic in nature—then it is all too clear that the metastatic second punishment cannot but have played a vital catalytic role.

If the private sector has been remiss towards the quested rehabilitation of the ex-offender, the disheartening truth is that the state itself is blameworthy tenfold more. Despite the semantics of a pretentious "second chance," the state has failed to set the supreme example and guiding precept of full forgiveness, and by its own myopic policy has systematically flouted the correctional will.

But the second punishment is a two-edged sword, which inflicts upon the state the far more grievous wound.

Consider the ex-offender whose application for a hack license to operate a taxi in New York was summarily turned down by the licensing authority of the Police Department. The file showed that eight years earlier, at sixteen years of age, the applicant had committed a robbery—a first and only offense, for which he had been mercifully adjudicated a "youthful offender," given a suspended sentence, and placed on probation by a circumspect court sensitive to the boy's unquestioned rehabilitative potential. Predictably enough, after he had completed the probation requirements satisfactorily to the very letter he had served two years in the armed forces, completing his stint with an honorable discharge. He was now married and had a child to support. And, like many other returning veterans, he was now unemployed.

Desperately, he turned to the Youth Counsel Bureau to intercede in his behalf. It promptly did so by vigorously protesting the police ruling as a patent flouting of the law's strict injunction that no adjudication as a youthful offender "shall operate as a disqualification of any youth subsequently to hold public office, public employment, or as a forfeiture of any right or privilege or to receive any license granted by public authority; and no youth shall be denominated a criminal by reason of such determination, nor shall such determination be deemed a conviction."

But the Police Department remained unmoved in its firm refusal to issue the license. Even the plea of the court's Probation Department fell on the muffled ears of the licensing agency.

Months passed. The distraught youth again implored the aid of the Youth Bureau, pleading for an opportunity to make a new life for himself in the only vocation he knew, if he only could get the taxi permit—begging that he could wait hardly any longer, as his wife was now threatening to leave him for nonsupport.

In the slowly grinding wheels of justice, the Youth Counsel Bureau finally turned to the Legal Aid Society, in one last throw of the dice, to institute court action in his behalf. But by this time the youth had simply vanished out of sight.

"I thus resolutely rejected a world which had rejected me," lamented Jean Genêt in *The Thief's Journal.* As our crime rate soars, one cannot help but wonder at the causal connection between our own stupendous folly and the rising graphs of crime and recidivism.

In the litany of the public safety and of deterrence, we have fallen short even in the prime virtues of consistency and coherence, suggesting that the conventional second punishment is grounded in random factors not only utterly alien to the public safety and security, but rather that an irrational lingering prejudice alone is the supreme mothering force.

"A basic dilemma that permeates penology is presented by the fact that the criminal law is still trying to ride several unruly horses running in opposite directions," declared Dr. Sheldon Glueck, eminent Harvard criminologist. "Retribution, deterrence, prevention, the teaching of the public a moral lesson, reformation, rehabilitation—all these aims are more or less entangled in the statutes and judicial decisions."

In the weird double standard we have been pursuing, a taxi driver blemished with the slightest police record can be summarily denied a hack license, but a taxi fleet operator of hundreds of cabs enjoys thorough immunity from all official prying into his own moral fitness. A street peddler is required to be licensed, but a house-to-house salesman is not. A cosmetologist and an embalmer are stringently subject to the screening process of licensing, but a psychotherapist, a moving picture operator, a blood donor, a marriage broker, an auto mechanic, a radio and television repairman, and audio-electronic technician are all exempted from official certification. A dealer in second-hand goods must pass the smudgy good character muster of fingerprinting clearance, but the fingerprint experts themselves, the handwriting analysts, and the polygraph examiners are safely beyond the pale of official overseership and regulation.

In the classic ministrations of bureaucratic ambidexterity and disingenuousness, the civil service commissions of every state run head on into the untouchable discretion of appointing officers who would peremptorily reject an ex-offender without so much as assigning a credible reason—even though the candidate had already passed full muster as to moral character and fitness.

And, despite the lofty liberalization of civil service opportunities for persons with police records, the status quo ante still reigns supreme. "It seems very hypocritical for the Government to urge private employers to hire ex-convicts when they themselves are the greatest offenders in hiring discrimination," said the knowledgeable Fortune Society at public hearings held by the New York City Commission on Human Rights in May, 1972.

In the topsy-turvy, zigzag course of the second punishment, a real estate broker engaged in the buying and selling or renting of property must satisfy authorities of his moral qualification, but the managing agents and superintendents of the sprawlng real estate developments dotting the land gaily meander among all the temptations without any trace of licensing, supervision, or official controls whatever.

Contrarily, though New York's labor law circumspectly prohibits the fingerprinting of employees as a condition of obtaining or holding private employment, the state itself and all its municipalities run wild with fingerprinting requirements that effectively operate to exclude even the first offender on strictly "moral" grounds.

In a rare technical knockout of the second punishment, Muhammad Ali finally prevailed upon a federal court to restore his lifted license after proving that the same New York State Boxing Commission that had deprived him of his championship title for draft evasion had nevertheless licensed hundreds of others during the past decade although they had committed far more serious crimes, including murder, rape, and arson. Some licensees had even been court-martialed and dishonorably discharged for military-related offenses—and among those licensed was the heavyweight champion Sonny Liston, though he had been previously floored with a conviction for armed robbery and assault with intent to kill.

Notwithstanding the ceremonial charades of the written law

under which the physical fingerprints are routinely returned to the successful defendant or destroyed in his presence on demand immediately upon acquittal or dismissal of a criminal charge— the indelible arrest record remains a mark of Cain that will linger on for a whole lifetime.

Behold the case of the hapless New York arrestee who had been caught entering a grocery store while in a diabetic fit, frenziedly seeking something sweet to gulp down in order to calm his seizure. These facts having been amply established in court, the case against the diabetic had been promptly dismissed, and the fingerprints were ordered removed from the damning records.

Six years later, however, after the ambushing second punishment had begun to take its toll against him both professionally and in his efforts to obtain government employment, he categorically petitioned the court for the removal and destruction of the arrest card from the records of the village of Lynbrook and the Nassau County Police Department.

Constrained to deny the application, the court decried its lack of statutory power to grant the relief requested, noting, "It may well be that legislative consideration should be given to establishment of means of limiting access to an arrest record when no information or indictment is returned."

In the irrational prescription of New Jersey's disenfranchisement of citizens convicted of certain crimes, embezzlers have long been deemed ineligible to vote, while those convicted merely of larceny are not.

Typical of the wild incongruities, the licensed port watchmen within the sensitive jurisdiction of the New York–New Jersey Waterfront Commission constantly labor under the sharply watchful eye of the licensing authority, but the company that supplies the same watchmen, at an annual payroll cost of $8,750,000, is itself totally beyond reach of security investigation.

"In Colorado, for example," stated Wayne K. Patterson, director of the Colorado Department of Parole, "we have a parole system for which the state spends a quarter of a million dollars a year in rehabilitation of men paroled from the prisons or reformatories. We spend endless time in the search for jobs for parolees and attempt to convince employers of the social and moral values to be gained by giving jobs to men released from prison. But the state government itself, probably the largest employer in the state, is prohibited by the Constitution from giving men paroled from prison a job in any capacity."

In the conventional fixations of the administrative agencies against the ex-offender, consider the former inmate of a women's reformatory who was denied a license to operate a beauty parlor even though she had satisfactorily completed a vocational training program as cosmetologist and hairdresser in prison. More than eight years had elapsed since her final discharge, she had fully qualified to pursue her chosen profession, and as her court papers convincingly showed, she had demonstrated a sincere atonement for her past transgression.

Here, in one of the rare instances of conclusively proven arbitrary action, the prudential mediation of an activist judge finally induced the issuance of a license to her.

But yet, for every case advanced to court action, hundreds of others disdain to sue. For, all too often—apart from the overwhelming odds against overturning the octopodous discretion of the administrative agencies—the great cost of newspaper notoriety is a price too high to pay.

With such as the recently headlined story "Police Applicant Wins Court Fight"—where the successful suitor's complete identity, including name, residence, and Children's Court background were fully laid bare in the public pillory—one can only repeat with Pyrrhus of old, "Yes, but if we have another such victory, we are undone."

In the dizzying doublethink of arbitrary bureaucratic action, the New York City Police License Division recently disqualified an applicant for a tow-truck driver's license because of his drug-related misdemeanor conviction—notwithstanding his successful emergence from a two-year methadone treatment program, implemented by the judicial grant of a "certificate of relief" from the disability of his conviction.

Angrily pleading for reconsideration in her son's behalf, the youth's widowed mother wrote Mayor John V. Lindsay: "How long can a 24-year-old man live on welfare at $77 a week? How long before someone really cares about my son and others like him?"

Again, nothwithstanding the salutary rule laid down by an appellate court that the discretion vested in an administrative agency to grant or withhold a license must be "consistent with the policy of the State to assist in the rehabilitation of persons convicted of crimes"—the very same court, by a three-to-two vote, deemed fit to uphold the denial of a license to a longshoreman applicant whose only criminal offense was committed over fifteen years ago.

In a ringing dissent, Mr. Justice Owen McGivern wrote the following opinion.

> I feel that since the Legislature gave the commission the discretionary power to recognize rehabilitation, it should have done so here, at least to the extent of giving the petitioner a probationary status. His last criminal offense was over fifteen years ago. Actually, he worked on the docks, as copper, until 1960 without incident; and had worked as a longshoreman until 1958 having started at the age of seventeen years. It was the only way of life he knew and loved. Said he: "Well, I have been down here most of my life. I was contented with the work. It's a good income for my family. It's my whole life since I have been a kid."
>
> It thus seems particularly poignant to me, and a social and an economic waste, to deny this ablebodied veteran an opportunity now to do hard labor because of some misdeed done in the long ago under the stress of temptation about which we know not. He petitions us now not to work in Tiffany's, nor at Fort Knox, nor as a cashier in a bank. He begs the privilege of wield-

ing a bale hook on the open piers, in cold of winter and the heat of summer, in order to put bread on the family table. I vote to give him a chance.

We have before us a family man, forty-five years of age, whose only skills are attuned to the waterfront. For ten years he has been forced to scrounge around, unsuccessfully, for odd jobs as a janitor, trucker, bartender, to support an ailing wife and child, getting by only by help from Veterans welfare. He has stayed straight and clean for fifteen years. He comes supported by attestations by professionals in social work, by the family physician, and by neighbors. And there is nothing in this record to controvert these representations that the applicant is completely rehabilitated. Society cannot possibly suffer from an extension of mercy by permitting this man to do hard work, on the unrefuted evidence of his rehabilitation. Quite the reverse.

In Las Vegas, New York City, and elsewhere, a slew of musicians, entertainers, and nightclub personnel—many of them gifted and reputable artists—have been literally padlocked out of employment under the screening gauntlet aimed at ex-offenders by the licensing authorities. Among other notables, the talented Billie Holiday and the blind blues singer Ray Charles found themselves victimized into ostracism by the fingerprint barriers. The nightclub comedian Lenny Bruce was exiled from the New York scene following his obscenity conviction in 1964 only to die of a drug overdose in Los Angeles a short two years afterwards. The situation was such that Frank Sinatra insistently boycotted all New York City nightclubs since 1957, in symbolic protest against the demeaning rules.

"Why must I stand for the humiliation of being fingerprinted before I can get a card to work New York night clubs?" asked one girl singer. "I don't have to be fingerprinted like a common criminal to get a job as a cashier handling money. Are my songs that dangerous to the public welfare?"

Typically, another famous musician, who had become addicted to narcotics as a result of medical treatment for an illness, and who had adamantly refused to submit to the screening requirements for a New York City cabaret license, voiced his feelings. "I will not go through the degradation of groveling before some ignoramus in the police to plead for the right to play my music in public," he said. "Thank God there are other states and cities with a little more enlightenment than that shown by New York's notorious blue-nose night club rules. I have not used narcotics in years and I refuse to consider myself a menace to society, particularly saloon society."

When the late lovable humorist known to the entertainment world as Lord Buckley made the fatal mistake of misrepresenting his past criminal record to the cabaret licensing authority, the police abruptly called the curtain on his career, right at the end of his performance. He had been convicted nineteen years earlier on a drunkenness charge and had been arrested (but not convicted) two years later for possession of marijuana.

In the midst of a long legal wrangle to recover his lifted license, Lord Buckley suddenly died of a massive stroke—and his death touched off a bitter public controversy.

The president of the American Guild of Variety Artists, Joey Adams, enraged over the "martyred" Buckley, publicly stated: "I think the police would do better if they fingerprinted some of the customers who show up in the cabarets." The redoubtable Ed Sullivan, on whose television program Buckley had been featured on nine different occasions, and who had been preparing to testify as a character witness for the beleaguered entertainer just before his death, delivered this eulogy: "He was a wonderful, decent man. During the war, he was part of my troupe that entertained in hospitals all over the country. Nobody found it necessary to screen him then and have him carry a police card." And Buckley's own aroused lawyer publicly avowed, "We intend to get Mr. Buckley's card back posthumously, so he can be buried with it."

Not long after, all licensing and fingerprinting requirements of nightclub entertainers in New York City were finally abandoned.

Witness the pathetic case history of a medical doctor who had forfeited his license following his conviction for an abortion. Paroled after serving a prison term of two to four years for the crime, he had been granted a full pardon by the governor. Then, in the midst of World War II, he promptly offered his services to the Medical Corps of the United States Armed Forces, but was rejected because of his record of conviction, despite the pardon. To maintain his family, he obtained a night-shift war job with the American Locomotive Company as a checker and storekeeper at $45.00 per week, charged with the duties of keeping records of all cars coming in and out and checking out the material transported in the cars of the company.

In the meantime, he applied to the Board of Regents for restoration of his license but was curtly turned down. Two years later, still hopeful, he applied again—bolstering his petition with commendatory letters from seven reputable doctors of his own community, all urging his restoration to the profession. The commissioner of public safety, as well as the city judge, joined in approbation of his petition, as did the principal of the school which three of the ex-doctor's children attended, as well as the foreman of the war plant in which he worked during his exile from the medical profession, all ardently adding their voice of support. Even the assistant district attorney who had prosecuted him and the trial judge who had presided over his sentence further documented his plea with weighty letters of support in his behalf.

Again, without even the formality of a hearing, his application for restoration was once more summarily rejected.

Turning to the courts in a last desperate bid for vindication, he commenced a mandamus proceeding for an order to compel the Board of Regents to issue the license. Throwing himself upon the full mercy of the court, he bared his very soul.

> I have lived and breathed medicine and surgery. That is all that I in my heart know and understand, and I humbly request

that this court will give me another chance to serve in my permanent vocation, mankind, my country, my family, my state, my community and myself. Since my release, I have rehabilitated myself and I bear no grudge or malice toward society but I find myself diverted from that type of service to which I had formerly dedicated my life's work, namely in the practice of medicine and surgery for the benefit of mankind.

At long last, the state supreme court finally granted his petition. In an opinion expressing grave doubt as to his guilt, it held that the Board of Regents had acted arbitrarily and directed the restoration of the license.

But the triumph was short-lived. The Board of Regents quickly appealed the decision to an appellate court. By a divided vote, the court upheld the Board of Regents and declared, "If, in this instance, the sinner is to be forgiven, this absolution must come from the Regents and not from the courts."

Witness the plight of a youth who ranked first in a written examination for appointment as educational director in the Department of Correction. In his personal history to the Municipal Civil Service Commission, he had trustingly declared that he had been convicted some seven years earlier on a larceny charge in Philadelphia, now dimmed in the aftermath of his later achievements.

What he had disclosed was that, after serving the minimum sentence and gaining his parole, he had assumed a position as director of research in an educational bureau of Columbia University. While thus engaged, he had enrolled as a student of the Columbia University Extension Department, avidly pursuing his studies into the summer sessions and winning the degree of Bachelor of Science. And by the time he graduated, he was in charge of a correctional project involving inmates of the New York City Reformatory.

To top it off, he had also won a full and unconditional pardon from the governor of the state of Pennsylvania.

Notwithstanding this formidable background of credentials,

the Civil Service Commission disqualified him on moral grounds of his criminal past. The fact that the commissioner of correction specially interceded for him with the civil service authorities, fervently urging a reconsideration of its action, availed him nothing.

Thus was lost to the service of the state, and to the cause of correction, one of its most promising fighters for the reconditioning of minds broken by a criminal record.

In the case files of the Probation Department of the Brooklyn Supreme Court is the saga of a nineteen-year-old high school graduate who was drawn into the vortex of the second punishment through the joyride theft of a car. Donald had never been in trouble before. His father was a retired policeman, now working in a bank. His mother was an IBM supervisor; an older brother was a graduate civil engineer.

Predictably enough, he had been favored with a "youthful offender" status—thus anesthetizing his criminal act against future stigmatization; and, of course, he had completed his probation satisfactorily. He then obtained a commitment to a promising job with a public utility. But suddenly and abruptly, the offer of employment was withdrawn because—he was told—he lacked the necessary experience. But Donald knew differently.

The probation officer immediately contacted the utility's personnel manager. Stonily obdurate, the organization man simply stated that though he was personally sympathetic, company policy rigidly forbade the hiring of any ex-offender. Again the probation officer argued that Donald had committed no crime in the eyes of the law. The effort proved futile, for the company absolutely couldn't assume the responsibility of permittting Donald to visit customers' homes. Undaunted, the probation officer finally prevailed upon the personnel manager to submit the issue to the executive office for a last-ditch policy decision. At long last, the ramparts fell; the utility finally did yield.

Here, it was the evangelical fervor, the dogged perseverance, and the abiding faith of a correctional officer that had helped restore a youthful ex-offender into society, under the balm of a protective law.

But droves of other beleaguered youths attest otherwise. There are too few probation departments in the service of these deprived offenders. And in the sparse areas where true probation is functional, the hard fact is that the impossible demands of the oppressive caseloads they normally carry have diluted their strength and effectiveness.

Literally hundreds of messages have come to me from convicted offenders sincerely pleading for the opportunity of a genuine chance to start anew. Common to all is the bitter mosaic of endless frustration, and a deep, deep longing for forgiveness.

One of them goes in this vein.

I am an ex-convict and an ex-alcoholic. I started drinking while serving honorably with the United States Air Force during World War II and until recently had been drinking ever since. As a result of my extensive drinking, I had trouble holding a job and was arrested on several occasions for being drunk and disorderly. Last year, while under the influence of liquor, I committed my first major crime. I wrote a letter to a man trying to extort money from him. The Postal Authorities picked me up and I made a statement immediately confessing my crime. I was sentenced to serve 6 months in a Federal Institution and was released after serving 5 months at Federal Detention Headquarters in New York City. While serving time I became interested in prison work and some of the guards suggested that I apply for that type of work after my discharge.

I have been completely rehabilitated in more ways than one. Not only would I never do wrong again, but I haven't touched a drop since leaving prison and never intend to drink again. But, it appears, I am the only person who believes this.

Recently, I took a Civil Service examination for the position of "Correctional Officer." I knew that if I could land such an important position, I had an excellent chance of getting my family back. My wife left me after my arrest. I passed the examination very easily but the Civil Service Board in Leavenworth, Kansas, rule me "ineligible because of suitability." I am not the dramatic type, but I sincerely believe I would make a better Correctional Officer than a man without a record. "A scalded cat flees from water." That is the way I feel about it. I am actually afraid to commit even the smallest infraction of a law or regulation.

I am applying to you as a last resort for help but even if I never hear from you, I shall not hate anybody. I am not the vindictive type. I believe the Penal Institutions are for rehabilitation purposes. I wish that the people who set up these institutions believe in it. They certainly don't practice what they preach.

Though good intentions abound everywhere, the fulfillments are few and far between. Profoundly symptomatic of the macabre letdowns was the aborted attempt by the public-spirited *Saturday Review* to open the gates of employment to ex-offenders, offering its own columns to the business community as a clearinghouse for available jobs.

Five months later, the editorial pages poured out a rueful confession of failure.

No more than half a dozen people have had bona fide job interviews as a result of the project. Many promising beginnings have failed to bear fruit, since for one reason or another prospective employers have found themselves unable to hire an ex-convict after all. One business executive telephoned immediately after the project was announced to say he would welcome any ex-convicts he might interview. But a few days later he called back in embarrassment to report that top management had, on second thought, vetoed the idea on grounds that it might be bad for business if customers found out. Another businessman, at first eager to participate in the project, had to bow out reluctantly after his partner turned thumbs down.

And, in a parting shot, the magazine bluntly declared:

In the end, the answer may lie in our understanding the cost to a society of supporting more than 200,000 men and women behind bars, many of whom follow the tragic circuit from prison to crimes on the outside and back again. Some of us flinch and blanch when it is suggested that we welcome those men and women back with no irrelevant reservations when they are finally freed. But the risks inherent in this approach are slight in comparison with the danger and desperation attendant on the present situation.

A chilling foretaste of the second punishment hovers over every candidate for parole from the prisons and penitentiaries of the nation, as the standardized letters of rebuff from potential employers keep coming back with appalling regularity.

"I still never met a guy coming out who didn't have one thing going for him at the beginning, namely the will and determination to try and go straight, to get a job and settle down," stated Melvin Rivers, ex-offender and past president of the prison reform–minded Fortune Society. But yet, to hear Mr. Rivers tell it, the closing circle of a criminal record kept him out of construction work because he couldn't get a union card, turned him back as a singer with a choral group because he couldn't get an entertainer's cabaret license for work in any place where alcoholic beverages were served, and most ironic of all, barred him from a license to engage in the one occupation he had mastered in prison, barbering—thus forcing him back into crime and into prison, over and over again.

In a revealing study of a group of federal prisoners who had been test-paroled without the ready availability of a suitable job, Professor Donald Glaser and a University of Illinois team of researchers found that fully one-third of the group had failed to attract any employment whatever during the first three months of their release. And as to those who did find jobs, the disheartening discovery was that the median income for the entire group was only $80 for the first month, $179 the second, and $207 the third.

The respected Prison Association of New York asks, "Why this recidivism? The answer lies in the inadequate correction programs and the sad fact that our correctional system does not correct. It is not enough that we house prisoners under decent living conditions, with decent clothes and adequate food. We must also feed their minds and spirits. Our failure to do this will result in a merry-go-round of criminals."

Warden Lawes of Sing Sing Prison declares, "We know now why men come back to prison a second, third or fourth time. It is because society lacks faith in its own measures for rehabilitation. It is because the prisoner, on his discharge from prison, is conscious of invisible stripes fastened upon him by tradition and prejudice."

"The last thing I wanted was to see the inside of a prison again," says Carmelo Soraci, the life-termer who finally won parole after his gifted hands had fashioned the beautiful stained glass windows of Sing Sing Prison. "I wanted no part of crime or the law. I just wanted a job and to live a normal life."

Yet Soraci did return to prison after being fired by an art director from his first post-prison job solely because of his record. In quick succession, two other openings vanished from under him for exactly the same reason. "This went on for two months. I became bitter and didn't care about anything. I wanted a job, any kind of work," he said. "I was again arrested for forgery, and this time to buy food for my family, and sentenced to Sing Sing."

Disadvantaged as they are at every turn, there is not even the oasis of a self-help sanctuary to which the reform-minded ex-offender could turn for moral uplift or mutual encouragement. If one were a chronic alcoholic, the open arms of an Alcoholics Anonymous would readily rally behind him in spiritual and material succor. If he were a drug addict in search of therapy, he would be warmly welcomed into the confraternity of his peers in Odyssey House, Phoenix House, or Synanon. If he were a compulsive gambler, he would soon hear the beckoning call of Gamblers Anonymous in the friendly outreach by the saved towards the sinners.

But there dare not be any communion of "Ex-Offenders Anonymous," where even the truly reform-minded denizens of the second punishment could congregate together for mutual encouragement and empathy. For, in the conditioned reflex of our own warped attitude towards ex-offenders—as already shamefully manifested in the community's reaction to the rehabilitative half-way houses—the chances are that they would be assailed for consorting with criminals.

Enigmatically, we would spare no effort or expense to assure a fair trial to any accused, yet, grotesquely, we turn our backs on the ex-offender once the judicial curtain is finally drawn.

Witness the four-month-long Calley court-martial growing out of the My Lai massacre, the longest trial in military history; or the grindng wheels of justice in the Bobby Seale six-month-long murder prosecution, distinguishing itself at its very inception with a jury of seven blacks and five whites ultimately chosen out of a total of 1,035 veniremen examined. Compare the painstaking fifteen-month-long trial of the Black Panthers in New York, at an estimated cost of well over two million dollars to the state; the nine-and-one-half-month trial of Charles Manson in Los Angeles, cost-figured at about one million dollars; the Angela Davis trial resulting in her final acquittal at the hands of a white jury; the freed Edgar H. Smith, Jr., who walked away from the death house at Trenton State Prison after a total of nineteen appeals had been filed in his behalf by state-appointed counsel— these are truly living testaments to our unswerving passion for justice to all until a fair verdict of guilt is finally sealed.

The riddling anomaly is that we would grant American citizenship to a man merely upon a showing of good moral character for five years preceding his petition for naturalization—let bygones be bygones as to his criminal past—yet we slam the door permanently shut against the resocialization of anyone who had faltered but once against the rules anytime in his life.

Though we would not subject any man to the barbarous double jeopardy of multiple trials or punishments for the identical offense, we acquiesce in the endless gauntlet of the second punishment—amounting to an infinity of jeopardy, reaccusation, retrial, and repunishment, over and over again for a whole lifetime.

Though there is a cut-off statute of limitations firmly imbedded in our civilized law, beyond which the state may not go in exacting retribution for any offense short of murder or kidnapping, there is no statute of limitations against the never-ending stigmata of a criminal record.

A rule of law that withholds the finality of forgiveness after punishment is ended is utterly indefensible, either in the logistics of correction or in morality. We audaciously seek the forgiveness of humankind for our own first flubs, of whatever nature, criminal or otherwise, yet so far as the first offender is concerned, diffidently deny our reciprocal forgiveness in kind to the equal entreaties of others. We blandly beseech the pardon of the Almighty for our own sins of trespass, yet we will not deign to pardon those whose trespasses against us have long been expiated by due process of law.

To those who misguidedly hold that the lifetime stigma of a criminal record is, and must remain, a fixed necessity in the constellation of punishment—to the first offender and the hardened criminal alike—one answers in the words of William Pitt: "Necessity is the argument of tyrants, it is the creed of slaves."

To the few diehards who would stubbornly cling to the second punishment of the rehabilitable first offender, let them at least be true to themselves—let them candidly strike the term "rehabilitation" from the lexicon of correction and frankly proclaim the brutal truth that there never has been, nor will ever be, a genuine second chance for the first offender. Rather, let the watchword again openly be: Once a felon, always an ex-felon; once a convict, always an ex-con; once an offender, always an ex-offender; once a criminal, always a criminal.

Thus, at least, it would absolve their minds of the sins of hypocrisy and fraud against the ex-offender, and it would deliver their souls from the myth that one can punish and correct at the same time.

The choice before us is clear; there is no middle ground. If, in Webster's definition, rehabilitation means the "full restoration of one's former good name and capacity," there is no piddling alternative to the complete, unequivocating obliteration of the second punishment.

Bad enough in the scheme of punishment are the envenomed bitternesses engendered among politicized prisoners because of an undeserved or unnecessary commitment to imprisonment, or an excessively harsh or disparate sentence at the hands of an insensitive judge.

It is not easy to cool the rage of those sentenced to five-, ten-, or even twenty-year prison sentences commonly meted out for the mere smoking of marijuana—stacked against the suspended sentence of a police detective for selling heroin in a bargain plea to the reduced charge of "official misconduct."

"It is hardly reassuring when one man goes to prison for years for theft while another man involved in a conspiracy to steal our freedoms is in and out of jail in a wink of an eye," observed Attorney General William B. Saxbe as to the standardized soft sentences spooned out to the Watergate convicts, in a speech recently delivered before the National Association of Attorneys General.

Hurtful enough in the battle to reclaim men's minds is the thumbs-down against a timely release at the whim of a thin-backed parole board, or the systemic brutalities and animalistic treatment accorded prison inmates in the infernos of riot-torn prisons, lock-ups, and jails throughout the land.

If stone walls do not a prison make, then surely, the eight-by-five-foot sorely constricting cells, and the sheer dehumanization of incarceration, remain an awesome imitation of the real thing.

All these grievances cry for the rectifying hand of a just society—without refueling their smoldering resentments with the lethal second punishment awaiting them at the very threshold of the prison gates into the community-at-large.

The bromidic theorem of penological revisionism is that prisons have failed in their essential mission of rehabilitation and reform because so many of their inmates do repeatedly come back. But in truth it is we rather than the keepers of the prisons who are the real gremlins. It is not the prisons so much that have failed in their essential mission of deterrence through humane incarceration, but we ourselves—in the post-prison syndrome—who are the real catalytic agents of their continued criminality.

If the crime of punishment is the irreversible, raw lifetime sentence underlying every criminal conviction, the crime of "correction" is our benign neglect of the first offender at the very cradle of criminality.

"Since ninety-eight percent of all state and federal prisoners will return to walk the streets of our communities again, there is little hope for the future unless we provide the necessary programs to change their life-styles," declared Norman A. Carlson, director of the Federal Bureau of Prisons in a recent speech before the Houston Rotary Club. "Without some place to go—without some concerned citizen willing to provide a second chance—all correctional programs are meaningless."

The tragedy is that the lifelong punishment of social degradation was never meant to be—for we do not in our hearts will it, nor has anyone in the official seat of correction, in the tribunals of justice, or in the rule of natural law ever sanctioned it or condoned it as such. In the stark words of the criminologist Edwin Sutherland, it is an "unintended consequence of punishment."

The chief judge of the Court of Appeals, the ranking judicial tribunal of the state of New York, long ago expressed it as follows.

> We would never go so far, I am sure, as to say that because a man had been in prison he remained a criminal all his life. Some men, as we know, with no criminal propensities at all have made mistakes, been overtaken by temptation and paid the penalty the State demands. We would not add to their burden

by saying or even intimating that they shall be shunned or classed as criminals. . . . Persons who have been convicted of crime and served the sentence imposed are not thereafter barred from society or intercourse with other human beings; they are not outcasts, nor to be treated as such. The Legislature did not intend to close the door to reformation, repentance or a new try at life.*

Chief Justice Warren E. Burger, in his very first public statement after assuming office as the head of the United States Supreme Court, stated: "We take on a burden when we put a man behind walls, and that burden is to give him a chance to change. If we deny him that, we deny his status as a human being and to deny that is to diminish our humanity and plant the seeds of future anguish for ourselves."

The intolerant criminalization of the first offender—the unremitting denigration of his natural right to regain the self-esteem and trustful respect of others—the lasting repression of his basic prerogatives of citizenship: to vote, to serve on juries, to hold public office, to engage in the licensed occupations and professions, the systematic blacklisting from employment—all add up to a wondrous witch-hunt clashing head on with the highest teachings in the curriculum of correction.

The price we pay in retributive recidivism is frightful enough. But the price we really pay runs far deeper—in the gut of the national welfare. By criminalizing scores of millions of our people with the ineradicable scar of a criminal record, we have undermined the very pillars of our democracy. For the quintessence of our democracy inheres in the individual self-esteem of each and every member. Our strength and vitality as a nation stems, seed and root, out of the mutual respect and inwrought equality that is the birthright and patrimony of every American.

An egalitarian society that suffers the permanent criminalization of its people on so massive a scale—forcing its neophyte

* Chief Judge Frederic E. Crane, in *People* v. *Pieri,* 269 N.Y. 315, 327, 199 N.E. 495, 499 (1936).

offenders into a dead end of hopelessness, with no chance to undo the past, and offering no outlet for reparatory relief from lifelong degradation—cannot but draw of its own lifeblood and, in the final reckoning, cannot long endure.

Under the heel of the ailing Weimar Republic, the criminal outcasts were among the first to emerge from the woodwork as the charter storm troopers of Adolf Hitler.

"Those who see in the preservation of the existing social order the ultimate purpose of their lives will not come to us," admitted the führer in *Mein Kampf*. When urged by General Ludendorff to expel the criminal undesirables from the budding Brown Shirt movement—those who, as William L. Shirer described it, "flocked to the party as if to a natural haven"—Hitler candidly wrote in the *Voelkischer Beobachter*, on February 24, 1925, "I do not consider it to be the task of a political leader to attempt to improve upon, or even to fuse together, the human material lying ready to his hand."

It was hardly surprising that the ultra-rightist Minutemen of California, girding for guerrilla warfare against our democratic society, had been originally spearheaded by two ex-convicts who, in their blatant bid for new recruits, cannily announced that "even a felony record is not a bar to membership."

Nor is it pure chance alone that, after a marauding gang of 154 youths had been caught in the early 1960s desecrating the outer walls of many New York City synagogues with swastika smearings, it was found by Professor Martin Deutsch of the Department of Psychiatry at New York Medical College that over one-half of the youths arrested had previous police records.

It is worth pondering that more than two-thirds of the 3,927 Watts rioters taken into custody by the Los Angeles police were found to have had previous arrest records. In the same familiar pattern, a profile of the Detroit riots that rocked the nation in the summer of 1967 revealed that 48.6 percent of the 7,223 arrested had previous criminal records.

The gnawing question is: What subliminal nexus is there

between the stigmatic record and their common antiestablishment rebelliousness against the system, under the banner of any cause?

For the black casualties of the second punishment—the truly hard-core unemployed trapped in the self-perpetuating circularity of poverty, criminality, and tenured stigmatization—the oppressions are infinitely compounded. The bill of rights we offer to the black masses of convicted offenders—many of them victimized by purely discriminatory arrests and convictions—is but an empty dream in the face of the impassable barrier of the criminal record.

"Unemployment and underemployment are among the persistent and serious consequences of disadvantaged minorities," grimly acknowledged the National Advisory on Civil Disorders in 1968. "The pervasive effect of these conditions on the racial ghetto is inextricably linked to the problems of civil disorder."

It is small wonder that the Presidential Riot Commission urgently recommended to the nation that "artificial barriers to employment and promotion must be removed by both public agencies and private employers."

It is an intriguing thought that practically all of the saber-rattling separatist revolutionaries in the vanguard of the black liberation movement had been each shadowed by criminal records long before their anarchic spleen had exploded into uncompromising warfare against the existing order.

Looking backward, who can really tell whether Malcolm X, the embittered protagonist of the pro-African movement, or Huey Newton, the "supreme commander" and founder of the nihilistic Black Panther Party, or Eldridge Cleaver, the self-exiled plenipotentiary of its "International Section," or the terroristic Donald D. Freeze, self-styled general field marshal Cinque of the Symbionese Liberation Army, or the intractable anarchist of Soledad Prison, George Jackson—to name but a few ex-offenders in the forefront of revolution—might not have more readily aligned themselves within the system, had society seasonably tendered to each of them a true second chance?

Was it pure accident alone that Bobby Seale finally emerged

as cofounder of the renegade Black Panthers—rather than as a leading partisan of nonviolent change within the established framework of the democratic ethic—right in the wake of a court-martial conviction and ruinous dishonorable discharge from the Ellsworth Air Force Base, which, as the sentencing court had correctly foreseen, would forevermore hound him out of the main-stream of civilian job and equal rights opportunities for a whole lifetime?

Consider Robert Collier, the revolutionary convicted of crim-inal conspiracy to blow up the Statue of Liberty, the Washington Monument, and the Liberty Bell, who revealingly unburdened his own inner distress in the autobiographical *Look For Me in the Whirlwind.*

> And I had to make a living, of course. I lost it because of the Air Force Discharge. It wasn't exactly dishonorable, but it had a jive wording of "discharged under other than honorable con-ditions." If I told the truth, I wasn't hired in the first place, and if I didn't, then the people who hired me found out about it and I was automatically fired. So I took to the streets—gambling, hustling, using my wits to make a living.

In the vacuum of untested suppositions, who can really tell what course this country might have taken had we with foresight focused our compassion, our concern, our forgiveness towards the prison inmates of the nation—in the very infancy of their criminal careers—in time to have reached and turned around even such seasoned criminals as the escaped ex-con of Missouri State Penitentiary, long before he had finally pulled the trigger against Martin Luther King?

Who can safely say that the second punishment of every one of these convicted persons, even from their very first offense onwards, had played no role in the metamorphic destiny of such as the turned-around Tania, twenty-year-old Patricia Campbell Hearst; Patricia Soltysik, college-bred theoretician of the Sym-bionese movement; Camilla Hall, daughter of a Minnesota minister; or of such cohorts as the brainy Nancy Ling Perry, erstwhile Barry Goldwater conservative; Angela Atwood, education major at Indiana State University; and William L. Wolfe, "Amerika"-obsessed son of a straight Pennsylvania doctor?

In retrospect, one cannot but flinch at the official report of the National Commission on the Causes and Prevention of Violence, following the sickening train of assassinations that overtook this country in the 1960s: "We need not resolve the interminable hen-and-egg debate over the primacy of nature versus nurture to conclude that man has the cultural capacity to minimize his recourse to violence."

The agonizing and haunting truth is that, in the never-never land of what might have been, we have never even tried.

Among the endless spin-offs of the second punishment, the evidence is persuasive that there is an interconnection between the blight of a criminal record darkening the homes of so many troubled American families—fifty million strong—and the tidal wave of juvenile criminality now engulfing every section of the nation.

It is undeniable that the tenured criminalization among scores of millions of ex-offenders cannot but have contributed a dominant causal part in undermining the economic security, the personal welfare, and the structural stability of millions of our families. The tragic proof is all around us in the chronic fatherlessness of countless broken homes.

Former Attorney General Ramsey Clark, in *Crime in America*, offers the estimate that approximately three-fourths of all prisoners at the federal youth centers had come from broken homes.

The research team of Sheldon and Eleanor Glueck found that 80 percent of the delinquents in a group of one thousand families in the underprivileged back streets of Boston had been chronically handicapped by a parentage of criminal background, with a pattern of a deserting father predominating. Summarizing their findings in *Unraveling Juvenile Delinquency*, a study com-

paring five hundred delinquent boys with a matching control
group of five hundred nondelinquents, the Gluecks stated:

> An old truism rediscovered by modern psychiatrists, psychol-
> ogists, educators, and workers with youth is that the family is
> the cradle, not only of most of the ideas, sentiments and attitudes
> of the growing child, but also of most of his insecurities, anxi-
> eties, tensions, and other emotional distortions. . . .
>
> It would seem obvious that parents who themselves had been
> reared in an atmosphere of intellectual and educational inferior-
> ity, of physical and mental disease, and of drunkenness and
> crime would not be likely to bring to the rearing of their own
> children the security, the happiness and the sound moral stan-
> dards which constitute so necessary a culture medium for whole-
> some emotional and intellectual development, especially in the
> competitive and exciting environment of underprivileged urban
> areas.

The burning corollary, then, is: In the character-molding
incubus of the parent-child relationship, what can one reasonably
expect the criminalized, stigma-laden father to transmit to an
impressionable and reactive child when he himself has been
psyched out of contention by a debilitative punishment that society will never let him undo?

Where have we failed from turning the ex-offender—in Dean
Roscoe Pound's words—into "a happy asset to society, and not
a discouraged potential liability"?

Most sinister of all among the feedbacks of the second punishment is its heavy impact upon the drug scourge. The vicious
circle of drug addiction and drug-connected criminality—compounded by the job-denying police record of every convicted
addict—has not only subverted the public safety for every one of
us but, by the very same stroke, has created the artificial barrier
of a criminal life sentence against all real hope of full rehabilitation, particularly for the convicted addict.

Consider the outlook. Over 50 percent of all serious crimes
against person and property are now drug connected.

All the signs point to an increasing incidence of addiction among our population, with all that it portends against our national safety and security, and there is no end in sight. "This state has spent three-quarters of a billion dollars in pursuing every possible approach to drug abuse that showed promise, more than the federal government and the states put together," reported Nelson Rockefeller to the New York legislature in his 1972 state message. "Still, no real answer to the drug problem has been found."

In January, 1974, New York's special State Commission to Evaluate the Drug Laws dramatically confirmed that more than 90 percent of rehabilitated addicts have criminal records. "The grave risk presented by a failure to absorb these people into the job market is threefold," it said. "The money expended for treatment will have been wasted; that instead of returning upwards of $1,000 per year in taxes, these rehabilitated addicts will be receiving over $2,000 apiece in welfare; and, through forced inactivity, some of them are bound to slip back to unlawful drug use and conduct associated with such drug use."

An astounding 25 percent of all Vietnam veterans have been reported addicted to hard drugs, practically all now enslaved to a costly fix, and practically all peculiarly vulnerable to a drug-connected criminal record.

To the explosive mix of that background, add the ingredient of tens of thousands of Vietnam veterans who were officially stripped of their uniform because of drug addiction—all now circulating in our midst under the millstone of the second punishment.

With all the current modalities of methadone treatment, or the new experimentations in heroin maintenance and other trial projects, we will never attain the ideal of a drug-free, inner-directed, fail-safe cure until we grasp the basic truth that the addicted offender must also be effectively detoxified of his stigmatic record.

Harlem spokesman Livingston L. Wingate, former director of

the New York Urban League, put it thus: "Now what good would
it do to detoxify him and send him right back out to the same
community, the same environment which knocked him down in
the first place?"

Right on target was New York City's commissioner of Addiction Services Agency, Graham S. Finney, who urged the prompt
"removal of all artificial restrictions on the employment of the
former addicts in order to assure their reentry into society,"
candidly adding: "Let us be quite honest. America is today losing
its race to conquer addiction, its manifestations and its causes.
Worse still, as a nation, we are not even yet trying to do so."

The case-wisened Drug Abuse Council, powered by the Ford
Foundation, the Commonwealth Fund, the Carnegie Corporation,
the Henry Kaiser Family Foundation, and the Equitable Life
Assurance Society, reported to the nation in August, 1973, its
salient findings that there was a vital link between employment
and addiction. "Given the absence of training and employment
opportunities," it said, "all the clinical talk of changing the addict's
life-style through counseling and therapy, seems absurd, if not
vicious."

It is not too often that the twain shall meet between a willing
employer and a convicted ex–drug addict genuinely motivated
towards the straight world of rehabilitation.

Just such a synergistic happening did unfold when Tom, a
twenty-one-year-old bearded youth—who had spent a half-year
in a drug treatment program after a drug-related criminal conviction—applied for a job opening at a small burglar alarm
company in Brooklyn, operated by an empathetic twenty-eight-
year-old decorated Vietnam veteran. Without too much ado, the
owner hired the youth as an installer of alarm systems. "Tom was
very straightforward about it," the owner later recalled. "All my
life I spewed liberal thinking, but this put me on the spot." And
he added: "It was the best thing I ever did. He's trustworthy,
dependable, the customers love him."

It was not too long, however, before the screws of the second punishment began to close in on both of them. In short order, the state's Department of Motor Vehicles lifted Tom's license to drive for his past conviction of driving under the influence of drugs. For eight long months, until the license was finally restored, Tom's employer was forced to hire a surrogate driver to accompany the grounded ex-offender on his appointed rounds. "Needless to say, during that period, we lost money on him. The thought that was going through my mind was not Tom, but other people like him—there must be thousands of them—and how difficult it must be for them, how hopeless if they tried to do it alone. One state agency will spend millions to reform them, and then another will go out of its way to hinder them."

But even at that, the trials and tribulations for Tom's benefactor were far from over. In quick succession, his insurance company abruptly canceled his auto liability policy after a routine check on the seven drivers in his employ had turned up Tom's drug-driving criminal record, throwing the insurance coverage into a high-risk assigned pool and a doubling of his premium. For good measure, the insurance company served notice that it was canceling his workmen's compensation policy as well.

And, in tactical response to the outraged public protests, the public relations office of the insurance carrier purred out a sanctimonious news release assuring the general public that the cancellation of the policies had "nothing whatsoever to do with Mr. ———'s use of drugs."

Rehabilitation, anyone?

3

Anatomy of the First Offender

Surely, one would surmise that a tactic of oppression so consumingly destructive to the human psyche as the second punishment has to be vindicable by some such compensatory value as deterrence, or at least, by some other overriding concern for the public safety—for, certainly as to the first offender, it would be utter madness to suffer a scourge of such dimensions for any lesser rationale.

The irony is, however, that when the bird-dog scent of a criminal record is most needed to signal the presence of the dangerous offender in our midst, it is far beyond our grasp; but where it is least vital to the public security, as in the case of the inherently redeemable first offender, it is always around. While the self-immunized recidivistic criminal roams freely undetected, his opposite number—the genuinely redeemable first offender—remains constantly exposed in the pillory of the second punishment.

The lesson we have learned is that no hard-core criminal has ever been kept out of circulation by his criminal record. The barriers are too easily bypassed, the detours too plentiful, the back doors of self-absolution practically without limit. Though we ritualistically fingerprint, polygraph, and brainwash the first offender, we casually expose our very homes and business enterprises to the really dangerous criminals in our midst. Though their fingerprint records may be in the far-off archives of the FBI, or data-banked in a sophisticated computer, or their dossiers or criminal files formally lodged in the repository of the local police, the criminal behind the record remains inscrutably at large.

The recidivistic offenders may be effectively channeled out of the mainstream of some legitimate businesses or governmental operations through fingerprinting devices and security clearances, but their unrestricted access to opportunity elsewhere has left little to comfort public security.

Though we have purged the crime-infested waterfront and the houses of Wall Street by fingerprinting and licensing of all securities personnel, the thefts and peculations abound as ever before. While the FBI combed the land for its most wanted criminals, practically every one of them remained substantially mobile.

No criminal record stymied the daring ex-convicts who had executed the million-dollar Brinks robbery.

Bank robber Willie "the Actor" Sutton, five-time felony loser, methodically moved past bolted steel doors by posing as a Western Union messenger, a letter carrier, a firemen, and even as a policeman.

The convicted swindler Philip Musica, years earlier, successfully palmed himself off as the impeccable F. Donald Coster, president of McKesson & Robbins, until a scandalous discrepancy of eighteen million dollars in assets led to his discovery.

Bruno Richard Hauptmann, convicted as a four-time robber by the time he illegally entered this country, quietly ensconced himself in a Bronx carpenter shop shortly before he was picked up as the prime suspect in the Lindbergh kidnap-murder.

It was not until fifty-eight members of the underworld had been flushed out in secret conclave in Appalachia, New York, in 1957, that Senate investigators discovered that though the elite of the criminal kingdom were all ostensibly legitimate businessmen—mostly engaged in the operation of restaurants and taverns, manufacturing, the export-import business, and the trucking industry—no less than thirty-five of them had criminal records. Their host, a beer and soft drink distributor, had been the prime suspect in two unsolved murders.

In sum, indispensable as the criminal record is in the retainer of law enforcement—certainly as to the incorrigible and dangerous offender—it is naïve to suggest that it has proven to be an effective deterrent. The dismaying fact is that at least 80 percent of all serious crime is recidivistic in nature; only one out of every ten major crimes is ever cleared even by so much as an arrest; only one out of every fifty ever results in a punishable conviction.

It is not the spectral threat of a criminal record, nor the club of a possible criminal sentence, nor even the chancy backlash of the consequential second punishment that really deters the potential criminal. "The hard fact is," observed the eminent criminologist Austin MacCormick, "that so small a percentage of the total number of offenders are caught and convicted in America today, that legal punishment cannot be considered a major factor in the control of crime."

What does deter the criminal offender is the certainty of detection and arrest and the unswerving swiftness of condign punishment.

It is not the muffled sound of a criminal record but the blast of a police whistle, the wail of a burglar alarm, and the roar of a patrol car in active pursuit that are really decisive in the ultimate values of deterrence.

"Most criminals go into crime on the basis of a calculated risk. Most offenders, I believe, know what they are doing and do it because they think they can get away with it. If anyone wants proof of this, it might be instructive to look at the cases of those who have pleaded guilty to charges stemming from Watergate," declared Attorney General William B. Saxbe of the

Nixon administration, to an audience of wardens representting eighty institutions in the federal prison system.

Warden Clinton Duffy of San Quentin Prison, surveying the years of his stewardship from 1940–1951, noted that none of his condemned charges awaiting execution had ever given thought to the death penalty when committing the homicidal act, nor had any of them ever expected to be caught.

The Loeb–Leopold thrill murder of fourteen-year-old Bobby Franks in 1924 had its diabolical origin in the detached self-assurance of two brilliant classmates of the University of Chicago that their genius in plotting the "perfect crime" would absolutely foil any possible detection.

If the climactic penalty of capital punishment doesn't frighten off every would-be murderer, if a ninety-nine-year maximum sentence for mere possession of marijuana in Texas is not enough of a deterrrent to discourage any potential pothead, if flogging at the whipping post doesn't always daunt the Maryland wrongdoer, if a possible twenty-five-year prison sentence doesn't give pause to every budding burglar, or the heavy hand of a life sentence disincline the habitual offender out of his lifestyle of criminality —then it is only because of the smug assurance that the average criminal offender will not ever be caught, let alone convicted or punished.

Where we have gone wrong in the public security is that we have failed to differentiate the first offender from all others in the deadly ministrations of the second punishment.

The backlash against the public security has come only because we have bludgeoned the ex-offender out of his inalienable birthright to a fair and decent chance to live down his criminal past.

This is an amazing thought, considering that every unregenerate criminal now mired in an irreversible course of criminality— the second, third, fourth, and umpteenth felony repeaters in our midst—were at one critical time but first offenders in the infancy of their criminal careers and prime candidates for rehabilitation and reform. There's a mighty difference between a man's first and second offenses, Judge Curtis Bok of the Pennsylvania Supreme Court reminds us, in *Star Wormwood*. "The first offense should be regarded as a regrettable happening. Once it has been committed, devices should be applied so accurate and sure that it will not be repeated."

"Recidivism is recycling, and it is promoted by the system itself more than by any other aspect of social environment," declared Professor Marvin E. Wolfgang, chairman of the Department of Sociology at the University of Pennsylvania. "The irony of it all is not that we fail to reform but that we *cause* the return to criminality by the way we treat, handle, and process individuals. Our successes (the non-recidivists) come out that way by chance; our failures are the direct result of our methods of processing. The criminal justice system is not responsible for new clients—that is, first-time offenders. But the system *is* responsible for second and multiple offenders."

The late Monsignor Francis J. Lane, dean of American prison chaplains and beloved patron of "Father Lane's Gang," who served as spiritual adviser to the youthful inmates of Elmira Reformatory for a span of thirty-six out of his thirty-eight years in the priesthood, and who long befriended the first offender as the "neglected man" in penology, stated over and over again, "I am firmly convinced that the reason we have so many repeaters in crime is because we fail them as first offenders."

The anatomical tracing of a criminal career from the incipient stage of a first offender to the final stage of a four-time loser could be a fascinating and rewarding basis for research in recidivistic behavior. If ever an in-depth clinical study is undertaken, I offer as Exhibit 1 the case subject of Lifer No. 25558 of the New Jersey State Prison: "Please accept my sincere congratulations as I heard your answers on the Night Beat program of May 8th, in regard to giving a second chance for a first offender," he wrote.

"I hope and pray that the bill that you have sponsored in regards to this matter will pass with flying colors. I assure you that if we had a bill like this in New Jersey some twenty-five years ago, that I would not be serving a life term sentence under the habitual criminal laws. I hope that you never lose your interest in the youth of today."

And, in similar vein, the unabridged testimony of a respected New York City contractor, who must here remain nameless:

> After listening to you on the John Wingate–Night Beat Show, Thursday, May 8, 1958, I was very much impressed by the significance and importance of the arguments presented by you and the ex-convict from Elmira. I felt it my duty to write, because I am in a position to substantiate your views in more ways than one.
>
> In my youth, I also spent a term in Elmira. However, had your bill been in effect at that time, I may have avoided spending six additional years in Sing Sing Prison, because a parolee really has a very difficult time. It took six more years of my life to overcome that handicap.
>
> The proof of the pudding is that I haven't had any trouble for over 21 years now. Presently, I am a well established businessman and respected in my community, have been married 17 years and have 2 children.
>
> You have my permission to use this letter in the public interest if you so see fit. I would also be glad to appear personally to testify to that fact.

The more one probes into the anatomy of the first offender, the clearer it becomes that we have been chasing the wrong shadows in the quest for the public security.

A Spartan clean record, of itself, is as grossly misleading a yardstick of one's moral fitness and probity as is a black-bordered criminal record an incontrovertible demonstration of the very opposite. For, in too many cases, a criminal record in absentia is but the false veneer of a master criminal too skilled, too cunning, too influential, or just plain too lucky to be caught.

Some of the worst criminals in the book have led charmed

lives to their very last, untarred by the slightest blemish of a criminal record. The mockery is that an Al Capone and a Costello had to be hauled into prison, at long last, only through the back door of an innocuous federal income tax violation. Valachi, by his own admission, had served a kingpin role in a murder combine for thirty long years before he was finally bagged on a marginal narcotics charge. The septuagenarian Meyer Lansky, who surfaced almost a quarter of a century ago during the Kefauver crime hearings as a leading Mafia henchman, closed the book in sum with a mere gambling sentence in 1953 and a piddling fine for bootlegging and disorderly conduct.

Many are the unpunished guilty who have attained the windfall of escape from all prosecution simply because of the laxity or the venality of law enforcement; many have emerged neatly unscathed through the spinning turnstiles of justice only because of a faltering identification, a suborned or coerced witness, a false alibi, or a tampered jury. A study of 7,849 criminal cases in Washington, D.C., during the first six months of 1973 revealed that 37 percent of all witnesses who did come forward and testify for the prosecution "were so afraid of what might happen to them that they felt they needed protection," according to the head of the federal Law Enforcement Assistance Administration, in a speech delivered to the New York State District Attorneys Association.

Many are the plainly guilty who have won an undeserved acquittal or dismissal through due process, through the fortuity of an illegal search and seizure, an unreasonably delayed arraignment, or an involuntary confession blurted out to a blundering constable. Many have been grudgingly whitewashed with immunity in exchange for the fingering of a guilty accomplice; many have emerged Mr. Clean only through the loopholes of some technical failure of proof in the necessary corroboration of a crime, or because some hung-up jury could not unanimously agree that guilt had been proven beyond a reasonable doubt; many have escaped simply because they have been denied a speedy trial.

The notorious Jesse James and his brother Frank, whose escapades in train robberies and bank hold-ups stirred the headlines in early America, each ended their active criminal careers with nary a conviction for so much as trespassing—Frank expired in peace on a farm in Kearney, Missouri, still wearing his long-barrelled six-shooter, and Jesse was finally gunned down at the hands of an assassin gang member.

What real difference is there between the convicted first offenders against whom we harbor permanent obloquy and distrust and the unconvicted, unscarred criminal wrongdoers freely circulating in our midst?

Person for person and dollar for dollar, there is unquestionably more criminality among the nonconvicted, showily respectable white-collar thieves, swindlers, and con-merchants than there is among all the convicted elements of the population put together under the crippling stigma of a criminal record.

In the realm of tax frauds, it is estimated that unreported income each year ranges from twenty-five to forty billion dollars. "Some of this is inadvertent," states a recent task force report to the nation on *Crime and Its Impact,* "but undoubtedly a sizeable amount is deliberate, criminal evasion."

"While no reliable estimates can be made of the financial burdens produced by white-collar crime," concludes the task force report of the President's Crime Commission, "they probably are far greater than those produced by traditional common law theft offenses—robbery, larceny and burglary."

The respected criminologist Fred E. Inbau of Northwestern University intones in similar cast: "I submit this to you fully confident of its validity as to the approximation of percentages—about 85 out of every 100 persons will 'steal' if the opportunity to do so is presented to them. I feel confident that this figure is about right and I base it upon the professional experiences some of us have had in the investigation of thefts and embezzlements committed by employees of banks, merchandising companies and other commercial houses. To be sure, I am not talking about large thefts and embezzlements, but thievery nevertheless."

If we were to line up all the guilt-ridden tax cheats in the land, all the false swearers in and out of the courts of justice, all the conventional swindlers in the marts of commerce, all the white-collar criminals coursing the woodwork of big business, all the intoxicated and reckless drivers careening the nation's highways, all the casual experimenters of the euphoric drugs, all the deviate sex offenders running the gamut from private homosexuality to swinging adultery, there would be few left among us to qualify at the pearly gates of moral judgment. "There is no man so good, who, were he to submit all his thoughts and actions to law, would not deserve hanging ten times in his life," declared the philosopher Michel de Montaigne.

Though the officialdom and underlings of the banking profession are undoubtedly the most thoroughly screened lot in the nation, the Surety Association of America reports that, in one single year alone, one bank out of every eight reported frauds, forgeries, and embezzlements committed by its own impeccably finger-printed and bonded personnel; more than 8.5 percent of the losses was the work of bank presidents themselves, and almost 20 percent the handiwork of specially trusted bank managers and vice-presidents.

According to the American Bankers Association, the nation's banks suffered $16.9 million in embezzlement losses in 1969, more than double the take from all bank robberies and burglaries combined during the same year.

In the acid test of the public security, is society more victimized by the filcher of the church poorbox than by the major drug companies found guilty of conspiratorially cheating the medically indigent of $1.7 billion in the unlawful price fixing of antibiotic drugs?

Does the single conviction of a man for perjury stamp him as more obnoxious to the public safety, more to be distrusted, more chronic a liar than the carloads of unconvicted false swearers of fraudulent income tax returns, or the multitudes of unpunished perjured witnesses who sully our temples of justice day after day in every court of the land? Are all those who systematically defraud insurance companies with fictitious claims and losses, all the gluttonous swindlers lavishing padded expense accounts in our economy, more susceptible to truthfulness and veracity than the erstwhile one-shot perjurer now bound hand and foot to the lifetime second punishment?

Are the outwardly respectable entrepreneurs who recklessly pollute our waters with lethal waste, or the car manufacturers whose flimsy product is unsafe at any speed, or the tobacco tycoons who suavely tout their death-dealing cigarettes behind a Madison Avenue smokescreen, more to be trusted than the offender forevermore buried in the morass of permanent criminalization for a single brush with the law?

Is the transient dishonesty of the common thief more erosive of the public ramparts than the collusive price rigging and larcenous consumer mulcting systematically practiced by the minions masquerading under a cloak of respectability who, in the words of a sentencing judge, "have flagrantly mocked the image of the economic system of free enterprise which we profess and destroyed the model which we offer today as a free world alternative to state control and eventual dictatorship"?

Is the handcuffed first offender—be he convicted briber, bigamist, or business cheat—any more menacing to the common weal than the free-booting corporate mafia that venally funnelled fistfuls of bribable cash to the political coffers of the Watergate-scarred presidential election committee of 1972?

"In the balance sheet of moral values," editorially asked the *Christian Science Monitor:* "which is the greater crime, shoplifting or wholesale larceny through the sale of fraudulent goods?"

In bottom truth, we are all ex-offenders, who, but for the

chancy lottery of fate alone, could have been equally outcast long ago as full-fledged pariahs under the lash of the second punishment.

So blissfully ignorant are the unschooled youth of the lasting sting of a criminal conviction, so vastly do they misperceive the lifetime impact of an arrest record, that legions among them have taken the fatal plunge of their first brush with the law without the faintest idea of the interminable penal consequences.

Simply because of our own default in teaching them the rules of the game, many have ruefully learned—too late to turn back—that the misappropriation of a car for a transient joyride, or the casual smoking of a marijuana cigarette, or the mere fleeting possession of a switchblade or flick knife, blackjack, slingshot, or souvenir handgun, are among the myriad don'ts explosively lying in ambush throughout the penal codes.

Many an unwary youth has had to walk the plank of a police bust or suffer the hassle of a mind-bending prosecution for criminal possession of dangerous drugs—booby-trapped into a criminal record under catch-all statutes creating a sweeping presumption of guilt against each and every individual occupying an automobile, a room, or anywhere else where they may happen to be in close proximity to the illegal drug.

Many have learned to their eternal sorrow that even the eager consent and willingness of an underage "victim" to an act of sexual intercourse is no legally excusable defense to the invidious charge of statutory rape committed against the peace and dignity of the state. In New York, under a sleeper statute just recently enacted, even the harmless "heavy necking" with an under-seventeen female more than five years his junior could net a romantic male a cooling-off period of up to three months in jail for the misdemeanor of "sexual abuse."

Millions of our youthful first offenders have been unfairly convicted after trial under proof no longer acceptable to modern juvenile courts, now superseded by the fundamental rule that guilt must be established beyond a reasonable doubt in every case.

Literally tens of millions of our youth have fallen into the trap of a ruinous criminal record through an improvident plea of guilty, where a trial might have won an immediate acquittal or outright dismissal of the charge. They have rushed into judgment if only to spare a family from the grief and shame of scandal and notoriety, or to relieve anguished parents or wives from the emotional wastage and economic drain of a battering trial.

Countless numbers among them have copped out to the hidden life sentence of the second punishment, soothed into a guilty plea by overzealous police, abetted by the indifference and neglect of case-weary judges, win-happy prosecutors, and derelict defense counsel—and led down the primrose path of bargain justice with the promises of a suspended sentence, a grant of probation, or an unconditional discharge—all attractively giftwrapped in the simulated forgiveness of a euphemistic "second chance."

Until the precedent-shattering *Gault* decision of the United States Supreme Court in late 1967, ushering in a new era of protection for the juvenile offender, unnumbered millions of our youth had been regularly euchered into an improvident on-the-spot guilty plea, without benefit of counsel standing at their side. Considering that a plea of guilty is generally dispositive of over 90 percent of all criminal prosecutions with assembly line proficiency, one shudders to dwell on the frightful toll of miscarried justice in all the juvenile courts of this nation.

Where is there the youth who, but for the fluke stroke of fate or the chance intercession of others, has not narrowly escaped the crushing stigma of an arrest, or an irreversible adjudication as a youthful offender or juvenile delinquent?

Where is there the mature adult who can now avow upon his conscience that he has never willfully offended against the criminal laws? Who is there in all the world to say that, but for the grace of God, he too might not have suffered the second punishment of a lasting criminal record?

Astronaut Scott Carpenter, who by his own account as a

youth "stole things from stores and was just drifting around, sort of a no-good," would be the first to admit that the stamp of a police record might have grounded him forevermore from the orbiting Mercury that did eventually net him the admiration and esteem of all America.

Pat Boone, veritable idol of unspoiled manhood to millions of adoring teenagers, startled his fans with the stark revelation that when he was barely sixteen years of age, "four or five of us guys did our shoplifting. Each of us took a downtown store in Nashville at Christmas time . . . we did it for excitement, but we did it."

"Almost all youths commit acts for which they could be arrested and taken to court," reported the President's Commission on Law Enforcement. "But it is a much smaller group that ends up being defined officially as delinquent."

The shocking findings of the National Commission on Marijuana and Drug Abuse are that 24 million Americans have already sampled marijuana at least once. An additional 9.3 million have flirted with hashish, 4.7 million with LSD, peyote, or mescaline, 2.6 million with cocaine, and 2.2 million with heroin.

If the penal laws of "criminal possession" were to be strictly applied to the estimated 50 percent of all teenage Americans who have tripped with marijuana and hashish, roughly half of all our youth between the ages of sixteen and twenty in the schools and campuses across the nation would now be saddled with an arrest or conviction record which no euphoria could ever wish away.

Said a former commissioner of New York's Waterfront Commission: "I was a member of a tough gang of street fighters when I was a kid. Plenty of the fellows in the gang went on to Sing Sing and Leavenworth. These are things that stay with you. Whenever a longshoreman with a criminal record comes before me in this job, I can never escape the thought: There but for the grace of God go I."

A pilot study of hidden delinquencies among our youth revealed that of a total of over six thousand admitted offenses committed by a group of selected subjects, a scant 1.5 percent had actually been brought to public attention by arrest or juvenile court proceedings.

The criminologist Austin L. Porterfield of Texas Christian University, examining the pattern of covert misbehavior among a group of purportedly "clean" college students as compared to a group of delinquents who had come to the attention of the juvenile courts, found that every one of the 337 college students tested, of both sexes, admitted that he or she had committed one or more of the 55 offenses listed; one theological student among them confessed to a total of no less than twenty-seven acts of classic delinquency. In all, the derelictions of the unarrested college group were found to be actually far greater in number, and no less serious, than whose which had brought the less fortunate group into conflict with the law.

Sociologist Mabel A. Elliott concluded:

> Data from these studies, partial and limited though they may be, give us rather significant evidence that many lawbreakers in favored economic and social groups (probably the majority) receive no penalty at all for their offenses but instead escape punishment completely. Most of these nonconvicted offenders seemed to be leading pretty decent lives as respected citizens in their communities. We are therefore forced to speculate as to what might have happened to those persons who were prosecuted and given penal sentences if they had likewise escaped detection and conviction. Might they too have profited from the opportunity to maintain their self-respect and have become decent law-abiding citizens? Certainly it is well for us to keep in mind that the so-called law-abiding have many offenses to their discredit. Furthermore the man who escapes penal sentence escapes far more than the sentence. He escapes condemnation and stigma in the community as well.

Ponder the implications of a test study recently made of some of New York's finest by undercover police agents of the Internal Affairs Division of the New York City Police Department: Of fifty-one randomly selected patrolmen to whom had been handed "lost" wallets containing twenty dollars or more with instructions to turn them in to superior officers for possible identification of their rightful owners, a whopping total of no less than fifteen pocketed the money without so much as turning in any official report whatsoever.

Consider, too, the classic study undertaken by the Randen Foundation of New York, probing the extent of undetected criminality among the adult population in general. It circulated a questionnaire entitled "Have You Ever Committed a Crime?" to a representative cross section of citizenry consisting of the relatively crime-free intellectuals, professionals, and businessmen.

Of those who responded to this questionnaire, cataloguing a total of 49 specified offenses of the garden variety in New York's penal code, a total of no less than 91 percent—1,020 men and 678 women—admitted to the commission of one or more criminal offenses, each punishable by a maximum prison sentence of one year. More, 64 percent of the males and 29 percent of the females admitted to the commission of at least one felony. Nor have they been wanting in self-confessed recidivism, for the summary tabulation revealed that the average male committed a grand total of 18 criminal acts during his adult lifetime; the mean average for the female was a staggering 11.

Summing up, criminologist James S. Wallerstein of the Randen Foundation, in a report entitled *Our Law-Abiding Law-Breakers,* bluntly stated, "Perhaps the principal conclusion to be drawn from this study is the revelation of the prevalence of lawlessness among respectable people. The absence of a police record for many citizens arises not from their individual virtue but from sheer accident and from less than one hundred percent law enforcement. From this angle, the punitive attitude of society toward the convicted offender becomes not only hypocritical but pointless. In time to come, men may be rated not by their past mistakes but by their assets and potentialities."

By his own autobiographical confession, Mark Twain narrowly escaped criminal prosecution and a maximum two-year penitentiary term, after jumping town via the first exiting stage-coach from Nevada—a dozen paces ahead of the pursuing con-stabulary—for the criminal offense of hurling a duel challenge at a rival.

It was only by the bare skin of a hung jury that the indomita-ble Clarence Darrow was saved from the ignominy of a convic-tion for jury tampering.

Arthur Garfield Hays, the famed libertarian in the annals of the law, often told how he had unwittingly blundered into the commission of a federal crime during the early years of his legal practice, while handling a creditor's lawsuit against a bankrupt estate. "I have often wondered what my future would have been had this matter come to public scrutiny," he wrote in his own autobiography. "Things like this make one hesitate to pass judg-ment upon his fellow-men and justify skepticism of the storybook reasons for success or failure. How many men of mature years would be out of jail if all about them were known and if every infraction of the law led to punishment?"

Blessed are the favored cadres of marked offenders who have escaped the second punishment, at least in degree, through the back door of some labyrinthine corporate camouflage, or through the expedient anonymity of some trade or business pseudonym.

Luck-starred indeed are the targeted men who have managed to dodge the invidious employment quizzes and the fingerprint-ing inquisitions of bonding or licensing through the safe detours of independent free-lance salesmanship or retail enterprise, or through the privileged sanctuary of the unlicensed occupations and the unskilled jobs.

Fortune has indeed smiled upon the uniquely endowed ex-offenders whose presiding genius and virtuosity in the arts and sciences have wrought an orbital thrust powerful enough for a liberating lift-off from the constricting gravitational pull of their second punishment.

The literary talents of O. Henry far outshadowed the shackling barriers of a five-year federal prison term at Ohio Federal Penitentiary for embezzlement, circa 1898.

Art Linkletter, famed television raconteur, candidly revealed in an autobiographical spread in the *Saturday Evening Post* that he had been indicted by a federal grand jury during World War II for falsely claiming American citizenship—a "disastrous experience" he noted, "which could have ruined my career," adding: "My press agents have omitted this troublesome experience from all my biographies, of course, but there is no reason for not talking about it now."

Beloved Harry Golden miraculously emerged unscathed only because his literary reputation and personal goodness had been too deeply rooted to be hobbled by a malicious tipster who—on the very eve of a scheduled national telecast featuring the celebrated author—dropped the bomb that Harry Golden was the same Arthur Goldhurst who had been imprisoned for a federal offense a quarter of a century before. "I did everything humanly possible to avoid becoming a 'success,'" Mr. Golden later revealed. "I resisted it as long as I could hold out. Beginning in 1952, I turned down at least six of our most famous publishing houses who sent men down to Charlotte to see about a book from me. I wouldn't budge. The fear of success and popularity, no matter how remote, with the publication of a book, was too great a risk for me to take. Finally, in 1958, I permitted World to publish *Only in America,* with terror in my heart. I had to do it because I was faced with the loss of my newspaper due to the South Carolina advertising boycott."

But not all are invested with the exceptionality of superstardom capable of lifting themselves by their own bootstraps out of the quagmire of the second punishment. The scores of millions of remaining ex-offenders—the average, down-the-middle, thronging plebeians among us, preponderating over all others—will, alas, never rise clear of the overhanging pall of their criminal record.

In actuality, all men are first offenders upon the very commission of their first criminal act, even if they escape the condemnation or stigma of arrest or punishment. A criminal is no less a criminal simply because he remains undetected or unscarred.

The youth who has puffed his first marijuana reefer, or burgled his way through the first window, or thefted his first auto joyride; the embezzler who has siphoned off his very first dollar in an inaugural binge of lust or temptation; the forger who has altered his very first check—all these, in the authentic reckoning of criminality, are indeed "first offenders," though they are uncaught, unconvicted, unpunished, and untagged.

The abortionist ultimately brought to book on a manslaughter charge, who confessedly had performed no less than twenty-five thousand illegal abortions in his thriving medical practice, surely was no novitiate first offender in the arithmetic of criminality. The corporate vice-president who failed to file a federal tax return continuously for almost twenty-five years until the Internal Revenue Service finally flagged him down in 1970, certainly was no "first offender" in the nomenclature of wrongdoing. Common experience teaches us that the motorist finally bagged for intoxicated or reckless driving could easily have escaped detection dozens of times before the first arrest.

But there is a mighty psycho-legal difference between the uncaught, unstigmatized offender and the newly pegged first offender caught at last with his hand in the till.

Just as the criminal law measures its heavy punitive sanctions against the habitual offender by the delineating criterion of the "second" or "third" conviction—the number of legal *convictions* rather than the number of offenses committed in between—so does the criminal law now unleash its stigmatizing sanction against the *first* offender upon the critical moment of his very first contact with the law.

These, then, are the first offenders coursing through the criminal courts day after day—the high, the low, and the in-betweens of our society, running the whole gamut of the willful, the reckless, and even the unwary in the versatile mill of human frailties—

the recognizable peers of our own communities and of our culture, the progeny of our own homes and families—yesterday's recurring headliners, but today's "ex-cons" and "ex-offenders."

The first offender is the kid across the track busted as a car thief for the thrill of a single joyride in his neighbor's car.

It is the gang of seven high school and college youths in an affluent suburban community arrested for the burglary of some five hundred homes and businesses; the coterie of students from a minileague suburban college caught stealing some one-thousand-dollars worth of personal watches, radios, and clothing from the dormitories of nearby Princeton University.

It is the college instructor found guilty of criminal contempt for willful refusal to answer questions by a grand jury investigating the illicit use of narcotics on the campus grounds of Stony Brook College.

It is the den mother of a cub scout pack and PTA president of an upstate New York community, arrested as a common gambler for operating a wheel of fortune at a charity carnival.

It is the young couple and the doctor charged with infanticide in the mercy killing of a thalidomide-deformed baby.

It is the usury victim charged with perjury who lied to a grand jury probing his loan from an underworld banker to avoid risking his family's lives.

It is the playful mother of three children, convicted by a federal jury for causing a fake bomb scare at the New York International Airport, after flaunting a suitcase with a "time bomb" aboard a Miami-bound plane.

It is the past national commander of the American Legion fined five thousand dollars for willful failure to file an income tax return; the law school professor who pleaded guilty to tax evasion; the El Paso County judge given a five-year suspended sentence for willful failure to file federal tax returns for five successive years; the former United States commissioner of Internal Revenue sentenced to a five-year jail term and fined fifteen thousand dollars for filing a string of fraudulent income tax returns.

It is the police sergeant in charge of the Juvenile Aid Bureau and treasurer of the PAL, under grand larceny indictment for stealing two thousand dollars of the entrusted funds in his care.

It is the hospital director of food services, charged with bribery in a seventy-five-thousand-dollar kickback racket; the rock-and-roll disc jockey fined three hundred dollars after pleading guilty to accepting payola from favored record companies to plug the most popular tunes.

It is the motorist sentenced for short-changing the toll basket on the New York Thruway, unsuccessfully contending to the last that the flashing "thank you" green signal had entrapped him into a false security of absolution.

It is the exemplary columnist Murray Kempton and comedian-activist Dick Gregory, arrested on disorderly conduct charges for demonstrating near the International Amphitheatre during the 1968 Democratic National Convention.

It is the ex-reporter for the *Philadelphia Inquirer,* sentenced on a perjury conviction arising from a shakedown of businessmen by threatening to print unfavorable articles about them; the Hollywood movie producer of *King of Kings,* fined two thousand dollars and placed on six months probation for lying in a bankruptcy case that he had no Swiss bank account; the practical jokester who wound up with a six-year-to-life sentence in Los Angeles County for sprinkling LSD on potato chips at a party caper which convulsed fifty guests into an hallucinogenic nightmare.

It is the retired major general, ex-provost marshal general of the United States Army, recipient of the Distinguished Service Medal and chief of United States marshals by presidential appointment, who pleaded guilty in federal court to fraudulent embezzlement of firearms from the Chicago police for his own personal profit.

It is the trio of male faculty members of a girls college of the State University of New York who pleaded guilty to a morals charge for possessing obscene pictures.

It is the president of the Association of Process Servers, fined and placed on probation by a federal judge under the civil rights law for signing false affidavits of personal service to induce the entry of fraudulent judgments against defaulting debtors.

It is the pair of volunteer firemen, arrested after setting fire to a twenty-room mansion, sounding the alarm, and then joining seventy-three fellow volunteers in a vain effort to quench the fire.

It is the airline hostess held in fifty thousand dollars bail for smuggling four-and-a-half pounds of heroin from Paris, secreted in her girdle and brassiere.

It is the doctor arrested on a bribery charge for attempting to squelch the prosecution of his teenage son for selling marijuana; the superactivist history professor of New York University, indicted for threatening to destroy a thirty-five-million-dollar computer unless the administration agreed to furnish bail of one hundred thousand dollars to a Black Panther awaiting trial on similar charges; the Los Angeles dentist charged with draft-evasion conspiracy for supplying scores of draft-age youths, including his son, with unneeded orthodontic fittings; it is the New Jersey physician who forcibly raped a patient after putting her into a submissive hypnotic trance.

It is the son of a retired brigadier general of the United States Army, the son of a governor, the daughter of a congressman, the scion of a United States senator, all arrested for possession of marijuana and dangerous drugs.

It is the policeman stripped of his uniform after pleading guilty that he grew marijuana plants near the station house in Central Park where he had been assigned.

It is a pair of East Tennessee State University students arrested for desecrating the American flag, one of them a son-in-law of the secretary of defense of the Nixon administration.

It is the promoter of the aborted Powder Ridge Rock Festival, accused of perjury in connection with the rip-off of five hundred thousand dollars in unaccounted ticket sales.

In kaleidoscopic view, these are the one-shot situational

offenders, the singleton "criminals," the happenstantial misfits, the accidental transgressors, the once-burned-twice-shy individuals whose first arrest and conviction is, and will remain, the one and only blot against their names for a whole lifetime.

Happy experience has long proven that the first offense is the very last for the overwhelming mass of convicted first offenders. The lingering emotional shock of an arrest, the shattering ordeal of an arraignment, trial, or plea of guilty, the searing trauma of a sentencing proceeding, the agonizing wall-to-wall ennui of a prison commitment are more than most persons would care to endure more than once in any lifetime.

A recent United Nations study confirms the prevailing view that "crime and punishment remains the one unrepeated experience in their lives, whatever treatment has been awarded for the offender's first crime." In *The Criminality of Youth*, the noted criminologist Thorsten Sellin affirms, "Most persons are punished for offense against the criminal law only once in a lifetime." The British experience is similar, reported Right Honorable Lord Shawcross, Q.C., in the *American Bar Association Journal:* "Once caught, 85 percent of first offenders do not commit crimes again."

Knowledgeable wardens and "with-it" prison chaplains throughout the land will readily attest to the real resolve of every prison inmate never to return to the maddening wastage of imprisonment, and most do not.

For every inbred repeater like a John Dillinger or Al Capone or Caryl Chessman in the rank hierarchy of irreclaimable recidivists, and for every criminal psychopath like a Charles Manson or a Mad Bomber or a Boston Strangler, there are literally legions of anonymous, self-immunized, nonrelapsing, fully rehabilitated tyro offenders who will never see the likes of a court or prison ever again.

The commonly cited, uncritically examined, scary estimate of 75 percent purporting to be the recidivist rate of criminality is a hurtful and misleading myth, for it takes no account of the zero recidivism of most first offenders.

One can no more rationally measure the true recidivist rate through the prism of the turnstile repeaters in the prisons than can one generalize the true birthrate, say, from all those hospitalized for pregnancy with repeated readmissions, without taking into account all those who had left the maternity bed for the first, last, and only time.

The outsized 75 percent recidivist rate reflects only the repeater rate for those who have been recommitted to prison for a second or other multiple time—but it is far from the true repeater rate for all ex-inmates discharged from the prisons, for it fails to take into account the overwhelming number of former inmates who have never been rearrested for any new crime, nor does it reflect the recidivist index for all those never sentenced to prison at all.

Barely 15 percent of all those sentenced by the criminal courts are ever sent to jail, while the rest are either placed on straight probation or given a suspended sentence—or merely fined.

In actuality, the overall recidivist rate would hardly exceed 20 or 25 percent, at most, of all those convicted of crime. Were the fact otherwise, we would have been long overridden with a crime problem from which we could never have recovered; the jails and prisons of the nation would not have been nearly large enough to contain even the minutest fraction of their total input; the spiraling cost of recidivism, bad as it is even now, would have simply burst the economy asunder.

In a frank report to the nation, the President's Task Force on Prisoner Rehabilitation, in April, 1970, admitted: "Particularly little is known about either the amount or the causes of recidivism. Guesses about the percentage of prison-leavers who commit new offenses range from 30 to 70. No one even ventures to guess about the percentage of crimes that are committed by prison-leavers. And, most importantly, there is little or no hard information about which offenders repeat and why—or, even more to the point, which offenders do not repeat and why. Until some light is thrown on this last matter, the success of any correctional program will depend at best on intuition rather than on knowledge and planning."

"The fact is that most serious offenders never repeat their crimes," avers Sol Rubin, distinguished counsel of the National Council on Crime and Delinquency, in the authoritative *Law of Criminal Correction.* "Very likely the prisoner recidivism rate is closer to 20 or 25 percent than it is to 60 or 65 percent."

Given the extraordinary provocations of the volatile second punishment, the marvel is that the rate of recidivism, such as it is, has held to such remarkably minimal levels.

The answering clue lies in such countervailing forces as the normal maturation of the average ex-offender; the self-experiential revelation that criminal offenders do sometimes get caught and punished; and the forbidding odds against a new lenient sentence if criminally convicted a second time.

But withal, it is inarguable that even a soothingly modest 20 or 25 percent rate of recidivism nevertheless remains an awesome challenge to the public security. Given the enormous volume of which it is a quotient, and multiplied geometrically by the prolific spiral of repeated offenses, the inescapable truth is that the numbers game of recidivism can give little satisfaction. Whatever the percentage, it is altogether much too high—for it accounts for most of the serious crime inundating this land. "If it was true in 10 per cent of the cases of second offenders, then society bears a terrible load of guilt," wrote Murray Kempton in his column.

"The most important statistic on crime is the one which tells that 80 percent of all felonies are committed by repeaters," says former Attorney General Ramsey Clark in *Crime in America.* "We know further, indeed we have demonstrated, that recidivism —the repetition of crime by individuals—can be cut in half. It can be cut far more than that. But if only one half of the repeated crime we now suffer could be eliminated society would be free of 40 percent of all serious crime. If we are really concerned about crime, if we really care about our own character, how can we fail to make a massive effort?"

The fears and prejudices we harbor against the first offender are utterly without rational explication in terms of the public safety, or in the proven precepts of morality and justice, or in the tested ideology of correctional values.

Nor can our irrational biases against the first offender be palmed off as merely the innocent handmaiden of ignorance and misunderstanding. For in patent truth, if the Archie Bunkerisms of prejudice were that shallow only, the ready solvents of education and cultural reenlightenment would have long debunked them from our midst.

The fact is, rather, that our prejudices are ulteriorly nurtured in the seedbeds of exploitation and conflicts of interest. Put your microscopic eye to the pragmatic prejudices systematically practiced against all those branded by the tags of race, religion, national origin, or sexuality. Focus your gaze at all those in the vanguard of the second punishment against the first offender.

It isn't blind, unintentional prejudice but the hard ploy of profitability when an employer haggles with an ex-offender or a parolee over the going pay rate or working conditions of a suitable job. It isn't inadvertent indifference but fail-safe expediency when a buck-passing bureaucrat turns his back on an ex-offender's plea for a governmental job or a work permit or license. It isn't for lack of compassion or understanding, but a selfish conflict of interest, that a trade union would bar an ex-felon from apprenticeship, or discourage the competition of rehabilitative prison labor.

Wanton prejudice had a field day when no less than the vaunted "conscience" of the United States Senate, Margaret Chase Smith of Maine—unabashedly indulging her own caper of presumed guilt-by-association—deliberately slammed her mind shut against the forgiving concept of the second chance only because it dared enjoy the prized imprimatur of her nemesis, Dean Roscoe Pound of Harvard. "Inasmuch as Dean Pound was among the sponsors of a publication making an attack on me," she simply stated in words no more and no less, "I am not impressed with his opinion."

The master key to the whys of all human behavior is the dynamic of self-interest, the life instinct of self-preservation. It is the well-spring of all conduct, the supreme catalyst underlying man's motivation in all things. "It is an ingredient of everything that is good as well as evil in his behavior," averred the psychologist Gregory Zilboorg, in *The Psychology of the Criminal Act and Punishment.*

Dissect the criminal act of every wrongdoer and you will uncover every rubric of egocentricity churning within the criminal mind. In different molds, the primacy of self is overtly manifested in the internalized motivations of lust and acquisitiveness, the mean-spirited quests for hate, pique, power, or revenge, the compulsive drives for self-fulfillment or self-survival in myriad ways.

This inner governing passion of doing your own thing is as plainly native to the sophisticated forger and counterfeiter, the bank robber and safe cracker, as it is to the run-of-the-mill car thief or possessor of narcotic drugs. It is the seminal spur underlying the asocial action of the lawless thrill-seekers, the identity-starved destructiveness of the street gangs, or the national security caper of the Watergate burglars, as it is the central psychomotor force behind the mixed bag of all the prison rioters, the flag burners, the political assassins, and the assorted saboteurs against the existing order.

Apply the same acid test of self-interest to the graduate echelon of criminal recidivists and you will find the identical skein of self-serving gain and self-survival firmly interwoven into the basic pattern of their confirmed criminality.

It is time to recognize that this very same inner prod of ego-centeredness that intrinsically propels the criminal offender into the vortex of criminalization cum recidivism can now be effectively deployed by society, in reverse direction, to influence the ex-offender's homecoming to self-rehabilitation and reform through the talismanic redemptiveness of forgiveness.

The philosophers Jeremy Bentham and John Stuart Mill have dubbed this phenomenon of human behavior as the standard of utilitarianism; Freud alluded to it as the reality principle in behavioral modification. In the parlance of Skinnerian psychology, the magic carpet of the second chance for the first offender could work a meaningful manipulation of the social environment to achieve a revolutionary change-from-within.

"What I do say is," declared Dean Roscoe Pound, the chief exponent of the law's mighty influence in social engineering, in his *Introduction to the Philosophy of Law*, "that if in any field of human conduct or in any human relation, the law with such machinery as it has, may satisfy a social want without a disproportionate sacrifice of other claims, there is no eternal limitation inherent in the nature of things, there are no bounds imposed at creation, to stand in the way of its doing so."

PART II

A New Slate

"Though your sins be as scarlet, they shall be as white as snow."

Isaiah 1:18

4
Magic of the Second Chance

If all mankind had to pay the supreme penalty of an everlasting punishment for any of its first faltering flubs and failures, our civilization would have withered long ago into a forsaken malaise of hopelessness and sterility, without a candle for the future.

Our universe might have had a far different hue had Albert Einstein been permanently blackballed out of the scientific firmament after having flunked his first entrance examination to the Zurich Institute of Technology. Wilhelm Roentgen, discoverer of the X ray and Nobel Prize recipient in physics, and the trouble-jinxed Senator Edward M. Kennedy of Massachusetts, could easily have been counted out of serious contention as future doctors of the human condition after each of them had courted permanent expulsion from academia in their tyro years. Heywood Broun would never have risen to journalistic eminence had he not been permitted to bounce back from his scarlet letter F in college English for a second try.

The universality of the second chance, the inherent right of the grand comeback in all things, has coursed through every artery of human intercourse for time without end, sparking that magic of forgiveness that has brought triumph on the very heels of a disastrous debut and a redemptive fulfillment out of the very heartbreaks of virginal missteps.

Even in moral lapses bordering on rank criminality, the largesse of the second chance has never been found wanting. Fresh in mind is the coddling reprimand, rather than the heavy hand of criminal punishment, spooned out to the trio of Apollo 15 astronauts by the National Aeronautics and Space Administration, for the smuggling of four hundred philatelic covers aboard the spacecraft for purely personal profit.

No lifelong stigmatization of guilt ever sullied the names of sixteen Air Force Academy cadets who were quietly permitted to resign from the academy with ostensibly honorable discharges, though they had been formally condemned by a student honor court for cheating their way into passing grades.

"They say best men are moulded out of faults," wrote Shakespeare, "And, for the most part, become much more the better, for being a little bad."

The baffling enigma is, however, that we have been so blind to the tremendous metamorphic potential of a compassionate second chance in the house of criminal correction. For there is simply no welcome mat marked "Forgiveness" at the correctional door, not even for the first offender after punishment is done.

The glimmer of "forgiveness" in the mantle of protection insulating the immature juvenile against the ravages of a criminal stigma has indeed spared legions of our youth from the thorny roadblocks of a raw criminal record. The intensely dramatic example of the now prominent New York physician who at sixteen committed an armed robbery but was saved from the brand of a felon through a merciful adjudication of juvenile delinquency is but one of many in the archives of the youth courts.

Meager as it is, the sprinkling of neo-forgiveness inherent in a suspended sentence, or in a probationary discharge in lieu of imprisonment, has surely helped blunt the blow of the second punishment for countless multitudes of ex-offenders.

Certainly there is a vicarious, crypto-forgiveness in the majestic scroll of a governor's pardon, or a presidential clemency, yet they neither truly pardon guilt nor defuse the second punishment. "We counsel, we grant probation and parole, and treat—not infrequently with success," avers law professor Aidan R. Gough, "but we never forgive."

What we have failed to grasp is that people are people, whether they are ex-offenders or anyone else, pulsing with the same yearnings for forgiveness common to all humankind. "Forgiveness is part and parcel of rehabilitation whether of criminals or anyone else who has erred, or who has, in fact, what all of us have— the defects of being human," stated Sol Rubin in his valedictory broadside in *The Law of Criminal Correction*.

One of the country's great apostles of the new horizons in criminology, Dr. Harry Elmer Barnes, pointing up the remarkable teachings of his wartime experience with "industrial parole" of prison inmates during his distinguished service with the War Production Board in World War I, reported:

> The excitement and fears of wartime at least slightly undermined the usual paralyzing effect of the convict-bogey. The populace, for the moment, became more fearful of foreign enemies than of escaped convicts. It was able for the time being to tolerate the idea that they were fellow human beings.
>
> For the first time in American history, it was possible for able-bodied discharged prisoners to secure employment in normal industrial channels without serious resistance and handicaps. Even more important was the fact that prisoners were made to feel that they were to some extent members of the normal civilian community, nation, state, and local. They felt that it was possible to pool their efforts with those of the outside public in behalf of the public weal and national safety. They came to believe that the public was beginning to take some constructive interest in them and to place some trust in them, rather than continuing to regard them as caged beasts, to be continued as outcasts even after release.

This graphic demonstration of correctional power should have drawn little wonder or surprise.

These ex-offenders had been welcomed, at face value, into the ranks of wartime labor as accredited citizens rather than as discredited ex-criminals. Their single badge of identification was a war serial number rather than a criminal history, for as Henry Ford once astutely remarked, "I hire a man, not a history." They were not stigmatized as ex-cons or ex-offenders but were regarded only as cocivilians. They were not thrust against an unbreachable wall of discriminatory employment practices nor subjected to the arbitrariness of a vengeful or indifferent society. Their unstinted democratization within the defense forces, as equals among equals, gave them a newly kindled sense of human dignity, personal pride, and self-esteem. And, in the rejuvenative climate of an egalitarian army, these erstwhile ex-offenders responded in kind by giving their best, comparable to all others.

In similar cast, the Pentagon's spectacular turnabout in granting retroactive amnesty to ex-servicemen who had been booted out of the army with nonhonorable discharges because of drug addiction heralded a significant rewriting of history for whole battalions of stigmatized offenders. This action cannot but return enormous dividends to the country in terms of a singular crime reduction and a massive rehabilitation for all thus rescued from the quagmire of the second punishment.

The poignant lesson for correction is that the supreme catalyst of forgiveness can truly achieve a miraculous redemption for tens of millions of ex-offenders.

The trail-blazing parole of 2,942 inmates from the Illinois Penitentiary directly into the army during World War II yielded a predictable dividend of a recidivism rate remarkably below the normal average. In a follow-up study undertaken eight years afterwards, it was found that the violation rate for this test group of army parolees was whoppingly less than 25 percent that of a matching control group of other parolees.

Totally unsurprising too was the glowing success rate of the United States Air Force Prisoner Retraining Program, where, since 1952, aproximately nine thousand prisoners from air bases throughout the world have been given a real second chance, through the rehabilitative program at Amarillo Air Force Base, Texas, to wipe the slate clean despite their conviction and sentence to confinement by courts-martial.

A profile of the convicted airmen showed that 92 percent of them were first offenders, half of them serving sentences of from six to twelve months at hard labor. Roughly half of their number had been stripped of their military insignia by a military court, doomed to be discharged from the air force with either a bad conduct or dishonorable discharge. Their offenses ran the whole gamut of the criminal scale: larceny, crimes of violence, use or possession of drugs, robbery, manslaughter, as well as purely military offenses.

The success rate? For the five-year test period from 1964 to 1968, 89.4 percent of all airmen who had returned to duty under the retraining program were still serving honorably following their restoration to duty. "In every instance the results showed that the average ratings for our former prisoners were average or above," noted Major Floyd C. Kennedy, chief of the Analysis Division for the retraining group.

The bellwether state of California, long in the vanguard of progressive penology, is now beginning to reap the golden harvest of its advanced humane treatment of prison inmates, reflected in the remarkable cutback of crime. "During the past decade in California, we have accomplished a 35 percent reduction in recidivism," pridefully noted Governor Ronald Reagan, ticking off the shining landmarks of his state's correctional thrusts:

> We have the nation's largest program of family visits; we have hundreds of convicts leaving their prisons on three-day passes; we have more than 1,600 prisoners participating in work furloughs and our prison population is less today than it was in 1962; our corrections system offers educational programs that range from literacy training to junior-college level subjects; we teach 43 trades; we conduct counseling and therapy programs and we have made a concentrated effort to enlist minority citizens as correctional officers and as counselors in our rehabilitation

programs. We believe that a man who has strayed but is determined to find his way back into society as a useful, productive citizen is deserving of society's help.

Spearheading an experimental venture to pry open the locked doors of employment for ex-offenders, the United States Department of Labor recently undertook the calculated risk of supplying a performance bond for a limited number of unbondable ex-convicts. In the end, out of the 2,600 persons bonded into gainful employment, only 2 percent had defaulted in the trust reposed in them—a percentage rate slightly higher than the default experience for all other bonded employees.

The Mormon Church of Jesus Christ Latter Day Saints, self-appointed brother's keeper to long-term inmates of the Utah State Prison, had provided a specially adopted "family" to each of 140 selected prisoners. These people's abiding commitment was to watch over the inmates' estranged families during the entire prison term and to maintain a loving care and unstinted concern for the wards in their charge long after they were released into the community. Glorying in this remarkable input of correctional voltage, Utah's prison chaplain lauded it with unexaggerated pride as "the most successful prison rehabilitation program in the world." Of the 140 discharged prisoners who had been blessed with adopted families during their terms, only two had returned to prison in the test period of five years.

It was a moment to savor in judicial brinkmanship when Judge Nannette Dembitz of New York's Family Court granted the request of two juveniles, fourteen and fifteen years old respectively, to expunge all court and police records relating to their unlawful arrests for unlawful assembly and riot after they had been taken into custody during a demonstration in front of a public school; the New York City Police Department had itself petitioned the court to drop the charges because of insufficient evidence.

In a courier decision of first impression in the judicial annals of the juvenile courts, Judge Dembitz found authority for its expungement order not in the statutes, but in the inherent power of the courts to prevent injustice.

Yet, she ruefully added, though the physical record be expunged, the incorporeal second punishment remained wholly unaffected. As the judge noted, "Employers frequently commence their investigation of any applicant by asking him if he has ever been taken into custody or appeared in court. Complete protection for respondents and other juveniles from unfair discrimination due to untenable arrests and dismissed charges, can only be afforded by a statutory prohibition on employers' inquiries or a statutory procedure for nullifying abortive arrests. Absent such legislation, job applicants who admit an arrest may be rejected out of hand."

Looking backward, the second chance was surely in its fullest flower when, in early America, the colonies became the melting pot for hordes of English convicts eagerly subscribing to self-imposed banishment and transportation to these shores in indentured servitude for seven years as a happy alternative to the barbaric death penalty prescribed for some three hundred offenses, many of them trivial in nature.

At least fifty thousand of these expatriate felons crowded into this continent "for the better Peopling of his Majesty's Colonies." The historian Samuel Eliot Morison dubbed them "His Majesty's seven-year passengers."

Countless others fled to these teeming shores by special dispensation of the crown of England, opting to escape all punishment on condition of taking an oath of abjuration and leaving the realm in self-exile forever.

Translated into modern times, the sizeable ratio of fifty thousand within the then colonial population of three million—approximately 1.6 percent of the total—would be equivalent to a tidal wave of over three million ex-offender migrants in proportion to the existing population of the United States.

The historian Arthur M. Schlesinger, Sr., impishly hinting in

his *Paths to the Present* that there may be far more skeletons in
our national closet than we can dare imagine, declared, "The
musty archives of Newgate and Old Bailey would undoubtedly
clear up questions as to the genesis of many a present-day family
of ancient lineage."

Rehabilitation worthy of the name is far more than the mere
hand-out of a merciful sentence or a timely parole, for these are
but part of the whole personhood of every ex-offender.

The commendably audacious project of 107 plastic surgery
operations performed in a single year upon inmates in custody
of the Texas Department of Correction—in which elephantine
ears were pinned back, parrot-type noses rebuilt, and disfiguring
scars removed—was, after all, but an ersatz exercise in reconstruction as compared to the ugly residual scar of the criminal record,
a handicap more deeply injurious to their psychological welfare
and future prospects of social reassimilation than the physical
stigmata could ever have been.

Promising indeed are the sophisticated correctional ventures,
now in vogue, of diverting selected first offenders from the lifetime stigma of a criminal conviction to the big brotherliness of
community intervention, or "adjourning" a criminal case in contemplation of ultimate dismissal upon proof of good behavior
in the interim. But withal, even at best, the ineradicable and
nondivertible arrest record, the unending flak of the second punishment, survives all these patchwork ministrations.

The half-way house of correction, advanced as it is in modern
penology, is only a half-loaf of replacement for the all-out, permanent sanctuary of forgiveness. The innovative work-release programs for selected prisoners, the weekend furlough plans, the
restoration of voting rights, the liberalization of job opportunities,
are certainly tremendous pluses in the humanization of punishment.

But more than all these is the right to the bone and marrow
of the respect and esteem of others. In Emerson's classic theorem,

"a man has a right to be employed, to be loved, to be revered."

One can no more "rehabilitate" the ex-offender without radical excision of the malignant record than can the surgeon arrest a spreading cancer without bold use of the scalpel.

Psychosomatic medicine, for all its impressive gains, has yet to yield the tranquilizing balm that will cure the neurosis spawned by the festering criminal record. "There are social dimensions of neurosis that cannot be dealt with by a trip into the inner hurts of the individual," declared the social scientist Sam Keen in *Psychology Today*. "Wilhelm Reich, Herbert Marcuse, N. O. Brown, and other left-wing Freudians have shown the degree to which neurosis is in part a political problem that must have a political solution. To adjust a person so that he does not struggle against the social structures that perpetuate disease is to achieve a 'cure' at the price of avoiding reality."

We have long learned the utter futility of sadistic punishment for its own sake. We have emerged from the long night of the horrors of emblematic mutilation and branding, the screw, the rack, the pillory, and the stock in the brutalization of the convicted offender.

We have long outgrown the grisly deterrence of yore when the perjurer commonly had his tongue torn out and the sex criminal, his genitals; when the counterfeiter was immobilized by physical severance of his hands and the spy by gouging out of his eyes.

The self-defeating second punishment is but the stubborn remnant of the discredited outlawry and attainder philosophies of feudal England, when death was in the throne of justice, and excommunication was the prince of punishment for all those spared from the hangman's noose—when the convicted felon was automatically declared civilly dead and condemned to eternal "corruption of the blood"—when the criminal offender suffered instantaneous forfeiture of all his assets to the Crown and was rendered legally incompetent to appear in court as a witness or as a juror, or to perform any legal function whatever.

The abhorrent era of past "correction" is now sternly behind us. The unconscionable tortures and the decivilizing rule of unyielding vengeance—that which has long been universally condemned by the modern enlightenment as the "crime of punishment"—have been supplanted by a new heartbeat of correctional norms. "Retribution is no longer the dominant objective of the criminal law," proclaimed the United States Supreme Court. "Reformation and rehabilitation of offenders have become the important goals of criminal jurisprudence."

In the final showdown, it is the cherished badge of human dignity, the decent respect of mankind, the untrammeled right to pursue a legitimate livelihood, the fair opportunity to live down the past—in short, the wholehearted reintegration of the former offender in the body politic as a full and equal member—that alone can spell out our sincere earnest of a helping hand and our real intention towards him in the fateful business of rehabilitation and reform.

"Criminologists have reason to believe that readjustment takes place much more readily when the ex-convict is given an opportunity to regain the respect of his neighbor and his own self-respect," wrote Dr. Mabel A. Elliott in *Crime in Modern Society*.

As the neophyte stands at the threshold of his first traumatic engagement with the criminal law, still malleable to the paternalism and statecraft of our society, ours is the last clear chance to send him afield towards the open horizon of reform—or, by our own insensitive regard for his future welfare, condemn him to a life of confirmed criminality.

Clarence Darrow, writing to Leopold at a time when it seemed that the doomed lifer-plus-99 years would never see the outside world again, said, "The day will come when society will accept the idea that somehow every debt must be considered paid."

Restoration of the ex-offender to a status of absolute equality with all others is the only workable sine qua non for lasting reformation from within.

The golden mean of penal treatment must be that it fully serve the cause of deterrence and yet at the same time be wholly free from the recoiling overkill of a self-depreciating vindictiveness.

The basic need of correction is for a just equilibrium in the counterforces of punishment and forgiveness. Mutually opposed as these seem to be, they can be harnessed together in ecumenical tandem towards inner rehabilitation and reform. "To everything there is a season, and a time to every purpose under Heaven" says the Scriptures. There is a time for ploughing and a time for harvest; there is a time for punishment and a time for reconciliation and forgiveness; there is a time for law and order, a time for justice.

The second chance I espouse would liberate the first offender from the life sentence of his stigmatic record, after punishment is done.

Its shining hallmark would be a rejuvenescent forgiveness.

It would be an amnesty of the dimensional magnitude of perfect redemption that the Supreme Court of the United States—more than a century ago, during the Reconstruction Era—had once ascribed to the presidential amnesty of all who had taken part in the Confederate rebellion against the government of the United States: "It releases the punishment and blots out of existence the guilt, so that in the eyes of the law the offender is as innocent as if he had never committed the offense; if granted after conviction, it removes the penalties and disabilities, and restores him to all his civil rights; it makes him, as it were, a new man, and gives him a new credit and capacity."

Under its aegis, the offense shall be deemed to be fully expurgated and forgiven.

In the sweeping regenesis of this true second chance, the amnestied beneficiary would be expressly sanctioned by law to affirm—in any oath, in any application for employment or a license or permit, in every aspect of his civil pursuits of whatever nature—that he had never been convicted, or arrested, or charged with any crime or offense.

Hand in hand with amnesty, all legal disabilities would be terminated, and every lost civil right restored, including, above all, the right to vote, to serve on juries, to qualify for public office, and to hold a public trust.

No longer shackled by the artifact of the criminal record, the amnestied individual would automatically qualify to apply for a professional license or vocational certification, to establish eligibility of good character and competence for the restoration of a forfeited license or privilege, and to enter the civil service of governmental employment.

To implement the all-out guarantees of amnesty, the criminal record would be deemed annulled and expunged. Every aspect of the police record—the arrest dossier, the fingerprints, the bookings, the court registry of every nature or description, the probation records and parole files—would be permanently sealed and separately classified, held forever secure and inviolate against any unauthorized disclosure or inspection, save only for the limited purposes of law enforcement in the actual investigation, detection, or prosecution of any crime.

On every correctional front, the rule of amnesty would inexorably revolutionize the conventional pathways of probation and parole, the sentencing and the custodial processes, and would insure the ultimate homecoming of every rehabilitable ex-offender.

Sentinelled by amnesty, the advent of societal absolution for the ex-offender would mark the dawn of a challenging adventure in the social engineering of self-correction.

It would inevitably strengthen the public security as never before. Its protective cast upon every first offender, every marginal backslider, and borderline potential repeater would instantly translate into a prodigious cutback of crime and recidivism.

The criminal record would no longer subjugate the first offender in the lifelong bind of the second punishment. Yet, at the same time, its traditional viability in the service of law enforcement and the public security would be left wholly unimpaired.

James V. Bennett, former director of the Bureau of Prisons for the United States Department of Justice, one of the top penal authorities in the country, put it this way:

> Legislation of this kind is long overdue. It seems inconsistent for the State of New York to spend so much money on its correctional institutions in rehabilitating the offender, and then as soon as he is released, to subject him to so many legal and social disabilities that he is severely handicapped in making good his rehabilitation.
>
> If New York would pass a law of this kind, it would be a tremendous contribution to corrections and the prevention of crime generally in this country.
>
> Other jurisdictions, as well as New York, some day will have to face up to the fact that the rehabilitation of the offender must be a primary objective of the administration of justice, and that all our laws and dealings with the offender must be consistent with that objective.

The distinguished dean of American correction, Paul W. Tappan, former chairman of the United States Parole Board, assessed it thus in his foreword to the original tract *The First Offender: A Second Chance* (1957): "To the adventitious or circumstantial violator, this would assure a chance to start again without the measure of bitterness that he so commonly feels in the face of continuing official and public rejection. To the true criminal, freshly but deliberately launched in criminal enterprise, this device would provide a positive incentive to a redirection of his course, without fear that his efforts will be persistently repudiated."

If, in the final countdown, the catalytic impulsivity of amnesty will have achieved but a fractional part of the 50 percent cut-back in crime reasonably claimed for it, we will have wrought an epochal breakthrough in our fight against crime, translatable in tens of billions of dollars years after year, and in the priceless returns of human reconstruction for tens of millions of reincarnated ex-offenders.

In fairly prospective view, the ultimate reward of amnesty would instinctively pace every eligible ex-offender in a sustained momentum of exemplary behavior and lawful conduct.

The compelling self-interest of every amnestied offender to guard the prized status of amnesty once conferred upon him, to avoid its forfeiture for any criminal reinvolvement of moral turpitude, and to obviate the inevitably hard penalty that would await him as a deliberately recidivistic offender, would enrich the correctional process with a mighty reservoir of positive reinforcements on the one hand and a fistful of aversive suppressions on the other that would practically insure an unparalleled success rate for future probation and parole.

"It is my impression that your scheme is the most practical, humane, and progressive correctional device to appear in the field of criminology and penology since the inception of probation and parole," declared William J. Cooper, chief probation officer, United States District Court, District of New Mexico.

The second chance of amnesty would inevitably exert a compelling psychokinetic force in every facet of correctional treatment.

It would inaugurate a new detente and rapport between the supervisory agencies and the clientele of the criminal courts and the prisons, establishing a new mutuality and a uniquely reciprocal concord of interests, all responsive to the central precepts of inner-rehabilitation and reform.

"The correctional tools of probation and parole would have a powerful ally in the form of a personal incentive for good behavior. Every probationer and parolee would in effect be his own correctional officer," stated the Grand Jurors Association of Kings County, New York.

"It is important for every citizen to understand that this new proposal involves no coddling of criminals. The nullification of the record is effective only after punishment is done. The conviction would be automatically reinstated in full vigor upon any subsequent conviction for any crime."

In substantial agreement is Norman G. Baillie, state probation and parole officer for the state of Wyoming: "Such procedure, I believe, would be very valuable in the matter of supervision. The probationer, or parolee, would have an added incentive to complete a satisfactory period of supervision and further incentive, after discharge from probation, or parole, to conduct himself in an acceptable manner."

Thus, at no financial cost to the public—indeed, at tremendous savings in sharply reduced caseloads for understaffed probation personnel throughout the country—the self-policing, inbuilt psychodynamic of amnesty would inevitably maximize the productivity of every correctional agency to its ultra-optimal levels. Predictably enough, it would instantly relieve the probation officer from substantially all active supervision of amnesty-eligible first offenders in his charge, permitting every caseworker to refocus his major attention on the marginal subjects more critically in need of sustained vigilance and supervision.

"The basis of the idea which impressed me most," remarked District Attorney Henry A. Fischer, Jr., of Franklin County, New York, "is that the burden of meriting the second chance is placed on the offender, and it is not a question of increasing the probation departments and personnel in the various counties."

As a natural corollary, the criminal courts would instinctively veer to far greater liberality in the dispensation of a probationary sentence and would more freely indulge the rehabilitative technique of an unconditional discharge, thus enlarging the corrective potential of prison-free sentences far beyond all preexisting norms.

Concomitantly, society's new precept of forgiveness, under the sanction of judicial amnesty, would generate a significant attitudinal change by the public at large towards the amnesty-bound, destigmatized ex-offender.

In the pervading spirit of this new dispensation, the availability of job opportunities for expectant parolees would expand to unprecedented levels. The hiring managers and bonding agencies in the private sector of the business communities would more freely cooperate in the shared "risk" of rehabilitation of the court-certified amnestied individuals. The civil service and public employment agencies would readily lift the artificial barriers of a criminal record in favor of the judicially approved amnestied applicants. And, under the magical prod of the legal and moral pressures undergirding the new climate of amnesty, administrative agencies far and wide would surely incline toward a healthier magnanimity in the bestowal of licenses and job permits in the professions and vocations.

The logistics of amnesty would inspire a soul-searching generosity in the dispensation of parole in every prison of the land. "The average offender who comes into the courts of the nation is a fit subject for the application of the doctrine of the second chance," declared William Shands Meacham, former director of the Virginia State Parole Board. "If he cannot be placed on probation, he may still be a proper subject for parole later."

The apocryphal case of a first offender up for parole consideration at a state prison, under the aegis of amnesty, illumines the exciting potentials:

Board Chairman: David Downes, age twenty-four, minimum time of one year fully served, expiration date of maximum sentence, two years hence. Prison record, exemplary. I fully concur that Mr. Downes should be granted parole at this time. If the board members agree, then the only issue before us now is our recommendation as to amnesty. We have the power to recommend that the probationary interval of five years be shortened or that it be waived altogether. What is your pleasure, gentlemen?

Board Member: If we do recommend that Mr. Downes be granted amnesty forthwith, what would happen to the unexpired parole time of two years?

Board Chairman: Amnesty or not, he would remain under the complete jurisdiction and supervisory control of this parole board until the full termination of his parole, just like any other parolee. But to the world at large, for every other purpose, he would be fully amnestied.

Board Member: It seems to me pretty plain that if he is worth paroling back into the community at this time, then we should not hesitate to back up our faith in this man with a recommendation for an early amnesty. With stakes so high in society's favor from every angle. I have no compunction whatever in recommending immediate amnesty in this case.

Board Chairman: I absolutely agree that the risk of an aborted parole would be minuscule compared to anything that we had ever experienced in all parole history. It is therefore the unanimous recommendation of this board that amnesty be granted forthwith.

In the leavening backdrop of the ultimate second chance, the sentencing judges would incline more confidently to the liberal use of a rehabilitative probationary sentence or an unconditional discharge, fulfilling the ideal of a prison-free sentence with minimal risk to the public at large. And, alternately, in the leverage of punishment as to other defendants less deserving of leniency at the bar of judgment, the courts would more freely indulge in a constructive prison sentence intrinsically tied to the olive branch of eventual amnesty.

In end result, the criminal courts under amnesty would enjoy a sustained and continuing role in the correctional experience, maintaining their hold against all offenders crossing the threshold of criminal justice.

The stylization of sentencing for a youth placed on probation would run typically along these lines:

The Court: Mr. Defendant, the court is now ready to impose sentence upon you. Because you are a first offender, and your record is otherwise without blemish, and because the court does truly believe that you are rehabilitable and that it would best serve the public interest to do so, I am placing you on probation for one year; further, the court is granting you amnesty forthwith.

Though the court has accelerated your right to amnesty, please take note that the conditions of your probation remain

in full force. You will fully adhere to all the terms of supervision until the termination of your probationary period of one
year.

If you fail this trust, and return to this court with a second
conviction at any time in the future, know now that you will not
only forfeit your status as an amnestied offender, but in addition,
you will be deemed a second offender, and punished as such.
The key to your future is now in your own hands. From this
day forth, the court has now rung down the curtain on your first
offense, and I am confident there will be none other. The rest
belongs to you.

To the hardened offender at the bar of justice, where an
exemplary prison sentence would more nearly vindicate the public
interests of retribution, incapacitation, and deterrence, a sentencing
proceeding would run along these lines.

> *The Court:* I have carefully examined the presentence report
> and can find no mitigating factor that speaks in your behalf.
> Though you are technically a first offender at the bar of judg-
> ment, your determined lifestyle of crime now impels this court
> to impose a sentence of not less than two nor more than five
> years in State Prison.
>
> Now, mark this well, I want to advise you that society stands
> ready to welcome you back, in complete forgiveness, after your
> sentence has been fully completed, if only you yourself will it.
> The very same good conduct that will earn you a reduction of
> sentence for good behavior, and will open the door to an early
> parole, will entitle you to apply for full amnesty after the prison
> doors will have closed behind you. The choice for ultimate free-
> dom and your return to society with a new slate is now yours
> alone to make.

Hearken to the view of Judge Samuel S. Leibowitz, the
estimable "Mr. Courtroom" of the criminal bench.

> This proposal to absolve first offenders of the lifelong stigma
> of their criminal record will have a far-reaching impact upon the
> administration of justice.
>
> The total cancellation of the offense, and the full legal and

moral exoneration of every first offender, after the completion of the punisment plus the passage of the five year "probationary" interval should serve as a powerful incentive towards self-rehabilitation.

The automatic revival of the original offense, for the purposes of increased punishment in the event of a subsequent conviction of crime, will insure the continuation of society's protection against the multiple offender.

These proposals by Assistant District Attorney Aaron Nussbaum will prove to be of major legal and sociological significance.

One basic cause of recidivism among the criminal element of our population has been the uncooperative attitude of society towards all efforts by the ex-prisoner to readjust himself to normal living. I have long felt that the right to earn an honest living is the very first prerequisite to rehabilitation and reform.

The great virtue of these proposals of "conditioned amnesty" is that it will effectively insulate the reformed first offender from the crushing stigma and handicap of his former record. It gives him a true second chance.

And the distinguished chief judge of the New York Court of Appeals, the Honorable Albert Conway, presiding over one of the most respected judicial tribunals in the country, stated: "It marks a wholly new approach to peno-correctional reform based upon a significant concept of 'rehabilitation-from-within'. These proposals may yield an effective answer to the growing incidence of crime, the high rate of recidivism and to the removal, under specified conditions, of the stigma attaching to first offenders who now constitute a very considerable number of persons in this country."

To the wardens of our prisons and penitentiaries, amnesty would establish a new anchorage in the custodial process, hovering protectively over every inmate first offender in the Atticas of this country. The pulsing heartbeat of forgiveness will be a counter-conditioning force of the highest magnitude in neutralizing the psychological pollutions of prisonization. The golden promise of the second chance would resolutely implant new hope in place of forlorn despair, and open new options of liberation in the self-interest of rehabilitation and reform for every prison inmate.

Let the wardens speak for themselves:

Warden Fred R. Dickson of the California State Prison at San Quentin, named warden of the year by the Warden's Association of America in 1956—who presided at the gas execution of Caryl Chessman, though he had been a strong opponent of the death penalty—stated, "Your ideas would be of much assistance to a rehabilitation program for first offenders in prison. Those of us who have been given the responsibility of administration of our prisons see the problems confronting the parolees every day, upon release. I am confident that many of the recidivists are back in prison only because of their prior records; had such records not been held against them, they might have coped with their employment and social responsibilities."

One of the country's foremost prison experts, Harold E. Donnell, superintendent of prisons for the state of Maryland—a former president of the American Correction Association—put it this way.

> After more than forty years in the correctional field, in an executive capacity for nearly all this time, and having served as President of the American Prison Assocation and the Southern States Prison Association, as well as having had much administrative experience, I can subscribe to the conclusion which you have reached.
>
> It has always been most distressing and disturbing to see the handicaps under which many first offenders, who have served their sentence and rehabilitated themselves, have had to face out in the world at large following their incarceration. . . . The recidivist is always before us and the press gives him wide publicity. The man who goes out and rectifies his life and makes good in the social life and in the business world receives little or no publicity which is as it should be. He overcomes handicaps and makes his way. He could do this all the more easily if he were given another right to a full chance by wiping the slate clean after he has redeemed himself and satisfied the authorities that he intends to live a useful and honorable life.

The Right Reverend William F. Wilkins, president of the American Catholic Correctional Chaplains Association, declared:

> It is a vital step in rehabilitation, which will support and implement the work now being done in our prisons and institutions to re-orient these first offenders and keep them from becoming second and third offenders, due to the harshness of our present penal policy.
>
> This is one of the most important and progressive steps in modern penology. It has the endorsement of the Chaplains of all faiths of the United States, meeting at the Congress of Correction in Miami Beach last August, and the endorsement of James V. Bennett, Director of the United States Bureau of Prisons.
>
> There are many first offenders in prison today, who want to go straight and make an honest living. Our present laws make that most difficult, if not at times, almost impossible. Amnesty, if enacted, will save the State large sums of money now spent on prison maintenance.

Warden Douglas C. Rigg of the Minnesota State Prison stated: "I find myself in complete agreement with your contention that the stigma attached to being an ex-convict is a tremendous handicap to men attempting to make a law-abiding adjustment. I know from my own experience that many inmates feel that they can accept the punishment of imprisonment, but resent bitterly the continuing punishment long after they have received their discharge from prison or parole."

Warden E. V. Nash of the Missouri State Penitentiary:

> I truly believe that most business and professional employers, if combined by agreement and understanding, would concur with many of your commitments dealing with first offenders. In discussing this problem of first offenses in civic meetings, I find that most people express an attitude of desiring to help, yet, when confronted with the reality they seek cover. We, as free Americans, must certainly be forced to realize that we cannot continue in our present frame of mind in regard to first offenders whom we are forcing into a life of perpetual crime. Our seeming disregard for

others in this great ultra-modern world may eventually be the barrier of our future.

Warden B. R. Reeves of Alabama's Draper Prison went on, "It has a great deal of merit, and if and when it is put in effect, it should have a great deal of influence in combating recidivism in the prison population."

George O. Parker, superintendent of the Federal Bureau of Prisons in Alaska, said: "It seems to me that your proposal is one of great importance, and one that we in the correctional field must support if we are to lend aid to the rehabilitation process. I am in full agreement with your view that our traditional antagonisms against those who are desirous of reformation must cease in the interest of a free and healthy society."

And finally, Warden Walter M. Wallack of New York's Wallkill Prison, who served as president of the American Correctional Association and as superintendent of schools of Kansas, said: "There has never been any doubt in my mind that society is morally obligated to give a first offender a second chance. Without a second chance as a goal, rehabilitation in the real sense can never be achieved."

There have been gnawing doubts of whether the Attica tragedy might not have been at least forestalled had Governor Nelson A. Rockefeller, in one last desperate move, deliberately opted "to walk that last mile"—as Commissioner of Correction Russell Oswald so graphically phrased it in testimony before the fact-finding panel of the McKay Commission.

In the agonizing aftermath of what might have been, one cannot but ponder in retrospect whether the Attica scene would have ended differently had the governor elected a reconciliation along these lines.

> You have demanded an "amnesty" for atrocities committed against guards and inmates which neither the law nor I as governor could rightfully or legally allow.

But I stand ready to offer to you an amnesty far more meaningful and far broader in scope than the mere whitewash of accountability for the crimes committed within these walls. It is an amnesty of complete forgiveness of your criminal past record, a chance for each of you to wipe the slate clean once you have left these prison gates for a new start in life. If you can prove your worthiness of amnesty by a sincere commitment to self-rehabilitation and reform, you can write your own ticket to freedom and liberation.

I will support such legislation at the very next session of the legislature—as your own official observers, Senators John Dunne and Robert Garcia, Assemblyman Arthur Eve, and Congressman Herman Badillo, have already done with respect to the Amnesty Law for First Offenders now pending in the state legislature and in Congress.

I will wholeheartedly support such legislation not only for all first offenders among you, but for all others in this prison and elsewhere who can sincerely demonstrate to a court that a grant of amnesty would be consistent with the public interest.

This is my offer of "amnesty" to each of you. The decision is now yours.

The revitalization of the administration of justice with this mighty reservoir of potential witnesses would inevitably help turn the tide of aborted justice in every court in the land.

The modality of amnesty would actuate a new viability on the witness stand, restoring to the courtroom multitudes of ex-offender witnesses, finally liberated from their prejudicial criminal record in the overall quest for truth.

Guilty men would no longer go free, nor would the innocent be entrapped in a miscarriage of justice because of the unavailability of reluctant key witnesses.

The grossly guilt-slanted record will no longer becloud the issues of guilt or innocence in any criminal case, whether for the prosecution or the defense. The presumption of innocence will no longer be sacrificed to the second punishment. Under the new rule of law and justice, the amnestied defendant would freely take the witness stand in his own defense, without the counter-productive constraints of a criminal record, in any fair test of credibility.

Dean Roscoe Pound, lauding the amnesty concept in the restructured evidentiary rules of criminal justice, pointedly declared the following.

> Weighed in terms of the cardinal purpose of deterrence and rehabilitation, the evidence of prior charges or conviction has no place in a modern trial as it is used. It defeats both purposes: The one because it hangs over the first offender who is struggling to regain his place in society—impairs his resistance to temptation by hanging continual dread of humiliation over him, and the other because he can never be assured that he is rehabilitated in public estimation however well conducted he continued to be.
>
> Indeed the idea of going into an item of past misconduct of a witness having no relevance whatever to the issue on trial is a left-over from crude beginnings of a law of evidence. It is not merely useless for any real purpose of today but, I repeat, it is mischievous in its effect upon a cardinal purpose of the administration of remedial justice today.

And, in the considered view of the court-wise Judge Leibowitz, "The course of criminal justice will be greatly benefitted. The nullification of the record, after the five year interval, would enable the accused first offender to take the stand in his own defense, without subjecting himself to the recriminations of the first conviction."

To the criminologist and social scientist, the audacious heterodoxy of forgiveness in the scheme of correction would stake out an exciting adventure in the social engineering of the law.

In the new mold of correctional reconciliation, the intrinsically warring ideologies of punishment versus rehabilitation would at long last be harnessed in tandem, as logical and sequential complementaries in the chronology of penal treatment—thus assuring society's self-protection against the criminal offender and guaranteeing him eventual vindication of the natural right to a chance for full redemption after punishment is done.

"I can see at once that you have made a contribution of real importance," wrote Dean Roscoe Pound on January 9, 1957. "I am going to take the liberty of bringing it to the attention of some people interested in legislation on the subject in this community."

"It presents a realistic appeal to reason in the treatment of the first offender," stated Gus Harrison, Michigan's director of the Department of Correction. "It brings into sharp focus the incongruity of an approach to crime and treatment of the offender which requires that we utilize advanced techniques and draw upon the cumulated knowledge in the field of human behavior and of social sciences, yet allows us neither to forget nor forgive."

"You have presented a sound case for what appears to be a plausible solution to one of the most vital problems in the correction field," stated Robert D. Patton, chairman of the Youth Commission, state of Illinois. "We who are engaged in this work recognize the limitations of our present rehabilitation system. If we have faith in modern penology, we should be willing to extend the goal of rehabilitation beyond institutionalization and parole."

"Your solution by legislative action rather than by continuing to rely on the good will of the public (which seems to have failed in many instances) is interesting, and I for one would like to see it tried out," declared Raymond W. Houston, New York's commissioner of the Department of Social Welfare.

Dr. Edward B. Bunn, renowned chancellor of Georgetown University, put it this way.

You have put your finger on a very real sociological problem —the restoration of unfortunates who have been led into their first brush with the law, for whatever reason. Theirs is often a critical situation, and on the treatment they receive may depend the direction of their future, as useful, rehabilitated citizens of society, or as repeaters, habitual offenders, and ultimately hardened criminals.

There is always a danger, of course, in sentimentalizing about offenders, of any degree. Your thesis avoids this, to be sure, in that it starts from the premise that justice has been served, in the punishment already meted out to the offender. But justice is not served, as you pointed out, by "over-punishment"—by stigmatizing the offender, and making it difficult, not to say impossible, for him to regain both his own self-respect and his good standing in the community.

I congratulate you for a very fine study of the delicate balance which exists between the rights of society and the rights of the individual, and I sincerely hope that its wide distribution among sociologists, penologists, and perhaps most of all among laymen, may serve to emphasize, and contribute to the solution of, a growing social problem.

"It would certainly be worthwhile to try out your proposals," declared Meyer Levin, knowledgeable student of the human condition and celebrated crime reporter of the Loeb-Leopold case. "Psychologically, it seems very sound to expect that an opportunity for complete social rehabilitation would help the first offender to reduce his resentment over the after-effects of punishment, and help keep him from further hostile acts."

"As we advance in our knowledge of human behavior," Mr. Levin added in his syndicated column "A Second Chance for First Offenders," "we learn that many persons of seemingly adult development are retarded in their emotional growth. Punishment for a first crime may jolt them into an adult sense of responsibility. There seems little to risk in Mr. Nussbaum's plan, and much to gain for society."

Impressively enough, a test evaluation of the "second chance" by the eminent sociologist, Professor Leroy Baumann, in the social laboratory of Brooklyn College, produced an illuminating reaction among the 120 students enrolled in the courses in criminology.

In the documented report of his findings, he stated:

1. Practically all of the 120 students agreed with the fundamental premise of amnesty. It met their often expressed sympathy for

the offender who, under pressure, goes wrong and becomes en-meshed in a syndrome of causes and effects that act in the manner of a vicious circle. They felt that this is a method of breaking up that circle early in the game.

2. We followed in part Bloch and Flynn's "Delinquency" and many in the classes had studied the field of the main emphasis of that text, namely the psychogenetic development resulting in delinquency. These students, as well as all the others who fol-lowed their arguments, felt that the legalistic aspects of correc-tional treatment should be minimized and the therapeutic stressed. They regard your thesis as excellent if the first offense can be the occasion for setting in motion a treatment process based in kind and length on the needs of the offender as a person who needs help in individual maturing and social adjustment.

3. Lastly the group in the classes which regards most seriously the damage and cost to society was also delighted with your pro-posal. They were convinced that it is a way to lessen delinquency, and especially that difficult aspect of the hard core of delinquents, namely recidivism, they are apt to ascribe to faulty treatment as much as to unfavorable social conditions.

4. A few raised points of practical difficulties in the establishment of the procedure you advocate and questions about the public policy involved in keeping what they called public information from public scrutiny. The answers to their points seem fairly obvious and cogent.

"If all this amnesty proposal did were to underline the awful consequences of a first conviction, it would have done a service by awakening us," remarked professor of law Samuel M. Fahr in the *Iowa Law Review* in the fall of 1958. "But it does more, it is a cure for this ill which is worthy of further consideration and perhaps a probationary try in a state willing to do a new thing."

Above all, our democratic society would reap the manifold blessings of a resurrected morale, and a restored dignity and self-esteem affecting fifty million of our citizens, forging a new hope and a new direction for a multitude of American families.

In reciprocal response to our humane forgiveness—as in

universal reaction to the psychodynamic of forgiveness anywhere —the delivered actuality of amnesty would rekindle loyalty and dedication to the democratic ideal on a scale such as this country has rarely seen before in all its history.

In this time of change in America, amnesty may well point the way to the exciting challenge of regeneration within the frontiers of the established order, serving as living demonstration and concrete reality of a radical transformation within the system without violent convulsion, of a peaceful reconstruction without nihilistic destruction.

In our bicentennial year of 1976, it would give new luster to the promise of the right to life, liberty, and the pursuit of happiness.

5
Questions and Answers

From the catechismal crucible of the lecture circuit among numerous audiences representative of every segment of our society —the youth on our campuses, the professional groups, the businessmen, the chaplains of our prisons, the probation departments and correctional workers, the bar associations, the fraternities— emerged these typical questions and answers to the challenging creed of the second chance.

Can the law legislate forgiveness?

Of course, the law can no more legislate forgiveness into the hearts and minds of the unforgiving than it can force honesty upon the morally depraved by mere dictatorial decree.

But it can set the guiding pace for the new morality by its own precept and example. "Our government is the potent, the omnipresent teacher," declared Justice Brandeis. "For good or for ill, it teaches the whole people by its example."

"The most important thing of all about the Watergate investigation is the extraordinary demonstration of the force of law," Archibald Cox told a cheering audience of Columbia University students and faculty members shortly after he had been fired as special prosecutor.

Contrast the changing pulse of the Deep South, in the shining aftermath of the law's convulsive prods, within the last decade alone. Look back at James Meredith's bayonet-backed bid for admission to the impregnably segregated Ole Miss Law School; the bars are now down in every campus throughout the nation. A black mayor has just been elected in the heartland of Atlanta, Georgia; the first black homecoming queen ever in the history of the University of Alabama—the scene of Governor George Wallace's doorway stand against integration—now receives the school's prized trophy at the hands of the same governor, to the frenzied cheers of 58,000 student fans.

It was the energizer of the law that gave impetus to the women's liberation movement. It was the law's persuasive power of the public purse that quickened the court-ordered racial desegregation blueprints for public college systems and reintegrated housing throughout the country.

The rule of law, with equal effectiveness, can truly help turn the tides of public opinion towards the ultimate forgiveness of the first offender.

Would you limit the right of amnesty to first offenders only?

There is no sound reason why the same amnesty should not be made ultimately available to the deserving second, third, or umpteenth offender as well—provided only that he is not within the excepted class of a "dangerous offender," and that he passes muster under the law's specific prescription that "such grant of amnesty would best serve and secure his rehabilitation, and would best serve the public interest."

Certainly, as quickly as possible, we would move to extend amnesty to all juvenile offenders, regardless of the number of prior offenses, so long as the standards of qualification are faithfully met in terms of rehabilitation as well as the public interest.

"I would not shut the door of hope on any one," declared the great Cardozo in an historic address at the New York Academy of Medicine in 1928, "though classified in some statistical table as defective or recidivist, so long as scientific analysis and study of his mental and physical reactions after the state had taken him in hand, held out the promise of redemption."

Aren't the terms "second chance" or amnesty rather suggestive of coddling the criminal offender?

The second chance I speak of is far from a giftwrapped whitewash of the criminal wrongdoer, or any blanket giveaway of the public security or safety, and any coddling of the criminal offender to any degree. Nor is the amnesty I speak of even remotely related to the free-loading politicized "amnesty" that has become the standard hallmark of every airline hijacker, guerrilla assassin, and flag burner in modern times.

No, the amnesty I espouse is rigidly keyed to the precondition of lawful punishment in every case. Further, it is tied to the completion of a fixed probationary interval following the termination of the sentence—five years for a felony, three years for a misdemeanor, one year for a minor offense. And, finally, to complete the trilogy of correctional tests, it is an amnesty earned only after the tour de force of a specific judicial fact-finding that its bestowal would not only advance the offender's rehabilitation but conserve the public interest in equal measure.

This amnesty would be no utopian dream of impracticability, for the desensitized criminal record would remain fully available to law enforcement in the actual detection, investigation, and prosecution of crime. And finally, to batten down all the hatches of the public security, amnesty would be automatically forfeited immediately upon conviction of a second offense.

So, far from coddling the criminal, the rule of amnesty would have exactly the opposite effect against the professional criminal element and potential recidivist, who would be uniquely vulnerable to the heavy hand of a harsh sentence as second or multiple offenders for spurning the hand of the second chance.

You have estimated that there are about fifty million first offenders in this country. Would all of them be eligible for amnesty if the law were put into effect now?

Practically all, excluding only a minuscule percentage of "dangerous offenders" and others disqualified under the "public interest" test.

Considering that over 75 percent of all first offenders receive no more than a fine, a probationary sentence, or unconditional discharge, it is evident that most in these categories would encounter no difficulty at all in passing muster with the amnesty court.

We are assuming, of course, that the punishment has been completed and that the probationary interval has been terminated in each case.

Fifty million first offenders in this country? Wouldn't that really figure out to at least one in every four of the population, excluding those in the under-teens?

It is estimated that one of every four persons in this country will develop cancer during their lifetime; one of every four marriages will end up on the rocks of divorce or annulment. By comparison, why should the equivalent figure for first offenders be any more exceptionally startling, given the massive number of criminal convictions generated each passing year? If at least six out of every ten American boys now growing up in American cities will be arrested sometime in their lives, as the President's Crime Commission report states, the one-of-four projection is not too wide of the mark, by any means.

You have stated that "dangerous offenders" are categorically excluded from amnesty. Can you furnish some concrete cases?

A "dangerous offender" is defined as one who, after due hearing by the sentencing court, shall be declared and adjudged to be suffering from a serious personality disorder indicating a marked propensity towards continuing criminal conduct or activity. The concept is one that has been adopted in the Model Penal Code of the American Law Institute, and in the Model Sentencing Code of the National Council of Crime and Delinquency in 1963.

In the current lineup of typical "dangerous offenders" would be such as the demented gunman convicted of the attempted assassination of Governor George Wallace, the Boston Strangler, the superstar madman who crippled Michelangelo's *Pieta* in the Vatican, the ruthless assassins Lee Harvey Oswald, Sirhan Sirhan, and James Earl Ray, and the self-styled field marshal of the Symbionese Liberation Army.

To add a few illustrative examples from the back files of my own experience as criminal prosecutor in Brooklyn: George Metesky, the Mad Bomber of the 1950s, committed to the Mattewan State Prison for the Criminally Insane; Roscoe Kazle Anthony, the cold-blooded gun and cleaver killer under life sentence for a triple homicide; Burton Pugach, the jilted suitor imprisoned for maiming in the acid-blinding of a former girl friend.

How would the convicted assassin of Martin Luther King stack up as a candidate for amnesty?

The prognosis is rather negative. Manifestly, James Earl Ray would have been automatically disqualified from amnesty eligibility right at the very sentencing level as a thrice-convicted convict, and additionally as an escaped dangerous offender.

And realistically, even if he were technically eligible to apply, amnesty would be practically out of sight for him, for it will be ninety-nine years before his maximum prison term will have been completed, and he will be ineligible for parole consideration until more than half of that sentence is served. Add to that stretch the probationary interval of five years. Above all, consider the extreme unlikelihood that any court in the foreseeable future would ever justify an award of amnesty in the public interest.

Would you grant amnesty even to persons convicted of murder or treason? Sex offenders? Traffickers of heroin?

If any ex-offender would meet all the preconditions and criteria of amnesty, my answer would be unqualifiedly yes; otherwise, no. That is to say, if they are not deemed excludible as "dangerous offenders," if they have completed their due punishment for whatever crime was committed, if the full probationary interval has been satisfactorily terminated, and finally if a court will prudently certify that the public interest test of amnesty has been fully met, then there could be no rational objection to their inclusion not only for their sake, but for ours as well.

Homicide and sex offenders? It may surprise you to know that these are among the least of criminal recidivists. "Certain types of offenders, such as those convicted of forgery and larceny," reported Ronald H. Beattie, chief of the Bureau of Criminal Statistics, California Department of Justice, and criminal statistician of the United States Bureau of the Census, in the *Journal of Criminal Law* (May–June, 1960, pp. 49, 63), "consistently show a much greater tendency to repeat their criminal behavior than do persons involved in certain crimes against the person, such as sex offenders and homicide offenders."

Treason? To heal the nation, didn't President Andrew Johnson proclaim full amnesty to hundreds of thousands deemed guilty of treason for having taken an active part in the Confederate rebellion against the United States of America?

Be that as it may, regardless of the plausibility of any argument in their behalf, the proponents of amnesty would readily accede to compromise on this issue and exclude, for the time being, an ex-offender in these categories, if it would only help speed the day for the final fruition of amnesty for all other first offenders.

Would it not be really lying or perjurious for an amnestied person to deny that he had ever been arrested or convicted of any crime?

It is neither perjury nor lying to assert as a fact what the law has expressly authorized one to do.

Under amnesty, it would not be lying, or fraud, or perjury, to permit the amnestied first offender to lawfully disavow his prior offense under the statutory dispensation of total forgiveness. What the state has taken away, the state can surely give back. It is the state, after all, that declared the crime in the first place, that mandated the arrest and the conviction, that fixed the sentence, and that perpetuated the stigma of the criminal record into a lifetime second punishment. Surely the state's power to forgive can be no less omnipotent than its sovereign power to punish.

Boiled down to its proper perspective, in asking the amnestied person whether he had ever been previously arrested or convicted, an employer would be implicitly telling him, in effect: "If you have been amnestied pursuant to law, you may answer in the negative."

Analogously, the situation of an amnestied person would be no different, in legal and practical effect, than that long reserved for juveniles or youthful offenders—every one of whom are lawfully sanctioned to deny that they have ever been convicted of any "crime," even though the very same offense would have been deemed a full-fledged crime had it been committed by any adult.

By the same token of public policy, the law specifically empowers a party to an annulled marriage to declare truthfully, even under oath, that he or she has never been previously married, for the rescinded marriage, as Cardozo simply described it, "is effaced as if it had never been."

As to fraud and perjury, there is another side to the coin. It is not the amnesty system that would put a premium upon lying or fraud, but rather the present policy of the second punishment that routinely goads most ex-offenders into a wandering morality of falsehood to keep their criminal records undercover, concealed from employers, social acquaintances, and even from families.

Moreover, legions of disfranchised ex-offenders have illegally voted in every election. Untold millions have deceptively practiced licensed vocations or bonded businesses through the sub rosa ruse of dummy fronts to provide legitimacy for their operations. And in the syndrome of all the lying and subterfuge, even the probation and parole officers sworn to uphold the law are ofttimes compelled to yield to the national pastime of white lies and benign falsehood simply to preserve an ongoing livelihood for the job-begotten wards in their charge.

As a practical alternative to the authorized negation of the arrest and conviction record, why not simply require that employment applications be limited to this form: "Have you ever been convicted or arrested for a crime or offense which had not been amnestied or expunged?"

The trouble with semantic gamesmanship of this sort is that it would surely lay amnesty open to all manner of artful dodges and subterfuges to undermine it.

Experience has shown that the juvenile offender laws, designed to protect the minor against the stigmatization of a criminal record, have been compromised through the years by abusive misapplications on the part of private employers and public agencies to circumvent their objectives. A diluted amnesty system would inevitably succumb to the same devices. To take the very question you propose, its patently open-ended ambiguities would invite a criminal offender who had actually forfeited his status of amnesty because of a subsequent reconviction to try to crawl through its loopholes by fraudulently attempting to answer it in the negative.

In alternate forms, hiring managers equally disingenuous would subvert the amnesty system with supplemental employment questions such as these: "Have you ever been granted amnesty for any crime or offense; if so, give details. Have you ever been detained or interrogated on any criminal charge? Have you ever been accused or informed against? Have you ever been fined or sentenced or placed on probation?"

The only fail-safe, foolproof method to guarantee the letter and spirit of amnesty against all evasion is to implement the public policy of all-out forgiveness with the all-out expungement of the offense in every aspect.

Why a waiting lapse of five long years after completion of punishment before a man can apply for amnesty? Doesn't a parolee or ex-prisoner really need the assist of amnesty most the moment the prison gates close behind him?

The probationary interval is purposefully flexible, to accommodate the public interest in each individual case. Thus, the five-year period in felony cases can be shortened to any lesser time, or amnesty granted forthwith, in any deserving case, either by the sentencing court, or any parole board.

I have no objection, in principle, however, to the reduction of the general probationary interval to a substantially lesser period in each category of offenses—say, from five years to two years for felonies, from three years to one year for misdemeanors, from one year to six months or three months for mere arrests or adjudications as a youthful offender or juvenile delinquent, after punishment is terminated in each case.

As to those who must wait the full length of the probationary interval, take solace in the fact that a period of five years is as nothing compared to the interminable life sentence under the prevailing system.

Would you personally have any qualms about hiring an amnestied ex-offender for any position of trust or fiduciary capacity?

If I were an employer, I would unhesitatingly entrust the amnestied ex-offender in any capacity of trust or responsibility whatever. To be more specific, I would have no qualms whatever in employing him as a bank teller, policeman, correction officer, social worker, or in any other position of trust.

Keep in mind that the amnestied individual will have passed the screening eye of an amnesty court under the touchstones of personal rehabilitation and of the public interest. To a matured ex-offender who has experienced an actual arrest, conviction, sentence, and attendant stigma, the odds against a relapse would be relatively far out of sight.

For each of them, the prized treasure of amnesty would re-main a constant incentive to lawful behavior. The forfeiture of amnesty for renewed criminal conduct, and the harsher penalties befalling a multiple offender so circumstanced, would be an option that only a scant few indeed would ever risk or elect.

Time and again, experience has proven that an ex-offender or parolee, treated with humaneness and dignity, will almost invari-ably respond in kind with loyalty, devotion, and integrity second to none. In the larger view, just think what amnesty could achieve by way of redemption for the ex-offender, in the context of for-giveness after punishment is done.

In the crystal ball of predictive behavior, one could plainly see that the amnestied individual looms large indeed as a potential exemplar of law-abiding conduct, even as against all others.

Wouldn't employers try to subvert the amnesty system by prying into the past residence and employment background of all job applicants, thus ferreting out information as to all ex-prison in-mates?

To a degree, the attempted sabotage of the amnesty system would be a real possibility as to the comparatively limited number of ex-prisoners, compared to the full complement of all other am-nestied individuals.

However, once the spirit of amnesty becomes solidified into the living law, it is fairly certain from past experience in the com-parable civil rights area that any circumventive practices would be quickly disowned by most of the responsible private employers and governmental agencies. Additionally, hand in hand with the leverage of moral suasion, the enforcement arms of the civil rights commissions and the injunctive powers of the courts would play a significant guardian role.

Would the licensing authorities be obligated to reinstate doctors or lawyers to their profession automatically upon attainment of a grant of amnesty?

Not automatically; but if they are professionally qualified by aptitude and good character to resume the practice of their profession, then the criminal record of the amnestied doctor or lawyer, architect or teacher, would no longer serve of itself as an artificial barrier to reinstatement.

Under the new dispensation of societal forgiveness, backed by the overseership and vigilance of the civil rights commissions, the licensing agencies shall have to account for a prudent exercise of discretion in each case.

Are there any teeth in the amnesty law to guarantee full protection to the amnestied offender?

Firstly, a watchdog civil rights commission would have the saber-toothed power and authority to enforce the forgiveness decreed by the amnesty law.

By cease-and-desist orders on the complaint of any aggrieved individual, backed by the contempt powers of the judiciary, any arbitrary firing or refusal to hire an amnestied individual in public or private employment could be summarily enjoined.

Secondly, to protect the right of privacy for every amnestied individual, the malicious disclosure or publication of the expunged arrest or conviction record would constitute an actionable criminal offense punishable by fine or imprisonment or both and, in addition, would render the violator reparationally responsible in punitive damages at the instance of any aggrieved amnestied individual.

Would there be any recourse if amnesty were arbitrarily withheld, or if anyone is wrongly adjudged a "dangerous offender"?

Any capricious action in either case would be quickly and appropriately dealt with by prompt appellate review.

If an amnestied person is subsequently arrested and placed on trial, would the prior criminal record be available to impeach his credibility?

No, neither the defense nor the prosecution would be permitted to refer to his previous conviction. The amnestied record would be simply kept out of evidence, for use by neither side, until the conclusion of the trial.

If he is acquitted, then his amnestied status continues unabated as heretofore; if convicted, he automatically forfeits his right to amnesty and is treated as a multiple offender for the specific purposes of increased punishment.

In sum, all that we will have changed under amnesty to insure a trial free of prejudice is to apply the rule of evidence that has long prevailed in England, where a criminal record may not be generally used for the purpose of impeachment of a witness. In fact, the trend in this country is now exactly in the same direction —the proposed uniform rules of evidence would prohibit the use of a prior conviction against a defendant unless he himself had introduced collateral evidence to support his own credibility.

Can the amnesty system be administered practically and efficiently?

The very same computerized science that can routinely transmit fingerprints across the nation in a matter of seconds, that can speed case histories through a master network for the proper identification of recidivist offenders, that can pinpoint a stolen car in Baton Rouge, Louisiana, as the getaway car of a New York bank robbery, and that can keep currently functional with sophisticated programming in such widely divergent fields as business inventories, credit dossiers, space probes, weather data, and a host of other applications, should have little difficulty, in this age of megatechnics, in adapting the relatively simple demands of amnesty to the practical service of the criminal justice system.

Wouldn't the amnesty network impose a serious strain upon the public treasury?

The financial costs for new judges and courtrooms, whatever

they may be, would be negligible compared to the infinitely greater dollar savings in the cutback of crime.

Consider: If the putative leverage of amnesty could help reclaim but one-fourth (some knowledgeable experts say one-half) of all potential recidivists, the dissolution of a commensurate mass of recidivist business now clogging the criminal court calendars throughout the nation would alone pay the full costs of the amnesty system.

Consider, too, the tremendous economies automatically inherent in the restructuring of the law enforcement and correctional services to accommodate the practical elimination of all amnestied ex-offenders and the greatly reduced need for new prisons, courthouses, and all ancillary facilities.

Consider, above all, the dramatic downturn of human victimization at the hands of all those turned off from recidivism under the impulse of the amnesty law.

Regardless of cost, the essential business of criminal justice is not an exercise in cost accounting but to do justice. If the amnesty brand of justice delivers its promise to the scores of millions directly affected—with all that it portends for the welfare of our country and the security of every one of us—then suffice it to say that for its price, whatever it may be, justice will have paid for and attained its finest hour.

Can our legal system absorb a new caseload of tens of millions of amnesty cases with our already clogged court calendars?

Undoubtedly the boom situation in the initial stages would call for the creation of a special amnesty court, or as an alternative, a separate administration amnesty commission, to relieve the courts of this avalanche of new cases.

In either case, most amnesty petitions would require no hearings or other substantial expenditure of court time, especially the preponderating number of eligibles who had received no more than a fine, a discharge on probation, or a suspended sentence.

Wouldn't the advent of amnesty tend to dry up the menial job, low-pay labor market of the criminal ex-offender? Who will be there to take his place?

Yes, the upgrading of the ex-offender into a higher level of employment opportunities will undoubtedly raise some havoc in the labor exchange of the exploitative employer.

However, the republic will surely survive the grand displacement—stronger even than ever before. Witness the historic comparisons of such past economic upheavals as the child-labor laws, the emancipation of the slaves, the minimum wage. Witness the new ferment in economic levels and social status affected by the massive racial restructuring and women's liberation.

Assuredly, the labor market will not run dry by any means. With competence rising to its own level, the inexhaustible reserve of yet untapped manpower will be constantly more than adequate to fill the demand for the bottom-rung, marginal, menial jobs.

Do you think that the pardoning power of the governors and the politicians would readily yield their goldmine of political patronage to the fierce competition of amnesty?

Undoubtedly not, but the counterpressures of the vastly outnumbering forces of amnesty, having a political base of some fifty million first offenders and their families, should be able to supply some quick answers in the realpolitik of reform.

Would a grant of amnesty by one state be recognized and honored in all other states?

Yes, under the full faith and credit clause of the Constitution, a person granted amnesty by the state that had originally criminalized him would undoubtedly be accorded the same rights, privileges, and immunities of amnesty in all other jurisdictions.

A complicating legal question would arise, however, as to a person amnestied by New York covering a conviction rendered in another state. Should that person subsequently remove to a third state, some knotty questions could arise whether the latter state would be legally bound to honor New York's amnesty of the "foreign" conviction under the interstate comity clause.

These and other practical difficulties could be effectively resolved by enactment of reciprocal amnesty legislation in all the states as well as in Congress to cover all federal crimes.

Is the impact of the second punishment the monopoly of the United States alone?

In the global panorama of crime and punishment, the ravages of the second punishment are of worldwide scope and of universal concern, leaving their sobering imprint everywhere. The Jean Valjeans of the international community have long shared a common cause of crippling victimization.

Is there any amnesty-type legislation now in operation in any other coun ry?

There are none that bespeak the direct and unequivocal forgiveness of total amnesty. Some countries, such as Russia, Switzerland, Sweden, France, and the Netherlands physically destroy or expunge criminal records after a specified period, ten or twenty years later.

Then again, some few European countries, such as Italy, specialize in purely politicized "amnesties"—totally divorced from any abstract principles of law or justice—in celebration of such state occasions as the inauguration of a new president, or even as a gimmick to unclog crowded court calendars.

The prevailing yardstick, however, seems to be little more than a pardon of punishment, without regard to such relevant criteria as rehabilitation or correction, or to the public safety, and with no distinction whatever between the incorrigible repeater and the first offender. And, atop all, though the formal record of the conviction be technically expunged in any case, the stark odium of the offense and the lingering fact of the arrest—as well as the expungement itself—abides forevermore in a never-ending second punishment.

Are there any amnesty laws now operative in this country, such as the one you have advocated?

Oddly, none.

Back in 1956, Professor Paul W. Tappan wrote in a foreword to my tract *First Offenders: A Second Chance:*

> Strangely little attention has been given either by the legal profession or by criminologists to the need for effecting such changes in law and community sentiment as may cleanse the status of the rehabilitated person so that he may start afresh. It is patent that change of some sort is peculiarly important to the first offender and for the young delinquent, not only out of humanistic considerations but for legitimate, criminological ends.

Ten years later, Professor Aidan R. Gough of the University of Santa Clara, writing in the *Washington University Law Quarterly* for April, 1966, also noted:

> Despite relatively widespread judicial recognition of the perdurability and disabling effects of a criminal record, scant attention has been given by lawmakers and behavioral scientists to means whereby the law might, in a proper case, relieve the first offender, juvenile miscreant from this handicap.

Remarkably enough, the signposts of amnesty for humankind, each to the other, have all along dwelled in the ancient *Talmud* (*Taan 25b*), where it is plainly written:

> Our Father, our King, forgive and pardon all our sins.
> Our Father, our King, blot out and remove our transgressions and sins from thy sight.
> Our Father, our King, cancel in thy abundant mercy all the records of our sins.
> Our Father, our King, bring us back in perfect repentance to thee.

What are the prospects for amnesty legislation at the present time?
Some fifteen years ago, I asked the late Professor Paul W.

Tappan how long it would take to mold amnesty into law. His educated guess was that it would take no more than two years, that the idea of the second chance for the first offender would generate a ready response everywhere.

What we hadn't reckoned with was the thorny opposition of the newspaper lobby to the amnesty upstart that dared challenge "the people's right to know.". . .

PART III

Breakthrough to Amnesty

The task of social engineering has outgrown the machinery we had devised in the past. We must build newer, bigger and more effective machines for today and even more for tomorrow.

Roscoe Pound

6
In the
Legislative Arena

Amnesty leaped into its legislative debut in the year 1958.

Close on the heels of its introductory demarche into the bill hopper of the New York state senate, the newspaper lobby suddenly zeroed in against this threat to the "people's right to know," setting the stage for a momentous confrontation between the untrammeled right of a free press to circulate all the news it deems fit to print and what Justice Brandeis called the greatest right of all in a free society—the right of privacy, in the fatalistic quest for criminological reform.

The sponsor of the amnesty measure was none other than the senate's foremost authority on penal affairs, a topmost member of the New York criminal bar, Senator Harry Gittleson of Brooklyn, New York.

What particularly stirred the ire of the organized press was the sharp-clawed implemental enforcement clause in all-out protection of the amnestied individual. It provided that any person, firm, or corporation—other than law enforcement officers actually engaged in the investigation, detection, or prosecution of crime—

who or which, directly or indirectly, shall wilfully disclose, publish or allude to the fact of said conviction or any record pertaining thereto, or of any information obtained from such records in any manner or for any purpose whatsoever shall be guilty of a misdemeanor and shall be liable to the amnestied first offender in a civil action for punitive damages, and any such disclosure, publication or allusion thereto shall be deemed libelous or slanderous per se, as the case may be.

On February 28, 1958, the *New York Herald Tribune* exploded with a Paul Reverian front-page, double-columned spread headlined:

BILL WOULD ELIMINATE 1ST OFFENDER'S RECORD. ALBANY MEASURE RESTORES RIGHTS IF NO 2D CONVICTION IN FIVE YEARS.

By-lined Albany, the capital of New York, the *Trib* solemnly issued its warning.

New York City officials expressed concern here today over proposed legislation now before the Senate Judiciary Committee which would have the effect of wiping off the record books a crime committed by a first offender, provided the second offense was not committed in a five-year period.

The bill, introduced by Sen. Harry Gittleson, Brooklyn Democrat, is designed to erase restrictions of a resident of the state who has been convicted of a crime and served his sentence. . . .

Although no one in the office of Police Commissioner Stephen P. Kennedy wanted to be quoted directly on the matter while it is still before the Senate committee, it was learned that the official feeling was that the law would have the ffect [sic] of erasing valuable police records.

Shades of Horace Greeley, whose honored masthead it bore— it could not possibly be that the austerely objective *Herald Tribune* would consciously stoop to discolor the news! For manifestly, as the *Trib* had surely overlooked, the bill had distinctly provided that the police records were to remain fully available to law enforcement officers.

With all deliberate speed, the city editor took due note of Senator Gittleson's voluble protest and quickly assigned one of its crack reporters, David Lysle, to pin down the salient features of the amnesty bill for a corrective story. With the facts now firmly in hand, Mr. Lysle filed his newly researched copy that very day for publication in the following issue.

Meanwhile, the *New York Daily News*—boasting the largest daily circulation in the United States—unexpectedly entered the fray.

"The Silly Season seems to have hit Albany with a vengeance," it said, editorially lashing out against a number of bills which it urged the legislators to "toss into the nearest ashcan."

"And, while they're at it," boomed the editor,

> an even sillier bill, introduced by Sen. Harry Gittleson (D-Brooklyn), might also get the heave. Gittleson proposes to erase any and all records of criminal first-offenses, provided the felon doesn't get caught again for the next five years.
>
> Thus cops would have no background evidence left in their files, and newspapers could be prosecuted for warning the public that today's convicted mugger or rapist was found guilty of the same thing five years ago.
>
> What's in that Albany air, anyway?

The *News* fusillade against amnesty was singularly flawed not only in its misstatement that the bill would "erase" police records, but in its palpable perversion of the bill's contents that the amnesty law would prevent newspapers from printing anything about a twice-convicted mugger or rapist.

What the *News* had uncandidly kept from its readers was that the measure unreservedly applied to first offenders only; that amnesty would be automatically lost to any "twice-convicted mugger or rapist" under the forfeiture provisions aimed at the criminal repeater; and that the criminal psychopath, first offender or not, was categorically excluded.

In reaction to the *News*'s "silly" editorial, Senator Gittleson promptly hot-lined the city desk from the capital district of Albany, but an iron curtain of secretarial outposts kept the legislator from getting through to the command post. And, injury atop injury, the *Trib*'s sanitized version of the amnesty story was quietly interred in the newspaper morgue.

It had now become painfully clear that the journalistic Mafia had given the people's right to know an awful beating.

Back in the legislative barricades, the New York Civil Liberties Union now firmly placed itself on record in favor of the amnesty bill. Entreating the chairman of the Senate Judiciary Committee of the state senate, it stated:

> The New York Civil Liberties Union wishes to be recorded in favor of this bill.
>
> We believe it is important to have some method whereby a person who has been convicted once of committing criminal acts —very often in his youth—will not be penalized for the rest of his life for this indiscretion. This bill will give added encouragement to the ex-criminal not to return to a life of crime, and will also supply at least one solution to the problem of refusal to grant licenses, permits and other privileges to persons who have a criminal conviction of many years past on their record.

In this setting, Senator Gittleson successfully moved the bill out of the Judiciary Committee onto the floor of the New York state senate. Thus amnesty's cause had now finally entered the public domain.

> *Senator Gittleson:* Mr. President.
> *The President:* The Senator from the 18th.
> *Senator Gittleson:* I suppose I should rise on a high point of personal privilege at first, but rather than do that, I would prefer to discuss this bill. In passing, I should like to refer to the matter

that has addressed my attention to the question of high personal privilege.

We have a metropolitan newspaper in the City of New York called The Daily News. A week ago last Saturday, I think it was, one of their brilliant editorial writers captioned an editorial and wanted to know, "How silly one can get," then proceeded to say that Senator Harry Gittleson sponsored a bill that I am sure they didn't have the slightest conception of, but did insist it was the product of "How silly can you get."

Now, it seems to me that we in this House have reached a state where we ought not to worry too much about what one man may think of a bill, even if he happens to be an editorial writer, that isn't to say, however, that nobody may criticize or disagree with me: I do insist that when that one man has the temerity to characterize another's mentality in the language indicated, it is high time that we stood up on our haunches and said, "Wait a minute"—particularly since the paper did not have the common decency to advise me who authored that brilliant piece of prose.

Whoever he is, I should like to advise him through somebody present in this Chamber that apparently his paper does not know its own record. As early as two years ago this same particular bill and concept was discussed in complimentary terms in two separate special articles in the Brooklyn section by a reporter named O'Brien. He opined that it was conceived as a pioneering venture in penology and recommended that the matter be given adequate consideration.

When I called the editor to find out—or the editorial desk— to find out who wrote the article, I wasn't even given the courtesy of being identified or having the man identified and up to this date I haven't had the opportunity to tell that gentleman precisely how I felt about the magnificent editorial.

The difficulty, of course, is they have a two million circulation; in my immediate area, I asume that they have at least a 50,000 circulation.

But let us get to this bill. First, we ought to set the matter straight. This is not a program for coddling prisoners. This program that we have enunciated in this bill is to insure rehabilitation of prisoners after they have served their sentence, not before.

We don't suggest in this bill that under any circumstances a judge should, in imposing sentence, take into consideration anything other than the normal channels of information. He shouldn't disregard the fact that this man, whoever he might be, committed a heinous crime, if that is the crime for which he is being punished; we urge after he is punished, and after he has paid his debt to society—not before then—that the person be given a second chance and, if he earns it, we say that he should be entitled to get and enjoy it, we say that he should be entitled to get and enjoy the same privileges that a normal man is entitled to receive at the hand of his fellow man.

Now, I am not accustomed to using the word Christian bill, but if there is ever a bill that should appeal to men's normal instinct, in my opinion, this is the bill, and for the benefit of that editorial writer, I may say that I am in pretty good company.

I shall give you just a few of the people who endorse this bill: Dean Roscoe Pound—perhaps "Mr. Jurisprudence" in the United States of America; Chief Judge Conway of the Court of Appeals; Judge Leibowitz—I guess all of you have heard that name. He prides himself upon being the toughest judge in the United States. Paul W. Tappan, used to be Chairman of the United States Parole Board; James V. Bennett, the Chief of the Bureau of Prisons of the United States Department of Justice. All universities in the country have given their endorsement to the concept. I have before me but a few letters—and I am not going to read any of them—but this only represents one-fiftieth of the file, just one-fiftieth—and I say it to you literally—containing letters of endorsement for the concept and intent of this bill.

J. Edgar Hoover did not endorse this bill itself nor the concept, but did confirm that there are fifty million first offenders directly affected. I am only confining myself to those who have actually endorsed the bill. Now, I haven't spoken about the universities that have endorsed the concept, either, except in passing.

Let me tell you what this bill does, gentlemen; I would first want to address your attention to those who are opposed to the bill. The papers are opposed to this bill. I don't like to dismiss them by saying we shouldn't legislate for newspapers only. Of course, if we actually did that, we would be doing a salutary thing. That might be a little too much to expect, but I do say that their objection is steeped in selfish motives, and they don't understand the bill or if they do understand it, they don't want to concede that they do.

Let us read the bill together. It provides that if a man is convicted for the first time of a felony or a misdemeanor (and if the latter they include those involving moral turpitude)—after he has completed his sentence and after the lapse of five years thereafter, if he has behaved himself, he automatically wins amnesty; it continues only so long as he lives a decent life. If convicted a second time, he forfeits his privileges and is sentenced as a second offender; not as a first offender at all. In other words, his record comes back to plague him. In the meantime, so long as he behaves himself, he has the right to vote, which he has lost if he was convicted as a felon. He has the right to actually serve as a member of a jury which the normal person possesses. He has a right to hold public office. In addition to that he can engage in any licensed occupation or profession if he had lost the right to do so, by reason of the conviction, provided, however, that he is otherwise qualified.

In fairness, the author of this concept should be identified. He is an Assistant District Attorney, by name Aaron Nussbaum, presently connected with the Brooklyn office. He is a learned and cultured chap. He wrote a book about the subject some two years ago. All of you received copies of it last year and you probably did what we do with most of our mail. You and I probably threw it in the wastepaper basket. We erred. The book was one well worth while reading. He circularized every university in the United States, every chief of parole in the United States, every person engaged in penology in the United States or in the study of criminology and every Chief Justice of every State in the Union. He got back glowing letters telling him that his concept was well conceived.

Last year he crystalized the thinking of hundreds upon hundreds of letters. A member of the Assembly drew a bill that didn't satisfy him, consequently he refrained from causing same to be introduced. This year Mr. Nussbaum came up with the product of his thinking.

The only persons that he found opposed to this concept were those who think once a person is convicted of a felony or a misdeameanor—either he is a social outcast or socially incurable. He emphasized that not only the individual involved would be benefitted but in addition the public at large would profit. He pointed to the frequent injustices resulting from a conviction suffered most frequently through one's formative years. He refreshes our recollection on the occasions when the District Attorney is confronted with the necessity of resting his case on the testimony of an ex-con, who more often than not has been completely rehabilitated only to have his witness demolished by the seasoned lawyer's "Have you ever been convicted of a crime?" In civil litigations, a rehabilitated ex-con finds himself completely frustrated when compelled to affirmatively answer the same question.

I don't think a person ought to be labelled or branded that way. I think by and large, that if a person has returned to a normal and honest way of life, the least that he may expect from society is to be permitted to regain the respect and dignity that his fellow man possesses.

The newspapers announced that they were opposed to this bill because the people through them have "the right to know" what goes on in government. We believe that if they mean they have a right to constantly publish the fact that a person has been previously convicted without the restrictions or sanctions set forth in our bill, then we have destroyed the measure's purpose.

The bill provides that once a man has won his amnesty all records are sealed, except to those who are legitimately engaged in the prosecution of crime.

We insist that the beneficial aspects of the bill will be completely lost if, so long as a person is enjoying amnesty, anybody may make reference to his guilt. We have tried to avoid an invasion of rehabilitated persons' rights by imposing sanctions and restrictions. The newspapers oppose these sanctions. Perhaps they do not understand the operation of the program. Let me illustrate. Suppose a person at age twenty is sentenced to five to ten years in jail. Before that person becomes eligible for amnesty, he must serve his five years in jail and then five more years must elapse before he earns the right to amnesty. In the intervening ten-year period, any time before the expiration of the sentence plus five years, every newspaper has a right to a person's record, say anything they want to, provided, of course, they tell the truth. The only time they are foreclosed, and that is the purpose of this bill, viz: that a man should not be plagued forever after the expiration of the sentence plus five years, and then only if the same person has not been convicted in the interim.

What is wrong with that philosophy? What is wrong with saying to the newspapers that they cannot refer to a person's record until he lapses, and is convicted again.

I think that the bill presents a worthwhile contribution not only to the person who lapses but also to a liberal minded society so that it receives a useful citizen.

One other objection is raised by the newspapers. They argue

that a person automatically resumes his profession even if that profession refuses a license. Had they read the bill they could not have fallen into that error. It provides that he may not resume his profession unless he is otherwise fully qualified.

Now, I submit I am not going to waste more time on this bill. I am convinced if there was ever a bill that deserved the commendation of this Body, certainly if there was ever a bill that should get the seal of this State as a pioneering State in forward-looking legislation, this is the bill. It may be that it is not perfect in detail. It may well be that a lot of things are in here that should be omitted but the concept is one that should be adopted and should receive the approval of enlightened people and members of this Senate.

I say it in all sincerity because I am thoroughly sold on the purpose of the bill. If there are any errors or omissions we would gladly remedy them. Frankly, I think we ought to get some encouragement from this body. Whether or not it is passed in the Assembly makes no difference to me. I should like to get an expression of opinion whether the thinking is right or wrong. I would be very happy to obtain your reaction for two reasons: first, whether the concept is right and secondly, to serve notice upon newspaper editors that they cannot say to us we are crackpots when they do not know what they are talking about: they should not characterize any of us in opprobrious terms. If we are in the company of honest, intelligent people of the type that I have indicated, they ought to know that they may be mistaken sometimes and they ought to know that if a concept is good even though the adoption might affect their circulation, they cannot come into a Legislative body and say, "We won't have it just because we have the power of the press. That is wrong."

Gentlemen, I submit it to you and I think it ought to pass this body.

Senator Erway: Mr. President.

The President: The Senator from the 36th Senatorial District.

Senator Erway: Will the Senator yield?

Senator Gittleson: Sure.

Senator Erway: I have expressed my views as to the general principle which this bill achieves, but the thing that disturbs me very much is—and the bill certainly should do it—it covers all past crimes. In other words, a man who was convicted of a felony 20 years ago and has lived 20 years, he gets the benefit of this bill. Now, what are you going to do—what will happen to the Correction Department? This would mean the altering and setting up of a complete new system in the Correction Department and this bill takes effect immediately.

How in the world would they go about it with the hundreds of thousands of fingerprints and records in the Department?

Senator, I think you have something there and I am in favor of it, but that disturbs me and I do not know how the Correction Department would do it.

Senator Gittleson: I understand that and I have an idea it may require further study in that direction, but there is nothing in the world to stop that arrangement because we have a provision in the bill that provides that when a person has won amnesty, the records are sealed. This will not set up new records, it is only projected as to the future.

It might require better language. Please understand me, I am talking about a concept, a rehabilitation concept. I do not think this is a perfect bill. I think it requires further study, but an expression from this Body to encourage that further study is what I am seeking today.

Senator Speno: Mr. President.

The President: The Senator from the 4th.

Senator Speno: Since we are involved in what appears to be a philosophic discussion here, and a matter of whether or not we should establish some new system of records with respect to crimes that have been committed, I am troubled with your bill in this respect and I have only read it for the first time as it applies to this—it seems to me that we, the public, are entitled to know that a man in his past somewhere has committed some hideous crime.

I take, for instance, the example of a man who applies for some position in which it is necessary that I know, as his employer, whether I can have the trust and confidence or whether I can place him in situations where the temptations to which he succumbed heretofore are present and he may succumb again.

I wonder if this is a drastic departure. It is a deterrent to a repetition of the crime where a man knows he has done wrong and the world knows he has done wrong. I know you have the answer to this and this is a logical question to raise. It seems to me that this is something in the public interest that of course you and I know as to what the cases are, we have had them in the office where a man was convicted of one mistake and is marked for life because of that one mistake. He cannot drive a car and there are many things he cannot do because he made one mistake. But, I submit, Senator, that the wrong done to that man who probably is a good man and will continue in a normal life, is far outweighed by the situations where the people would be whitewashed in their record because of this and we, the public, would be exposed to them if they were tempted again. This, I think, is the fallacy in the reason behind this bill as I think about it today.

Senator Gittleson: The difficulty with your argument is this: You are reasoning along the same lines as all of us have for years, that once a man is labeled an ex-con he must be ostracized from society. If that is the concept we want to follow there is no persuasive argument in opposition, but let me suggest this to you, that once a man pays his debt to society by going to jail, paying his full debt without the slightest diminution, and then for five years has lived an exemplary life, nobody has a right to say, "Let us plague him and ruin him," particularly when you have the right, if he is thereafter convicted, to come back and say, "You are a worthless character."

Don't you see, it is the concept that worries you and I can understand the differing views affecting the concept. I can understand that some people feel that—once a criminal, always a criminal and can be very sincere about it, but I do not subscribe to it and I do not think enlightened-thinking people subscribe to it. I think that under the circumstances we must take a step forward so that we should not have 50 million people in this country in another generation who are going to be tarred and feathered because they were once convicted. The concept, in my opinion, Senator, is unassailable. That is my opinion. Your opinion differs. I cannot criticize it.

The President: The Senator from the 21st.

Senator Watson: As the Senator from Nassau has said, this is the first opportunity I have had to read the bill. But in listening to the debate of the Senator from Kings County I was struck with the thought that this concept follows a concept that many of us here in this Chamber follow. This concept is related to a prayer that many of us say every day of our lives and that is one that we have learned from childhood, that is the Lord's Prayer and I refer specifically to, "Forgive us our trespasses as we forgive those who trespass against us."

For that reason, I am voting for the bill before us, Mr. President.

The President: The Senator from the 19th.

Senator Marchi: I wanted to add my remarks in support of this bill. I cannot think of anything of a constructive nature that would provide a more powerful stimulation to a return to good conduct than an opportunity to wipe the slate clean and have this enforced after a period of good conduct.

I think the Senator is to be complimented.

The President: The Senator from the 8th.

Senator Duffy: Mr. President and Gentlemen, aside from the laudable concept of this bill, one of the parts that I object to is the subdivision 3 on page 6 that the first offender shall have the right to disregard the facts of his arrest, apprehension, detention and other accusations and if he is asked at any time whether he has ever been arrested or convicted or indicted or informed against he has the right to say no.

If he is being tried for a second offense and he has taken the witness stand, he has a right under this bill if he is asked the question "Have you ever been convicted of a crime" to say no.

Now, under our system of law the man is under oath and has sworn to tell the truth. Now, if he is permitted to sit there and say he has never been convicted of a crime when the attorney knows, the District Attorney knows and the Court knows and everybody knows that he has been convicted of a crime, where is our system of law enforcement going to go? Where is our system of jurisprudence going?

If the concept is laudable, and it may be, this particular provision of the bill is not good because it encourages perjury. If you want to take care of that part of it, prohibit the District Attorney from referring at the trial to this question, prohibit him from asking the question, "Have you ever been convicted," and do not let him perjure himself on the witness stand in the presence of the Court and the Judge and everybody else.

Senator Gittleson: I appreciate the force of that statement, but I think again we misconceive the bill. If you will look at page 7, Section 5 of the bill, we do precisely prohibit the District Attorney from questioning the amnestied individual regarding his conviction.

We do not put a stamp of approval on this man to become a perjurer. What we are saying is, what you have done in the past—this is the first offense—is forgiven, and because it is forgiven you can truthfully answer no.

Now that holds true in politics. When you get a Presidential pardon or a Gubernatorial pardon, that is what happens. When you are asked a question under the law you do not answer "yes," but rather, "I have been pardoned." You say no, and that is permitted by law. Let me tell you something else. It isn't anything unusual in the criminal law for a man to get some sort of a favor as a result of a prior conviction. Have you ever heard of amnesty given to people who are co-conspirators? Those fellows get that advantage. Let me tell you about perjury, too. As a matter of fact, this bill would encourage truthfulness and not perjury and it is not inconsistent with what I say and I will tell you why. He is living under a state of amnesty. If he knows that is going to cause him to lose that amnesty he is not going to perjure himself. He will not do it because he is going to lose and be punished as a second offender.

Senator Duffy: If I can answer that, you approach this problem from the point of the problem of the fellow who has committed a wrong and has been convicted of a crime, and deserves amnesty, which is true. So what the question raised by the Senator from Nassau means, don't you think that when you give that back to a fellow and the fellow is subject to going out and committing another crime, if he knows of the existence of this law he knows that after the five years have expired that he is still a first offender?

Senator Gittleson: He does not know that.

Senator Duffy: The deterrent effect of the law with regard to second offenders is gone.

Senator Gittleson: Under the bill if he commits a crime a second time he is a second offender and is punished as such.

Senator Duffy: And this helps him not to be convicted because the prior record is not before the Court.

Senator Gittleson: Why should a prior record cause anyone to convict him if he did not commit the crime? Why should that happen?

When convicted, that fellow is punished as a second offender and not before.

Senator Duffy: The fact that amnesty for a first offense is given under this bill destroys the deterrent effect of knowing he is a second offender or will be if he is caught a second time.

Senator Gittleson: That is not true. As a matter of fact it would encourage him to go straight. He has something precious to safeguard.

Senator Duffy: Let me ask you another question. Why is it

necessary to put in this bill this provision that says that any firm, person or corporation which shall directly or indirectly wilfully disclose, publish or allude to the facts of said conviction or any record pertaining thereto shall be guilty of a misdemeanor and shall be liable to the amnesty of the first offender and an action for damages? Why is that necessary under this bill?

Senator Gittleson: You destroy the amnesty provision. It affects his dignity and respect in his community and that is the purpose to safeguard and rehabilitate him in his community. If you permit newspapers or anybody else to talk about his record you have destroyed the salutary effect of the measure.

The President: The Senator from the 27th.

Senator Gilbert: I support the principle of the bill but there is one thing that disturbs me. I do not do a great deal of criminal law, but I know that there are many instances where the nature of the indictment or the information is based upon whether or not the defendant had previously committed a crime.

Now, would the indictment or the information be affected by your bill?

Senator Gittleson: You are talking about two kinds of cases that might arise. One case I have a distinct recollection of is a case where a fellow was previously convicted under Penal Law Section 1897. By accident, I took care of that by a separate bill. It provides that a person who—upon arraignment—admits, "I am the person who committed the prior crime" and he is tried for the crime with which reference to said prior crime may not thereafter be made before the jury.

If a person was convicted under those circumstances this bill would not affect him.

Senator Harry K. Morton: Mr. President.

The President: The Senator from the 49th.

Senator Morton: Mr. President, I am in favor of freedom of the press as far as that is concerned but I cannot vote for a bill when the preface starts out and indicates that tens of millions of our people are criminals. I would hate to have my grandchildren look back at the preface and think that we were all criminals.

There are good things in the bill but I think it requires more study.

Senator Gittleson: That preface is language cut out of a Court of Appeals decision. The man who drew it has every particular paragraph properly documented indicating the source of each particular declaration and, unfortunately, it happens to be true.

Senator Edward J. Speno: Mr. President.

The President: The Senator from the 4th.

Senator Speno: I detected from your earlier remarks that you have no real hopes of passage of this?

Senator Gittleson: In the other house, no.

Senator Speno: You are soliciting an honest expression of opinion from the members of his body?

Senator Gittleson: That is right.

Senator Speno: It seems there are many of us who agree that there is an area where there should be, and could be amnesty in a given situation. The thing that disturbs me is that you make no distinction in the nature of the crime.

Senator Gittleson: Yes, I do.

Senator Speno: Hear me out, Senator.

I find this fault in your reasoning. I have in mind one or two cases in my own community of heinous crimes involving moral offenses and I have in mind that a man convicted of such a crime has something wrong with his mental makeup. But thereafter, if he is employed by one of us in our homes, and we interviewed him first, he does not tell us that he has been convicted of this charge in the past. So I hire him, or you hire him, and something happens in that unfortunate mind of his and he commits the same crime against a member of my family. To me, sir, if that happens just once, it is enough for me to feel that this bill goes too far.

Senator Gittleson: I cannot criticize the person who thinks it goes too far. I repeat that this bill may contain very many things that must be corrected.

Senator Speno: What about devising some method where an application could be made whereby you get clemency from the Governor or work out a method of probation reports in individual cases?

Senator Gittleson: This is amnesty gained as the result of a man's behavior in his community without the necessity of making an application to any tribunal.

Did you ever try to get a certificate of good conduct? It takes two years and they grant one-twenty-fifth percent of the applications and then only for a limited purpose. The purpose of this is to have the fellow resume his position in society.

Senator Robert C. McEwen: Mr. President.

The President: The Senator from the 40th.

Senator McEwen: Mr. President, I would like to ask one question on this. Let me say I am in agreement with what you have said as to the purpose of the bill. But I have one question. This depends on the first offender leading an exemplary life. Does the bill call for proof of such or is it merely the absence of a conviction for five years?

Senator Gittleson: The absence of a conviction for five years.

Senator McEwen: In other words, even though he turns up at meetings like we have heard of recently, he would be eligible?

Senator Gittleson: That is a very good observation but I may tell you this about that. You see, I happen to be one of those fellows who believe a fellow is innocent until proven guilty and that association does not make you guilty. Maybe you have a different opinion.

Senator McEwen: I agree with you completely but I do not think I would give amnesty.

Senator Gittleson: The fact that I might be seen one time or another with the biggest hoodlum in the country does not make a hoodlum out of me in my eyes. I may be wrong but that is my conception. Until I am convicted of consorting with criminals, I am a person enjoying the same rights as any other person in the community.

Senator Walter J. Mahoney: Mr. President.

The President: The Senator from the 55th.

Senator Mahoney: May I state that my party has no position whatsoever on this bill.

As a matter of information, I feel constrained to read excerpts from three letters—one from the district attorney from New York, Mr. Hogan. I am just taking a few excerpts. He said, "It is my belief that this bill is completely unrealistic. I think the proposed bill creates a completely false situation when it tells a person that something he knows to be true, namely a prior conviction, has ceased to be true."

His concluding paragraph is in brief that the bill now before you has the effect of over protecting a small minority of our citizenry at the expense of the security and welfare of the citizenry at large.

One other: From the chairman of the Parole Board, Mr. Mailler. For persons on parole he says the bill would present tremendous problems in supervision inasmuch as many parolees would have their records expunged years before the maximum of their sentence expires.

Senator Gittleson: He has not read the bill.

Senator Mahoney: I am just reading this—"This bill in my opinion should not be passed until every facet is thoroughly explored which conceivably would require a considerable length of time."

As I have one other letter which I will not read on behalf of the chairman of the Legislative Committee of the New York State District Attorneys Association.

Senator Gittleson: I might tell you, in passing, that the Grand Jury Association of New York and Kings County have approved this and Mr. Mailler has written a letter to Mr. Nussbaum—I have it here some place—in which he approves of the entire concept.

Senator Joseph Zaretzki: Mr. President.

The President: The Senator from the 23rd.

Senator Zaretzki: You have seen that there is a patent difficulty in your bill in regard to the records kept in the criminal courts and the district attorney's office and the Bureau of Criminal Identification as was brought out by Senator Erway. The same difficulty faces these newspapers. I do not know whether you are familiar with their practice or not, but they keep files on everybody whose name appears in the news.

Senator Gittleson: They have a morgue.

Senator Zaretzki: They consist of an envelope in which is placed the clipping—whenever this name appears in the newspaper.

Senator Gittleson: That is right.

Senator Zaretzki: Under your bill they would be at their peril reduced to the position where in reading of an old crime they would have to start figuring out what his sentence was—assuming they knew what the sentence was—the time when the sentence expired and then figure five years from that date and see if he was mentioned in the papers again for the five-year period. You are imposing an impossible task on them. When they say they object to that part of your bill there is substance to the objection because you make them liable for damages per se—a fellow does not have to prove any damages. He just has to prove the fact that they mentioned this prior conviction. It is a difficult objection. I do not see how you can overcome it even if you amend your bill in the years to come. I do not see how you can get around it. I think the suggestion made by the Senator here of making the obtaining of a certificate of good conduct easier has merit. I think it is much too hard for a man to get such a certificate today. There are too many technical objections put in his way. I think your objective can be obtained from making it easier for a man to get a certificate.

Senator Gittleson: I think we have discussed it too long.

There is one thing about newspapers, in my book, that may not be shared by you. A newspaper is not angelic and to my mind any man who runs one should be charged with the same obligations you and I are. If they happen to have a morgue where they have details of a man's conviction twenty-five years ago, if they are told they cannot print it, they ought not to print it because they do not contribute one bit to the welfare of society when they do. What they do is to contribute to screaming headlines and circulation. If I had to choose between their circulation and the rights of people who have one mistake, I am for the fellow who made the one mistake. If they want to take that chance, let them do it. Let them pay for it.

Roll call.

The President: Read the last section.

Senator Gittleson: Slow roll call.

The Secretary: Section two of this act shall take effect immediately.

(The Secretary called the roll.)

Senator Daniel G. Albert: Before casting my vote I would like to say that I agree thoroughly with Senator Gittleson in the concept of this bill. That is quite unassailable. I also believe in actual practice and before we put anything like this into actual practice that this whole subject should get a great deal more study. I believe that a bill that would go so far as this one should have a great deal more study. For that reason I vote no.

Senator Gittleson: I move to withdraw the roll call.

The President: Are there any objections to withdrawing the roll call? There being none, the roll call is laid aside.

Senator Gittleson: I want to star it.

The President: All right, we will star it.

Senator Walter J. Mahoney: The bill is laid aside and starred?

The President: Yes, laid aside and starred.

In a bright new mood of seeming reconciliation, the New York State Publishers Association shortly afterwards took the initiative in reopening the lines of communication. On April 1, 1958, General Manager W. Melvin Street now wrote me as follows:

> Senator Harry Gittleson has given me a copy of your book "First Offenders—A Second Chance."
>
> Newspapers in the State of New York are extremely interested in the philosophy of your thinking, and I feel your writing covers the subject very well.
>
> Kindly advise me where additional copies can be secured and the cost thereof.

At long last, the discretive press would now—even of its own accord—protect the anonymity of the amnestied individual in the larger interests of criminological reform and social justice.

After all, there had been honorable precedent and noble example of voluntary self-censorship for the public good. To its lasting credit, the benign press had long shielded the identity of immature juveniles from the lasting trauma of newspaper notoriety. And in the same affinity, the newsmen's own recent code of ethics had now enjoined their membership from publicizing a criminal record in advance of trial.

In the ongoing dialogue with Mr. Street, my diary for April 30, 1958, recorded that "he is definitely impressed with the 'tremendous importance' of the amnesty bill, but is still concerned about the stringent penal provisions against wilful disclosure." I suggested that the problem could be coped with by appropriate amendment. I reminded Mr. Street that amnesty and the press shared a common concern for the identical constituency of fifty million first offenders and their families, the bulk of whom constituted the very readership of the organized press. He agreed to have the association take "another hard look."

To soften the opposition of the newspaper lobby, the amnesty bill was now surgically redrafted to delete its provocative section sanctioning criminal penalties and treble damage suits against willful violators of the rights of amnestied individuals. In its place, all powers of general enforcement were securely lodged in the State Commission of Human Rights.

Hearteningly, the *Herald Tribune* readily assented to report this new major development in amnesty revisionism to its metropolitan readership. The city editor now assigned a reporter for the updated story and he, in turn, carefully garnered all the salient facts.

But despite all the honorable intentions, the rigid censorship imposed by the higher pundits of the press had burst the bubble of optimism once again. And as time would soon show, the implacable opposition of the newspaper lobby would spell rocky days ahead.

The spadework for amnesty now had to begin in earnest.

The tiny seed planted in Brooklyn, initially nurtured by the great Dean Roscoe Pound of Harvard, Chief Judge Albert Conway of the New York Court of Appeals, Dr. Paul W. Tappan—the dean of American corrections and the former chairman of the United States Parole Board—had finally spurted into the national scene, anointed with the unanimous blessing of the American Correctional Chaplains Association, representing the prison chaplains of all faiths, at the annual Congress of Correction held at Miami Beach in the summer of 1959.

Congressman Victor L. Anfuso of New York had introduced the amnesty idea into the *Congressional Record* on January 20, 1958, headlined AN ASSISTANT DISTRICT ATTORNEY'S VIEWS ON FIRST OFFENDERS.

> Mr. ANFUSO. Mr. Speaker, under leave to extend my remarks in the RECORD, I wish to insert a thought-provoking review on a book dealing with persons convicted as first offenders. The book, entitled "First Offenders—A Second Chance," is written by Aaron Nussbaum, assistant district attorney of Kings County Criminal Court. It is reviewed by Paul W. Tappan, pro-

fessor of sociology and law at New York University, and is published in the fall 1957 issue of Cornell Law Quarterly.

I have known the author for many years. In Brooklyn, Aaron Nussbaum is often described as "a prosecutor with a heart." He is one of the ablest and hardest working assistants on Kings County District Attorney Edward S. Silver's staff. Nussbaum is a good lawyer, a man of sound principles, a friend of youth, and one who is at all times most anxious to see that justice prevails. His thoughts on the problem of first offenders and how to deal with this problem should be of great interest to enforcement officials, the courts, and parents in general. It is for this reason that I commend it to the attention of my colleagues.

The review follows:

Assistant District Attorney Nussbaum, of the Kings County Criminal Court in New York City, has set down in this publication a product of his years of experience in dealing with criminal defendants. In particular, he offers here a critical and penetrating analysis of some of the most difficult problems encountered in the administration of justice and of correction: the legal disabilities, the stigma, and the socio-economic deprivations that harass the convicted offender permanently without regard to his efforts to lead a law-abiding life.

Mr. Nussbaum paints a bleak picture of the present and prospective prevalence of crime in the United States. He estimates on the basis of Federal Bureau of Investigation statistics, on criminal convictions and recidivist rates, that over the period of the next 30 years there will be some 50 million persons convicted as first offenders, including felons and misdemeanants. Regardless of the validity of this projected figure, it is quite clear that the cumulative total of first felony offenders alone is very large. Moreover, these are cases in which rehabilitative efforts are especially important: the individuals involved need the fullest ameliorative measures that the law and community can reasonably provide to dissuade them from persistence in criminal attitudes and conduct. A problem of peculiar difficulty is that involving the reduced status and privileges of these offenders who have paid the State's penalty but remain outcast. The perpetual loss of rights and respectability is a major deterrent to the successful adjustment of the one-time offender after his discharge from treatment. Our law and correctional measures, together with more that are hostile to the ex-convict, increase rather than mitigate the danger of criminal recidivism. The resulting dis-service to the State as well as to the individual offender, is made abundantly clear in Mr. Nussbaum's spirited indictment.

The problems here involved have not been entirely without attention. Our juvenile courts spare children criminal convictions (but with exceptions in most of the States). New York under its recent Youth Court Act also provides a non-criminal status to selected cases of youthful offenders of 16 and over and the Federal Youth Corrections Act provides for the setting aside of the convictions of offenders under the age of 22 who have been sentenced specially as committed youth offenders, a provision that does not, however, apply to probationers. In many States the temporary or permanent deprivation of civil rights occurs only where offenders are committed to prison rather than upon felony convictions alone, though the felony record itself results in persisting limitations on the offender. A majority of jurisdictions restore forfeited rights only through the governor's exercise of the pardoning power. However, some States provide for restoration either automatically or upon application for offenders who satisfactorily complete a term of probation, imprisonment, or parole. In a few places it is required that some time interval elapse without further misconduct after discharge from correctional treatment before rights are restored. The record of conviction itself may be annulled under special statutory provisions upon discharge from probation in several jurisdictions that have followed a proposal in the Model Act of the National Probation and Parole Association. For the most part, however, present law goes no further than to mitigate somewhat the position of selected young offenders and of probationers. Even this is accomplished in only a very few jurisdictions. Existing legislation in this field is varied and vague. It reveals policies that are conflicting, invidious, and unclear. By and large the first offender, as well as the habitual and professional criminal, is encumbered with an onerous and permanent burden that restricts both his legal and his social relationships.

What should be done about this? Mr. Nussbaum recommends a forthright remedy, a means designed to motivate first offenders to avoid repetition of crime. His views deserve the thoughtful consideration of law-makers and criminologists. He proposes that the criminal record of every first offender, felon or misdemeanant, should be automatically nullified after paying his full price in punishment for the crime committed and after living in obedience to the law for an additional probationary period of 5 years, provided, however, that such conviction and record would be reinstated upon any future criminal conviction. More specifically, the author intends the running of the 5 year period to begin from the date of discharge by probation or suspended sentence, or from the date of release from incarceration— either by parole, commutation of sentence, or expiration of the maximum term of imprisonment. This suggests that some offenders might be serving time on probation or parole after their convictions had been canceled, and it may be argued that a different method of calculation should be employed. There must be wide agreement, however, on the fundamental principle that first offenders, whether young or mature, should have fair opportunity to live down their single errors. To the adventitious or circumstantial violator this would assure a chance to start again without the measure of bitterness that he so commonly feels in the face of continuing official and public rejection. To the true criminal, freshly but deliberately launched in criminal enterprise, this device would provide a positive incentive to a redirection of his course, without fear that his efforts will be persistently repudiated.

It must be admitted that the limited measures that have been adopted in the past to relieve certain classes of offenders from the eternal odium attaching to criminal conviction have proved largely ineffectual. Society is retentive and ingenious in its efforts permanently to outlaw the felon. One may inquire whether any statutory method can be devised by which to start the offender clean and afresh, so far as community and official responses are concerned. It appears that law will not alone accomplish that end. Rigorous efforts must be exerted to modify public reactions to the one-time offender. Our experience indicates, however, that law can be a powerful instrument in changing attitudes as well as conduct. And it is clear that change is needed here, both on an official and an informal level. The reviewer hopes that Mr. Nussbaum will reduce his recommendations to statutory draft that may elicit careful study by our legislators. His submission promises a long stride beyond the limited measures that have been taken thus far to remove the stigma and record of the offender who wants to go straight.

PAUL W. TAPPAN,
Professor of Sociology and Law,
New York University.

The state of California immediately was among the very first to embrace the second chance for in-depth studies and evaluations for legislative action and criminological reform. In the vanguard, Adult Authority member E. W. Lester called for the tract *First Offenders: A Second Chance,* for dissemination among every member of the Adult Authority and other major influencers in the law enforcement field.

Shortly afterwards, in 1961, the state of California scored a historic first in amnesty legislation in the United States. Its statute proclaimed that "such conviction, arrest or other proceeding shall be deemed not to have occurred, and the petitioners may answer accordingly any question relating to their occurrence" (Penal Code, Sec. 1203.45).

Though the California breakthrough for the first offender was not nearly as sweeping nor as broad in scope as the New York model—lacking the all-encompassing forgiveness envisaged for amnesty's beneficiaries, and limiting its operation to minors under twenty-one years of age convicted of misdemeanors only—it did, however, mark the auspicious beginning of a quasi-amnesty in rehabilitation.

In parallel developments, District Attorney Frank D. O'Connor of Queens County, president of the New York State District Attorneys Association, now carried amnesty's gospel into the campus of the Yale Law School, as did Roscoe Pound into Harvard and Professor Paul W. Tappan into New York University and Cornell.

Notably, the eminent criminologist Walter Reckless of Ohio State University embellished his class curriculum on penology with the ideology of amnesty; Dr. Harry Elmer Barnes incorporated the "second chance" into his classic *New Horizons on Criminology;* Professor Leroy Bauman, chairman of the Department of Sociology, put amnesty under the microscopic test of classroom dissection at Brooklyn College.

Concomitantly, the prestigious National Council on Crime and Delinquency now undertook the dissemination of a model am-

nesty-oriented annulment statute, under which the offender "shall
be treated in all respects as not having been convicted."

The legislatures of many states were soon prompted into a
flurry of holding actions to ameliorate the excesses of the second
punishment. Civil disabilities and forfeitures were now curtailed,
and restoration rights were liberalized. Wherever practicable, arrests in petty cases were supplanted by an enlightened system of
summons procedures in order to avoid the unnecessary hamper-
ing of our youth with police records.

Sparked by Dean Roscoe Pound's effusive support, a spate of
expungement statutes soon sprouted in a dozen states throughout
the country which—though far short of the fundamentality of forgiveness—nevertheless opened the way to at least partial remission
of the stigmatic record.

Hearteningly, the pollen of amnesty spread into Canada, New
Zealand, Australia, and the Republic of Korea, whose governments now solicited the blueprint of the "second chance" through
the agency of the United Nations. And, characteristically enough,
the indomitable freedom-fighter Menachim Begin committed himself to carry amnesty's colors into the Israeli Knesseth in the
evolving construction of its criminal justice system.

The way was now clear for a second try in the New York
legislature.

In 1964 there was a changing of the guard in the amnesty
line-up. Senator Harry Gittleson had ascended the bench, and his
colleague, the affable Senator Jeremiah B. Bloom, now assumed
command of amnesty's fortunes in the New York state senate. In
the fresh stirrings, the new sponsor quickly piloted the measure
into its maiden acceptance by the Senate Codes Committee.

Practical politics now demanded that the bill have the bipartisan backing of the Republican party, which had majority control. The influential speaker of the New York state assembly, the
Honorable Joseph Carlino, filled the gap by designating none
other than Republican Assemblyman Anthony P. Savarese, Jr.,

chairman of the Committee on the City of New York, to lead amnesty's battalions on the floor of the New York state assembly.

Two cosmetic changes were now made in the amnesty bill, rendering it more amenable to better administration. The one expressly excluded any "dangerous offender" or psychopath from a grant of amnesty, at the time of sentencing. The other change mandated the issuance of a formal certificate of amnesty to all those eligible, thus facilitating the management and reclassification of the criminal records of all amnestied offenders.

The amnesty bill now won the unanimous support of the Brooklyn Bar Association, surviving the triple wringer of three independent bodies: the Committee on State Legislation, the Committee on Criminal Courts and, naturally enough, the Committee on Human Rights and Freedoms.

Now, on the floor of the senate, the new sponsor briefly parted the opening curtain in the legislative saga ahead.

> *Senator Jeremiah B. Bloom:* Mr. President, I ask unanimous consent to make a statement.
>
> *The President:* Without objection, Senator Bloom.
>
> *Senator Bloom:* This bill is the work of Assistant District Attorney Aaron Nussbaum in Kings County. He has worked in conjunction with a number of organizations and received the approbation of the American Correctional Association, the Brooklyn Bar Association, the Kings County Grand Jurors Association and such prominent legal and penal authorities as Dean Roscoe Pound of Harvard University, James V. Bennett, Director of Federal Bureau of Prisons and Paul Tappan, former Chairman of the United States Parole Board.
>
> I have been assured by Mr. Bartlett that his Committee is greatly interested in this work. It is known as the amnesty bill.
>
> We have over a million people in the State of New York who are first offenders and who have been precluded from doing constructive work and becoming first class citizens again. This provides in the event of an offense, a one-year statute of limitations; in the case of a misdemeanor a three-year waiting period; and in the case of a felony, five years—after which time with proper supervision by the Court, they will no longer be required

to list their conviction in an application for employment. There is a great deal of sympathy for this.

Of course, it precludes those considered dangerous from getting this type of amnesty.

Due to the fact this Committee will give it more consideration and due to the sympathy evidenced by Mr. Bartlett and his Committee and the consideration given by Mr. Hughes, Chairman of Codes, I, at this time, ask that the bill be starred with the assurance that this bill will be given consideration in the future.

The President: The bill is starred.

The year 1965 was the breakthrough on the legislative front.

In the new season, the Democratic party had regained majority control of the New York state legislature for the first time in thirty years, and the Albany air was now electric with a spirit of reform.

Assemblyman Anthony P. Savarese, Jr., had donned the robes as a judge of the criminal court, and freshman assemblyman Noah Goldstein had succeeded him as captain of the amnesty measure in the New York state assembly.

The Bronx County Bar Association—which had previously disfavored the amnesty measure in 1962—now came out with a ringing endorsement.

> This bill is an example of constructive legislation which should be supported vigorously for both its social and legal effects. No longer would the "one-mistake" individual have to return to society and bear the stigma of conviction at every turn of his life. No longer would the conscientious but errant individual be restricted to a second class status and be deprived of full rehabilitation opportunities because of one encounter with the law. He would have available to him a process by which he could unshackle himself and become a productive part of the law-abiding world once again. Legislation of this type, with the proper safeguards provided therein, is a long step from the days of the "Scarlet A."

Now, promptly after the measure had dropped into the hopper, the New York State Publishers Association hurriedly circulated a memorandum in opposition, expressing its "particular concern" with the strong criminal and civil penalties affecting newspapers, arguing that "it would be virtually impossible for news media, at any given time, to ascertain the status of amnestied offenders," that "there has been no proven need or justification for this revolutionary concept," and spicing it all with the dire specter that among "some of the obvious revolutionary provisions of this bill are the outlawing of a father telling his daughter of her intended husband's past conviction."

Any lawyer could have quickly reassured the misguided press that the amnesty bill had no such ludicrous intention, but was aimed only at the *willful* disclosure or publication of the amnestied record. *Black's Law Dictionary* defines "willful" as "premeditated, malicious, done with evil intent, or with a bad purpose, or with indifference to the natural consequences; without legal justification."

Spearheading the attack against the amnesty bill, his flanks strategically secured by an allied press, was the glib Assemblyman Dominic Di Carlo, a former assistant United States attorney who was to distinguish himself in succeeding sessions of the legislature as the super law 'n' order apostle for the draconian penalties of the marijuana laws.

> *Mr. Di Carlo:* Mr. Speaker, I believe most of us feel with Mr. Goldstein that there are times when a person who has committed a criminal act should not bear a stigma throughout his life. On the other hand, we also have a public policy as Mr. Goldstein indicates, the public policy here being in his view that the criminal should not bear the stigma of conviction. On the other hand, we also have a public policy as to whether or not this would truly affect the rights of the people of the community.
>
> I am sure many of us have received mail dealing with crimes in our city, and many comments have been made about leniency. I believe in this particular case we may be at the wrong juncture in our history to pass a law which may take away one of the

crime deterrents to committing crime, that is, the stigma of the fact the crime had been committed.

This bill would increase crime rather than deter it in the case of a potential first offender.

I believe the bill has many provisions which, although well intentioned, could lead to harmful effects. In my own opinion I don't believe that we are at a time in our history where this legislation should be passed in this legislature.

Quickly moving into the stalemate, Assemblyman Max M. Turshen, the irrepressible dean of the assembly (with over thirty years of service) and chairman of the Judiciary Committee, now obtained the floor. With the thunder of Isaian righteousness, he turned to the hushed audience of fellow assemblymen.

> *Mr. Turshen:* Mr. Speaker, on the bill.
> *The Speaker:* Mr. Turshen.
> *Mr. Turshen:* Mr. Speaker, ladies and gentlemen of the house. First let me congratulate Mr. Goldstein on a very erudite piece of work in support of his bill. I think that every member got a copy of this. I want to congratulate you on a tremendous piece of work, both for its eruditeness, its learning and the wonderful effort that has been put in this bill.
>
> I also want to congratulate you, Mr. Di Carlo, for taking so much pain to make such an elaborate inquiry into all of the phases of this bill.
>
> I think this debate was worthy of a much fuller house than we have at the present time on an extremely important subject and a very serious proposition.
>
> I am for your proposition. This proposition was first enunciated by Assistant District Attorney Aaron Nussbaum of Kings County who has devoted upwards of fifteen years of intense study and research and who has written a book on this subject, and I have read the text. He has aided our distinguished colleague, Assemblyman Goldstein, in the drafting of this most humane, progressive and important piece of legislation.
>
> Now, let me say to you ladies and gentlemen, we must come to a time where we have to rehabilitate people. I know that Mr. Bartlett has done a tremendous job with his commission on revising our penal laws, and they have done an eminently wonderful service to the public in giving the particular time that

they did and coming forth with such an exhaustive and wonderful work in recodifying and revising our penal law. But I think there is a great lack in our whole treatment of the subject of criminology. I think this business of penology and its implication in punishment is horse and buggy, it belongs to an older age. We must come to a new concept in the treatment of criminals. We must recognize a different theory about criminals and crimes in general, particularly with the rise of crime today. There are those of the heinous nature, there are those of an anti-social nature where the people are definitely anti-social and incapable of being corrected, they are just incorrigible, they are anti-social and that's it. On the other hand we have those who are unfortunately driven by circumstances to commit something, then they will probably spend their whole life repenting that particular act.

Now this is a step in the right direction. This morning I passed a bill on the calendar which I have sponsored in the house for thirty years, from the day I first became an Assemblyman, and for thirty years I presented this bill annually and couldn't get the bill through, and today it passed this house unanimously, and it is a simple bill. It is a bill that says that we can separate and should separate in our penal institutions the first offender from the hardened criminal. Now a thing as elementary as that took thirty years to pass and it is funny this should be on the calendar the same day, and it is again a step in the right direction to help our society.

This bill will say to a man, "You have sinned," and this is the principle of religion, where a man comes in to confession, where a man comes to his confessor and tells about a transgression, commission of a sin, and he is granted immunity and told to go out and sin no more, because he has confessed his sin. Isn't that what we are doing here? Isn't that what we are saying to a man who was convicted of a crime, the man who has shown an exemplary life since the commission of the crime? The man has asked to be reclaimed and taken back into society, and this we need. We need a new approach. We need a new avenue to help people, help people to help themselves, to rehabilitate them and reclaim them for society instead of hardening their attitude and making them more anti-social as time goes by, because of our lack of knowing how to deal with these people who find themselves in violation of the law. Many of them are not even moral violations, as I say, it is just the circumstances, where so many times I have heard a man say, "There but for the grace of God go I."

I am sorry that we haven't got this house packed on a bill of this type, because this is a fundamental bill, this is a bill that goes to the very roots of the whole subject of criminology and penology, and I say to you ladies and gentlemen, if you pass this bill it is a step in the right direction, it is our duty to make new laws to take the place of those that are not workable and no longer serve our modern situations. So I plead with you, ladies and gentlemen, give this bill a chance, because we will make a great step forward in saving many people for society. This should be the purpose of all our laws, to help people get back on the right road, to show them the right way, and especially if they are interested and want it, by all means we ought to give it to them, and that is why I urge the passage of this bill.

In a parliamentary maneuver to thwart the impact of Turshen's stunning appeal, the opposition attempted a last-ditch effort to forestall a vote by offering study commissions and hearings, but presciently enough, Assemblyman Noah Goldstein refused.

Mr. Gioffre: Has this subject matter been discussed in your commission?

Mr. Bartlett: Yet, it has, Mr. Gioffre, but I must tell you that the proposal of the commission in connection with amnesty is not yet formulated. It would be part of the Code of Criminal Procedure on which we are just commencing work. It is not part of the penal law package before this house now.

Mr. Gioffre: Is it the intention of the commission to undertake studies on the subject?

Mr. Bartlett: Yes, we have made some studies already. I discussed with Mr. Goldstein this situation, and I think it is fair to say the commission favors the principle of some method by which amnesty may be granted upon a showing of good conduct for a period of years. I wouldn't want to say the commission favors five years or three years or one year, but the principle the commission does approve. It is fair to say that.

I personally have some misgivings about the mechanics of this bill. Again, I have discussed it with Mr. Goldstein. I would say this, that the measure, if it is not successful this year and the commission does formulate such a proposal another year, and I am still chairman—there are a lot of ifs and buts in there —we would be happy to ask Mr. Goldstein to sponsor it.

Mr. Gioffre: On the bill. I think that the thoughts which have been advanced on this bill are very well meaning, and I think most of us are in favor of doing something about it. However, it seems to me that the bill is a little bit premature, because of the fact that I am convinced that we should require some additional information and probably some public hearings on the matter, and therefore, I would suggest to Mr. Goldstein that possibly the bill ought to be put over another year to determine whether or not there are any other matters and any other provisions which ought to be taken into consideration in considering a bill of this type.

Mr. Goldstein: May I inform you that this delay is not going to help at all. I sponsored this bill three years in a row and I believe three years is ample time to wait.

With due respect to Mr. Gioffre, I cannot take his advice, as I do believe we should act now upon the bill, and I move the bill.

The bill passed the assembly by a thundering majority of 115 to 33.

Ranged on the side of amnesty was the whole spectrum of bipartisan political and social activism running the gamut from the independent Shirley Chisholm to the Republican minority leader, Perry Duryea, and the Democratic speaker of the assembly and majority leader, Moses Weinstein.

On May 5, 1965, an Associated Press dispatch reported that the New York State Newspaper Publishers Association would oppose the bill, voicing its particular concern with a provision that would make it a criminal offense for anyone to disclose the identity of an amnestied first offender.

The *Herald Tribune* moved into the lists of battle once again on May 10 with this editorial.

"Forgive and Forget" Gone Haywire

The Assembly passed a bill the other day, with hardly any public notice, that would automatically grant amnesty to criminal first offenders after a probationary period of five years for a felony, three years for a misdemeanor, and one year for the youthful offender. The conviction would be annulled, everything about it expunged, the offender deemed fully exonerated and even permitted to swear under oath that he was never arrested or convicted.

This "forgive and forget" bill is obviously filled with good intentions, but nevertheless unrealistic and unwarranted. It would, for instance, prevent a father telling his daughter of her intended husband's past conviction. No employer could determine a job-seeker's background. And any newspaper—or indeed any person, firm or corporation—would risk strong criminal and civil penalties by divulging the amnestied first offender's past history.

There is no need for this bill; its far-reaching implications are harmful. Such official secrecy is ridiculous, and can only succeed in causing far more trouble than it hopes to prevent. It is a mischievous interference with legitimate interests, another example of chaos under law.

The Senate should kill this monstrosity.

Frenetically picking up the journalistic hatchet, the upstate Hearst press likewise took off with a lead editorial in the *Albany Times Union.*

SOFT-HEARTED, SOFT-HEADED

An amazing proposal is half-way through our Legislature, and if citizens of good sense don't rouse themselves it might sneak all the way through. It's known as the "Amnesty Law for First Offenders," and having passed the Assembly when apparently no one was looking, it's in the Senate in the form of a bill offered by Senator Jeremiah Bloom, Manhattan Democrat.

The incredible idea is based in an assumption that everyone's entitled to one mistake, no matter how bad.

"Persons who have been convicted of an offense and served the sentence imposed should not be condemned as outcasts . . .," says the bill. "Particularly as to the first offender, there can be no meaningful purpose of rehabilitation or reform unless society tenders him a genuine second chance . . ."

So far, so good in the area of soft-heartedness. Surely the

matter of proper rehabilitation of the offender is one of society's major unsolved problems. Now for the area of soft-headedness to which, we are sorry to say, the Bloom bill then gallops toward. Here's what it would accomplish:

A first-offender, after serving his sentence and sitting out a probationary period, would have his conviction—and even the indictment leading to it—"annulled and expunged," and the offense "fully expiated and forgiven."

Then he would be able to deny, even under oath, "the fact of his arrest . . . accusation, arraignment, trial, and all other aspects of his conviction . . ." So, in effect, any kind of thug guilty of that one "forgiven" mugging or rape or manslaughter, perhaps, can thereafter swear—and be upheld by the law—that no such thing ever happened.

Then this forgiven thug could be "fully accredited as a witness," and be given the right to vote, hold public office, and hold any professional or other license.

His records will be sealed, and if you or any other citizen—or this newspaper, for example—were to mention that the thug had been guilty of any such crime, YOU could be jailed for a year. You might somehow come to feel that your own civil liberties had been abridged in such a case; in any event, there is a clear curtailment of free speech and free press inherent in this proposal.

Of course, it is recognized, even in this outlandish bill, that the forgiven first-offender might somehow go bad, and in that case, it would all come back to him. (Further, amnesty can be denied in the first instance to someone deemed a "dangerous offender," which means that he may be determined to be suffering "from a serious personality disorder indicating a marked propensity towards continuing criminal conduct or activity.")

On the other hand, "acceleration" of the amnesty is provided, so that it is possible for that first offense of thuggery to be expunged and forgiven very shortly.

It's a bad bill, well-intended though it may be in seeking to move to the heart of a thorny problem. The Bloom bill is no reasonable solution, it poses very dangerous side-effects, and must be defeated in the Senate.

In an exceptional display of objectivity and independence, some few newspapers stuck rigidly to the facts, without compromise and without coloration. Typical was the sweet reasonableness of the May 10, 1965, editorial in *The Daily News* of Tarrytown.

BILL TO UNDO WHAT'S DONE

"What's done is done" says Shakespeare in Act II of "Macbeth." But then he never came to grips with the New York State Legislature.

It seems to be on the verge of sending to the governor a bill which would permit most anyone who has been guilty of a single offense, misdemeanor, or felony, to get a certification of amnesty following a one to five year crime-free probationary period.

Once granted this certificate, the amnestied offender would be free under oath to testify that he had never been convicted. He could also deny such arrest or conviction were he to fill out any forms including job applications. And if some one were to go beyond his denials and discriminate against him on the grounds, he had been an offender, the State Commission for Human Rights could come to his defense.

Under a bill passed by the Assembly, 115-35, anyone who "shall wilfully disclose, publish, or allude to the former conviction" would have been subject to a year in jail, $500 fine, or trebeled damages in a civil action. But the Senate sponsor, Jeremiah B. Bloom, Brooklyn Democrat, is amending the measure to remove this triple-threat penalty. If he passes this version in the Senate, he'll then try to get the Assembly to concur.

If all this seems a bit "way out," it is.

No state has anything that quite approaches it. Nor does any other country, except possibly West Germany, which, in a way, goes further and expunges felony records after 10 years.

The legislation, however, is not a sudden aberration. It stems from a crusade that Aaron Nussbaum, long an assistant district attorney in Kings County, began 20 years ago. However, the legislation it inspired always died quietly in committee.

He got interested when a client, once convicted in a bankruptcy fraud case, "went straight," married, adopted two children, and had trouble explaining to the youngsters why he couldn't vote. There is a "certificate of good conduct" procedure by which felons can get voting rights restored but Nussbaum says it's not easy to get and only partly answers the overall problem.

He argues that the first offender, frustrated in getting a job, slips back into evil ways, commits another crime, and from then on is on the skids.

Objectors will argue that the offender should have known the consequences when he committed the first offense and that there is no point in telling offenders that society (once a sentence is finished) will "forgive and forget" once.

During the years, Nussbaum has written a brochure "First Offenders—A Second Chance" airing his ideas and picking up such amnesty supporters as the Kings County Grand Jurors Association (it thinks it would reduce crime), the director of federal prisons, various prison chaplains' associations, Supreme Court Justice Samuel S. Leibowitz, Dean Roscoe Pound of Harvard Law School, and, just recently, the Bronx County Bar Association.

Few would deny that Nussbaum has put his finger on a problem for which the state has long needed better answers. In theory a person serves his term, pays his debt to society, and begins all over again. In practice, of course, he often pays and pays and pays in many ways.

With Nussbaum's plan, there are certain safeguards. One gets amnesty only once and that's it. If the courts adjudge him a dangerous offender he doesn't get amnesty at all. If he commits a crime in New York or anywhere else, consorts with criminals, or becomes a vagrant or disorderly person his "expunged" offense gets right back on the record. Moreover for police purposes even the first offense isn't really "expunged." It remains in his record as "amnestied."

There is undoubtedly something to be said for legislation in this general direction. The trouble is that, unlike Nussbaum, most people haven't been thinking about the problem for 20 years. The mere fact that a bill on this subject has been introduced year after year doesn't mean people have been giving it much attention. It's the sort of thing that you might have thought the Legislature would have eased into more gradually with one or more public hearings. For this it would not seem to be too late.

Girding for the critical battle in the upper chamber, the amnesty forces eagerly sought to mollify the press by deleting the ironclad penalty clauses.

Suddenly, like a timed bombshell, the Association of the Bar of the City of New York entered the fray in staunch opposition to the amnesty measure, pitting itself against the solid phalanx of practically every bar association in metropolitan New York. Particularly dismaying was the association's cavalier disregard of assurances repeatedly given the author that it would solicit his presence and consider his views at forthcoming committee hearings before taking any final stand on the amnesty bill.

Curiously, the association aimed its disapproval at the very tenets underlying the amnesty concept—a sophomoric stance in diametric conflict with the proclaimed teachings of the United States Supreme Court and the accepted insights of practically every knowledgeable criminologist and correctional authority in the country, as well as of every leading light of the bench and bar.

> This Committee disapproves of the bills. We dispute the conclusions expressed in the declarations and purposes portion of the proposed legislation. We do not believe that the "impact of a criminal record . . . is a major contributing factor of criminality and recidivism." The appropriate subjects of a properly drafted amnesty bill are not members of a criminal class; fit subjects for amnesty will not become recidivists just because they have a criminal record.
>
> We agree that there is a "stigma attendant upon every criminal conviction," but we do not find that it is "an insurmountable barrier to the re-gained self-respect, dignity, and esteem of millions of our citizens and their families, and, as such, gravely undermines the essential values, attributes, and foundations of our democratic society."
>
> The bills correctly point out that one convicted of a crime may have his veracity impugned in a court of law. However, we disagree that the admissibility of such proof has resulted in "gross miscarriage of justice and with countless cost to all litigants, in civil and criminal proceedings alike." While there may be instances where a witness' criminal record should not be a proper subject for his cross-examination, these broadly written bills do not address themselves to the problem at hand. They would, inter alia, permit a witness who had been guilty of the most outrageous fraud or perjury to deny the fact of such conviction under oath, regardless of the issue concerning which

he was testifying. Such a situation, rather than the existing law against which the proposed legislation protests, would be destructive of our concepts of justice and fairness.

It was now the moment of truth on the senate floor.

The President: Senator Bloom.

Senator Bloom: Never have I been more proud to present a bill for consideration before our Body. We hear many people talk about rehabilitation, recidivism of offenders, talk about juvenile delinquency, talk about repetition of offenders, but comparatively little has been accomplished, although many well-meaning people and organizations and government have spent a great deal of money.

This bill proposes to give first offenders, in most instances, an opportunity for rehabilitation, a reason for rehabilitation, a desire for rehabilitation, because by virtue of this bill we tell the offender and the Court will tell the offender upon serving your term and your probation and if you behave yourself, get into no more trouble, you will be able to walk the street like any other normal human being without fear of not being able to get a job.

What is the greatest cause for recidivism? A man who has been an offender going to look for a job and being denied an opportunity, as any other normal citizen, to make a livelihood. What reason does he have to obey the law? How can he obey the law? Because he cannot make a livelihood. By virtue of this bill, we tell him, "Mister, you can make a livelihood like any other human being; you can be a father who does not have to fear coming home and have the kids in the neighborhood tell your son or your children that you are a felon. . . ."

I commend to you that this is a tremendous step forward in the rehabilitation of people who are first offenders and give them a chance to become citizens like everyone else. . . .

We have a year within which to study this and if there are any flaws, I am sure we will all be happy to correct them, because we are all concerned that there be no loopholes in this type of legislation.

Above all, I do think that it is high time that we showed everyone—New York State is supposed to be the leader—that we are taking a step forward in doing something really constructive in rehabilitation, because we can talk all day long about recidivism. We do not have the physical facilities to do it. We do not have the means with which to do it. We do not have the ancillary services in the Court with which to do it, and we do not have the programs with which to do it. Let us do something.

Undaunted by the propagandistic barrage, amnesty's minions now held firmly together. The bill sailed through the senate by a margin of thirty-nine to seventeen!

Remarkably, it had won the support of the chairmen of all standing committees of that body, including that of Senator John E. Quinn, chairman on the Committee on Penal Institutions—a correction officer by profession. Conspicuous among the ayes were the influential Republican Senator Edward Speno and the Democratic floor leader, Joseph Zaretski—both of whom had switched to amnesty in the afterthought of their earlier expressed reservations on the senate floor in 1958.

Notably, among the minority of negative holdouts were Senator George R. Metcalf, a journalist by profession, and Senator Leighton A. Hope, the president of an upstate radio station.

But there was a new parliamentary pitfall.

Because of the senate amendment of the original assembly measure, the bill had to be returned to the assembly for re-passage in its amended form.

Assemblyman Di Carlo, waiting in the wings, again honed his ax in a last-ditch effort to kill the bill.

Confounding the debate with pointed arrows of ridicule and derision of the second chance, Mr. Di Carlo literally twisted amnesty's terms beyond all recognition.

> *Mr. Di Carlo:* Will Mr. Goldstein yield to several questions?
> *Mr. Goldstein:* I will yield.
> *Mr. Di Carlo:* Mr. Goldstein, if this particular bill becomes law, isn't it a fact that we can have a situation where we have a person convicted of a morals offense, one year later could go and apply for a job driving a school bus, be in a day camp, children's camp, and this question is asked whether he has ever

been convicted of a crime and he can answer that question in the negative and be employed by that particular camp and agency?

What Mr. Di Carlo trickily sidestepped were the triple preconditions for any amnesty dispensation: (1) the completion of the fixed sentence prescribed for morals offenses, which could range all the way up to a twenty-year-to-life jail stint for rape; (2) the passage of the fixed probationary interval following the completion of sentence, extending up to five years additional in felony cases; (3) the absolute exclusion of any sexual psychopath from the benefits of amnesty at any time.

As a practical consideration, too, what Mr. Di Carlo had conveniently overlooked was that even now, under the existing system, no private employers could legally compel the fingerprinting of a convicted sex offender to ascertain his criminal background in any case.

> *Mr. Di Carlo:* Assuming you have a situation where a man is picked up for murder and arrested on the charge of murder. Let's assume that a key witness disappears for one year, and since this man has not been arrested in the course of one year, are you going to lower the statute of limitations of murder for one year?
> *Mr. Goldstein:* This has no effect in any fashion of lowering the statute of limitations, you are taking things out of context.

Mr. Di Carlo, a former criminal prosecutor, well knew that the crime of murder had no statute of limitations; that the disappearance of a key witness against a murder suspect would have stymied any prosecution, even under the existing system of justice, until that witness had been located. And, as a legislator, Mr. Di Carlo was keenly aware that a simple amendment, in any event, could have surgically disposed of any such contingency.

Once again, on May 24, 1965—despite Di Carlo's intimidating tactic of a demand for a roll-call vote—amnesty breezed through the New York state assembly by the overwhelming vote of eighty-nine to fifty-seven. The last legislative hurdle was now over.

The adoption of amnesty by the state of New York marked a breakthrough of social engineering in the law.

For the very first time, *forgiveness* was enshrined by statute into the tableau of rehabilitation, offering a genuine second chance to the criminal offender, the complete undoing of a criminal past, a fresh start in life free of the stigma of a criminal record.

It marked the dawn of a unique sovereign concern for the first offender in the schematics of correction, an epochal pathmark in the fight for criminological reform. "In my opinion," exclaimed publisher Marvin Lander of the *Criminal Law Bulletin*, "this is the most important piece of legislation in years."

The full flowering of amnesty at this historic session was no freak happening, but a natural in the fertility of a remarkably soul-filled legislature.

Characteristically, this same legislative body, with a record-breaking number of 1,644 bills passed, delivered the coup de grace to the death penalty; abolished the undemocratic blue ribbon jury system; adopted a radically modernized penal code—the first revision since the nineteenth century; established an updated criminal identification and intelligence system; burst forth with a no-fault divorce law; raised the minimum wage and unemployment insurance beyond all previous levels; inaugurated off-track betting in New York City; fleshed out new enforcement powers for the State Commission on Human Rights, the watchdog agency of all civil rights laws; authorized the loan of textbooks to students in private and parochial schools; prohibited the sale of pornographic materials to children under the age of seventeen; legalized the sale of contraceptive devices and the dissemination of birth control information; required printed warnings on cigarette packages that excessive use was dangerous to health; put new muscle into the women's equal rights law; directed that all motor vehicles sold in the state be equipped with an exhaust pollution control device and that all motor vehicles be safety inspected annually; created a two-hundred-million-dollar bond issue for slum clearance and low-rent housing; and clamped down on the sale of hallucinogenics, amphetamines, and barbiturates, in prophetic foresight of the gathering storms of drug proliferation.

In thrilling affirmation of the second chance, as if in defiant disdain of the Neanderthal views of the Association of the Bar, the legislature's action had solemnly memorialized the fundamental tenets of amnesty, graphically proclaimed in its very own opening section.

> The lifetime impact of a criminal record, productive of an unceasing burden of socio-legal restraints and inequities affecting career, livelihood and personal welfare, is a major contributing factor of criminality and recidivism.
> The permanent criminalization of every convicted offender is fundamentally inconsistent with and repugnant to the ideal correctional goal of total rehabilitation; the lifelong stigma attendant upon every criminal conviction is an insurmountable barrier to the re-gained self-respect, dignity and esteem of millions of our citizens and their families, and as such, gravely undermines the essential values, attributes and foundations of our democratic society.

Amnesty now faced the executive mansion. A vast outpouring of support, seldom before witnessed in Albany for size and quality, descended upon the governor.

Arrayed on the side of amnesty were no less than ten former presidents of the American Correction Association.

In addition, among those firmly in the saddle of support were such giants of the penal world as James V. Bennett, former director of the Federal Bureau of Prisons; Chief Judge Albert Conway of the New York Court of Appeals; and Paul W. Tappan, former chairman of the United States Parole Board.

And once again, amnesty had won the benediction of the American Catholic Correctional Chaplains Association, which now telegraphed the governor that the amnesty bill was "a vital step in Rehabilitation, and if enacted, will save the State large sums of money now spent on prison maintenance."

From the Correctional Association of New York came this message to the governor.

> The bill to provide amnesty under certain conditions to certain first offenders would remove to a very great extent both the hidden and existing legal blocks confronting many first offenders upon their return to the community.
>
> Regretful as it may be, serving a criminal sentence is not completed upon the individual's release to the community, for throughout the remainder of his life the individual continues to be "punished."
>
> It is felt that the above mentioned bill through the probationary period of five years for a felony and three years for a misdemeanor coupled with the exclusion of "dangerous offenders" and the retention of records for police purposes provides ample safeguards to the community.
>
> For the reason stated above, it is urged that the above bill be signed into law.

From the National Council on Crime and Delinquency:

> The New York Citizen Council of the National Council on Crime and Delinquency supports this bill which would add a new Article 9 to the Civil Rights Law so as to provide amnesty, under stated conditions, to certain first offenders.
>
> The Council believes that the stigma of a criminal record is not merely unjust to thousands of individuals but an actual bar to their future good conduct and therefore requests you to approve the bill.

From the New York Civil Liberties Union:

> This bill would provide amnesty for first offenders who do not run afoul of the law within specified periods of time after a first conviction and would thus spare them the lifetime impact of a criminal record.

With the rise in population between the ages of 18 and 25, and the decline in jobs available to people in that age bracket, we are experiencing an alarmingly high rate of crime. It is of great importance to society to insure that those who engage in criminal activity in that age bracket do not become enmeshed in a lifetime of crime.

The handicaps of a criminal record can frequently serve to make it difficult for first offenders to escape a lifetime of crime. This bill seeks to overcome such handicaps in order to rehabilitate first offenders so that they may lead lives as law-abiding citizens.

From Edward R. Cass, the governor's own-appointed vice-chairman of the New York State Department of Correction, the eminent president emeritus of the American Correctional Association:

May I urge your approval of Senate Bill, Print 5363, in relation to amnesty of first offenders. During my more than fifty years of active service in the field of correction I have urged during Legislative sessions, and nationally and internationally at other times as well, that first offenders—including as it does many youths—be given every reasonable opportunity especially after they have paid their debt to society to live a life free from stigma and hopelessness.

Therefore I believe the above bill, now before you, makes sound provision for administrative as well as necessary safeguards to deal with abuses or unwillingness of the beneficiaries to take advantage of the special consideration offered him as an aid to their future law abiding behavior.

From District Attorney Aaron E. Koota (now supreme court justice of Kings County):

It will give the first offender an incentive for self-rehabilitation, and consequently should be significantly helpful in reducing crime and recidivism. The Amnesty Law will be an effective correctional arm in the vital areas of probation and parole, adding a new dimension of self-interest to the continued good behavior of all those released on probation and parole.

The bill contains realistic safeguards to protect the public security against the professional criminal or the dangerous offender.

It does not coddle the first offender for it is effective only after punishment has been terminated. It is a conditional amnesty depending wholly upon the continued law-abiding conduct of the first offender.

I sincerely urge favorable action on the Amnesty Law for First Offenders.

From James Farmer, national director, Committee on Racial Equality (CORE):

> May I take this opportunity to urge that you sign the Goldstein Amnesty Bill (Senate Int. 703, Print 5363) into law.
>
> One of the major reasons for crime is the inability of those convicted once to obtain employment. Particularly is this true amongst youngsters from deprived homes, who do not believe that society cares about them. This bill, if made into law, gives such persons a chance, and hopefully may help them to understand that society in New York is concerned about them.

From the Committee on State Legislation, Brooklyn Bar Association:

> This Committee is informed that the above bill is before you for signature.
>
> While this Committee has not passed upon the precise bill, last year when a similar proposal was made the Committee reported favorably on the bill, and approved the principle of granting amnesty to first offenders under the circumstances contained in this year's bill.
>
> Likewise in 1964 the action of this Committee on the measure was approved by the membership of the Association at large. In addition this measure was approved by the Committee on Human Rights, and the Committee on Criminal Law of this Association.
>
> The Committee on State Legislation of the Brooklyn Bar Association urges your favorable action on this year's proposal.

From Hon. Adolf Berle, former assistant secretary of state; professor of law, Columbia University:

> Among your grist of laws passed by the Legislature is Senate Print #5363, entitled "Amnesty Law for First Offenders." It seems to me a vital reform and has wide professional approval. I hope it will have a little of your overtaxed time and that you may find it worthy of signature.

From District Attorney Edward S. Silver of Kings County, president, National District Attorneys Association:

> The bill is an example of constructive legislation, which I urge you to sign for both its social and legal effects. If you sign this bill, no longer would the "one mistake" individual have to return to society and bear the stigma of conviction at every turn of his life. The bill provides clear safeguards for the community. I strongly urge your signing this bill.

From John F. P. Passoe, Jr., director of Christian Social Relations, the Council of the Diocese of New York:

> I am writing to express my earnest hope that you will sign the bill providing opportunity for amnesty of first offenders, now before you after passage by the Senate and the Assembly.
> I must write as an individual since neither the Diocese nor the Department of Christian Social Relations has had an opportunity to adopt an official position on this measure, but I cannot imagine that the position would be anything other than fervent support. In addition to all of its other merits, the bill is almost a theological statement of forgiveness and reconciliation—a re-birth for sinners, if you will, wiping the slate clean after penance has been done. It does seem extraordinarily cruel punishment when a person who has paid the penalty for a single mistake must go through life with the haunting fear that that mistake will be revealed to jeopardize his job or his position in the community, and even more cruel when it serves to bar him permanently from the exercise of certain privileges.

From Alexander Bassin, Ph.D., adjunct assistant professor of education, Yeshiva University; director of research and education, Supreme Court Probation Department, Second Judicial Department:

> It is my considered opinion based on almost two decades of work in the correctional field, that the proposed measure will have a positive humanitarian and rehabilitative effect and I warmly suggest your signature be appended to the bill.

From Joseph A. Shelly, chief probation officer, Supreme Court of the State of New York, County of Kings:

> The Amnesty Law is a progressive piece of legislation and is heartily endorsed. It will free thousands of persons, of conviction, very often of many years duration and after they have paid their debt to society. It will help mend lives and encourage many who are deprived and disadvantaged through no fault of their own, to go straight. Among its real benefactors too, will be family men who, although leading law-abiding lives, have nevertheless lived under a cloud for years, because of a crime committed during their immature adolescence. These are not only first, but only offenders. Such legislation is long overdue and would likely be copied by other states.
>
> I hope that Your Excellency will sign this bill into law.

And, among many others, jurists and first offenders alike, pleading the cause of simple justice, Hon. Nathan R. Sobel, justice of the Supreme Court, Kings County, wrote the governor.

> This bill grants no wholesale amnesty. It is discriminating and selective. . . .
>
> I advance only one major argument. It is a matter of simple justice.
>
> I have been in charge of the largest study ever made into the causes of criminality. It now encompasses some 20,000 convicted defendants. We have learned a lot about the cause of crime. But we simply cannot put this knowledge to work unless we learn how to abolish poverty, ignorance and alcoholic and narcotic addiction. But even this would only put a minor dent in the total crime picture.
>
> But a few facts are pertinent.
>
> There is a large group of "accidental" offenders. The largest categories in this group are the (1) emotional crimes—anger,

jealousy, hatred; and (2) the "circumstanced" crimes mainly those committed by youngsters associated with compulsive criminals.

These accidental offenders are "one-shot" criminals, whether sent to prison or released on probation, these are never again "motivated" toward crime.

These can safely be amnestied as a matter of simple justice and for no other reason. This bill helps this large group who while never again committing crimes are forever embarrassed with their families, friends and business associates by the one "mistake." They are compelled to "invent" excuses for not voting. They do not change jobs even when it is economically advantageous to do so for fear of the previous conviction coming to light. They do not enter licensed businesses or professions nor apply for work in banks, insurance companies or even on the docks because of the disability. The bill is for this group.

The newspaper lobby again turned its heavy fire against the "right to lie" bill—a label about as tyrannically misleading as, say, the slick slogan of "right to life" would be in the mouth of Murder, Inc., for the repeal of capital punishment.

The *Herald Tribune* kept beating the drums for the newspaper combine, even to the extent of reading back into the bill the discarded penalty provisions.

THE "RIGHT TO LIE" BILL

Some strange bills can slip through the state Legislature in its closing days. One such, now passed by both houses, is meant to aid rehabilitation of criminals. It would do this by establishing complete amnesty for first offenders, five years after completion of sentence in the case of felonies, and after three years for misdemeanors. And what would this amnesty mean? Among other things, 1) that the offender could swear under oath that he had never been convicted; and 2) that for any one else "in any way whatsoever" to "disclose, publish or allude to" his conviction would itself be a crime, punishable by fine or imprisonment. Not only does it establish the ex-convict's right to lie under oath; it makes it a crime for others to tell the truth.

It's hard to believe that this monstrosity would withstand a court test of constitutionality. But it shouldn't get that far. It

ought to be squashed, promptly, by the Governor's veto. The
truth has a hard enough time as it is.

The orchestrated averseness of the press even filtered into the
hallowed precincts of the *New York Law Journal*. Under the
iron grip of its new editor-in-chief, veteran newspaperman Warren
Moscow, the *Law Journal* now gave featured front-page display
to the Association of the Bar's legislative report disapproving the
amnesty measure—but autocratically declined to open its columns
for a fair rebuttal, even though the bill was then awaiting the
decisive action of the governor. Moscow wrote:

> Dear Mr. Nussbaum, I am returning the enclosed for two
> reasons:
> 1. 11½ pages, single-spaced, would run approximately
> 5 columns in the Law Journal. We never print letters that
> long.
> 2. If the amnesty bill is signed by the Governor, you
> might want to recast this piece for our Notes & Views column,
> in which case I am interested in printing it. If the Governor
> vetoes the bill, I would not be interested. Meanwhile, thanks
> a lot.

This Alice-in-Wonderland legalese was something novel in
the mystique of the law, more peculiarly Moscow than Warren
by far. For not only had the editor denied amnesty its day in
court until after the ax had fallen, but even in such eventuality,
there were to be absolutely no requiems afterwards.

There were some honorable exceptions, betokening a philosophic break in the ranks of the newspaper guild.

The *New York Times*, ever faithful to its slogan, "All the
News That's Fit to Print," published a fairly objective spread,
headlined "Bill on Amnesty Awaiting Action," on July 8, 1965.

> The lives of at least 2 million persons in New York State
> can be deeply affected by a measure awaiting the signature of
> Governor Rockefeller. If he does not sign it by midnight

Thursday, the bill will die and with it widespread hope for a basic change in criminal procedure.

The bill, known as the Amnesty Law for First Offenders, was passed by the Legislature late in May. Awaiting the Governor's action nervously is the originator of the project, Aaron Nussbaum, assistant district attorney of Kings County, who has devoted 20 years to it. . . .

The independent *New York Post* editorially added its powerful voice to amnesty's legions, on June 11, 1965.

FOR FIRST OFFENDERS

A wise legal philosopher, the late Felix S. Cohen, once remarked that "just as all saints have a past, so all sinners have a future."

We commend this sentiment to Gov. Rockefeller in urging him to approve the "Amnesty Law for First Offenders." This bill has been approved by the Legislature and is now before the Governor awaiting his signature. Its purpose is to help first offenders rehabilitate themselves by total forgiveness after punishment is done. Their civil rights would be restored; their records would be deemed conldential.

The chief beneficiaries of this bill would be in the 18-25-year-old group. As the N. Y. Civil Liberties Union has noted, this is the "war-baby" generation now flooding into the labor market. The largest incidence of joblessness is to be found in this group; so is the largest incidence of crime.

Once enmeshed with the police and the courts, it becomes even more difficult for these youngsters to get jobs. The amnesty bill would help break this vicious circle.

As Aaron Nussbaum, the attorney who has pressed for this bill for 17 years, has written the Governor, the bill would set up a "workable method whereby the offender can have his debt to society marked fully paid after the termination of the punishment meted out by the court." We warmly endorse the wisdom and magnanimity of this principle.

And, notably among others, in similar mold the *Long Island Press* ran this article by John Greene on July 13, 1965.

NEW DEAL FOR FIRST OFFENDERS

A bill that directly affects more than 30 million first offenders in the nation and millions in New York State, according to FBI records, is awaiting its fate at the hands of Gov. Rockefeller.

A stroke of his pen will relieve them of a lifelong stigma, economic handicaps and the social ostracism of a criminal record.

Known as the Amnesty Bill, it is designed to safeguard and reinforce the public security by removing one of the major causes of recidivism stemming from the impact of a criminal record.

Its supporters say the legal redemption of a genuine second chance to the citizen ex-offenders will strengthen and reinvigorate our democratic society.

The bill is a pioneering approach in the concept of rehabilitation since it is addressed specifically to the first offender as society's prime hope and challenge for correctional re-direction.

It had its troubles in both Houses of the State Legislature. Only a dramatic plea by the veteran Max Turshen, chairman of the Assembly Judiciary Committee, saved it in the Assembly. A bit of surgery was needed in the Senate.

The bill will have plenty of supporters who will urge the governor to sign it.

Supreme Court Justice Samuel S. Leibowitz of Brooklyn said the proposal will have a far-reaching impact on the administration of justice. It should serve "as a powerful incentive towards self-rehabilitation," and "insure the continuation of society's protection against the multiple offender," he said.

James V. Bennett, director of the Federal Bureau of Prisons, Department of Justice in Washington, opined that "if New York would pass a law of this kind, it would be a tremendous contribution to corrections and the prevention of crime generally in this country."

"Legislation of this kind," Bennett said, "is long overdue. It seems inconsistent for the State of New York to spend so much money on its correctional institutions in rehabilitating the offender and then, as soon as he is released, to subject him to so many legal and social disabilities that he is severely handicapped in making good his rehabilitation."

The bill has the backing of the American Catholic Correctional Chaplains Association because it will support and implement the work now being done by the association "to re-orient the first offenders and keep them from becoming second and third offenders due to the harshness of the present penal policy."

A noted law professor stated the doctrine of evidence of a prior conviction "is one of the remnants in the law of legal procedure which still confront those who are seeking to make it conform to reason under the conditions of today."

A Kings County assistant district attorney actually is responsible for the bill. After 15 years of study and research, he wrote a brochure entitled "First Offenders—A Second Chance" in 1956, introducing the concept of the bill.

The essence of the amnesty measure is total forgiveness, granted automatically after the sentence for the first offense has been terminated, conditioned only on the passage of a probationary interval of five years in the case of a felony, three years in a misdemeanor case, one year for an offense, arrest, or accusation or adjudication as a wayward minor, juvenile delinquent or youthful offender.

Dangerous offenders are excluded from the terms of the bill. These are defined as persons suffering from a severe personality disorder indicating a marked propensity to continued criminal conduct.

Withal, this support was no match for the steely intransigence of the newspaper lobby. On July 21, 1965, the bell finally tolled for the amnesty measure.

The governor's veto message was one of the longest obituaries in legislative history.

> This bill would amend the Civil Rights Law to provide amnesty for first criminal offenders.
>
> Under the bill, a person who has been once convicted of any crime may, after the passage of a specified period of time not exceeding five years, appear in court and automatically obtain a certificate of amnesty solely by filing an affidavit stating that he has not been arrested or convicted of a crime in the intervening period. Such a person would be entitled to amnesty even though he is still subject to supervision by probation or parole officials. Once the certificate has been granted, the offender's criminal record would be erased and he would be authorized to deny the fact of conviction, indictment, arrest, or commission of the act itself. At the same time, he would

have the right (a) to testify anywhere as a witness without impeachment because of his crime, (b) to vote, (c) to hold any public office or other public trust, and (d) to the grant or reinstatement of any license to practice any profession, trade or occupation.

Apart from numerous technical defects contained in the bill, it cannot be approved because

(1) it is too broadly conceived and in many respects is conceptually unsound,

(2) it is internally inconsistent and would enable many dangerous offenders to be given amnesty, and

(3) it would enable unworthy persons—such as the embezzler-lawyer, the abortionist-doctor and the sexual offender-teacher—to return to their prior professional status without adequate protection to society.

The bill is too broadly conceived and in many respects is conceptually unsound because it treats alike all classes of offenders, without regard to (a) the nature or circumstances of the crime, (b) the character of the offender's rehabilitative efforts or achievements, or (c) the kind of legal disability which would be removed.

Thus under the bill, the murderer, rapist, non-addict narcotics seller, briber or extortionist would be treated the same, for the purpose of qualifying for amnesty, as the burglar or larcenist. Persons remaining or never subject to parole or probation supervision would be equated to those who have successfully completed parole or probation. The test of "rehabilitation" would be determined solely by the offender's statement that he does not have a subsequent criminal record, not as a result of an inquiry into his actual behavior or good conduct. The offender given amnesty under these conditions would be entitled to hold *any* public office—in the Legislative, Judicial or Executive Branch of Government—irrespective of the nature of his prior crime. A convicted embezzler would be entitled lawfully to deny his conviction upon application for a position in a bank, a sex offender would be free to deny his conviction when seeking employment as a teacher, and a convicted perjurer would be entitled to deny his conviction while testifying, as a witness in a criminal case, that he saw the defendant commit a serious crime.

In addition, the bill is internally inconsistent. It would grant amnesty to persons who have been previously convicted of crimes even though they have a "serious personality disorder indicating a marked propensity towards continuing criminal conduct or activity." But it would deny amnesty to such persons—hereafter convicted.

Finally, the bill would provide that an offender who has been granted amnesty has the right to reinstatement of any professional license previously suspended or revoked because of his conviction. In this regard, the language of the bill is mandatory. Under it a lawyer who has been convicted of embezzling his client's funds or a physician who has been convicted of abortion would be entitled to the restoration of his license after the passage of five years.

Among those recommending disapproval are the New York State Bar Association, the Association of the Bar of the City of New York, the District Attorney of New York County, the Division of Parole, the New York State Publishers Association, the New York State Bankers Association, the Commerce and Industry Association of New York and numerous public officials and private citizens and organizations.

The bill is disapproved.

(Signed) Nelson A. Rockefeller

The veto message was literally loaded with patent perversions of amnesty's real self.

It parroted the newspaper lobby's line that the criminal record would be "erased"—without mention of the ironclad mandate that the record would remain fully viable for law enforcement in the detection and prosecution of crime, and that it would be retained to impose multiple punishment in the event of a forfeiture of amnesty for repeated violations.

It superciliously asserted that the amnesty bill was "too broadly conceived because it treats alike all classes of offenders"—nimbly blinding itself to the built-in classification that the law applied to first offenders as a class, and that it differentiated among the different classes of first offenders in the fixed variables of punishment meted out for each particular offense—for the flat precondition of amnesty was the completion of that punishment. What is more, the probationary interval likewise varied according to the degree of the crime, five years for a felony and three years for a misdemeanor, before amnesty could become effective.

Again, the governor's veto blandly declared that the bill "mandated" the reinstatement of a professional license "after the passage of five years"—entirely ducking its specific caveat "provided he is otherwise qualified and eligible," and dismissing out of mind the standard period of punishment confronting a lawyer convicted of embezzling his client's funds, up to seven years maximum.

In holding that the amnesty bill was "conceptually unsound" because the test of rehabilitation would inhere solely in the absence of repeated criminal conduct rather than in an actual inquiry into his rehabilitative behavior, Governor Rockefeller entirely ignored the empirical precedent that this very same standard of rehabilitation had been successfully utilized by the New York State Board of Parole in automatically granting an absolute discharge from parole to all those who merely demonstrate the completion of five successive years of "unrevoked parole," without more, under New York's Correction Law.

What is more, the same automatic test of rehabilitation had long been prosperously employed under the Federal Youth Correction Act, which authorizes the vacatur of a judgment of conviction as to all youthful offenders merely upon the presentation of an unconditional discharge by the Youth Division of the Federal Board of Parole.

The veto message faithfully set forth the honor roll of all those recommending disapproval, but there was a thundering silence as to the overwhelming forces in the polar extreme of enthusiastic approval.

As against the opposition of the Association of the Bar and the New York State Bar Association, conspicuously missing were the earnest pleas for amnesty that had crossed the governor's desk from the Brooklyn Bar Association, the Queens Bar Association, the Nassau Bar Association, the Suffolk Bar Association, the Brooklyn Women's Bar Association, the Kings County Criminal

Bar Association, the Association of Lawyers of Criminal Courts of Manhattan, among others in the topmost who's who of the New York Bar.

Neatly shoved under the chief executive's rug was the sharply contrasting view of the Bronx County Bar Association, reflected in its *Advocate* of June, 1965.

> "Pardon's the word to all," said Shakespeare's Cymbeline, little thinking that it would provide a text for our Association's Committee on State Legislation, as our readers may see by looking at Mr. Lynch's report on amnesty to first offenders on page 150 of this issue.
>
> Those who wish to see the other side of the case discussed will find it set out on the front page of the "Law Journal" of May 10th, which summarizes the basis for the City Bar Association's "strongly worded disapproval."
>
> I suggest you can start an argument more readily by introducing this subject among your friends than with almost any other.
>
> For my part, I am pleased mightily with our Committee's stand. We boast that the offender has paid his debt to society by his sentence, but in point of fact we have merely exacted a downpayment. In an economy in which so much of employment stems from government or governmental licensing, or from the large industrial complex, the bar of a single conviction rests more heavily than ever.
>
> It is easy to say that the proponents are mere sentimentalists, but the hard way has been used, and to no avail. Perhaps we should try loving-kindness, not only because Scripture enjoins it, but because providing an incentive is also good sense. Society should say with Posthumous, "Live, and deal with others better."

Not a word was mentioned in the veto regarding the unqualified support from the National Council on Crime and Delinquency, the Correctional Association of New York, the Osborne Association, the American Correctional Chaplains Association, the New York Civil Liberties Union, the NAACP, and CORE, to name but a few in the forefront of dissent from the governor's veto.

District Attorney Hogan of New York County was cited in the solitude of disapproval, but nary a word of whisper that the bill carried the unreserved encomiums of Edward S. Silver, district attorney of Kings County and president of the National District Attorneys Association; Frank D. O'Connor, district attorney of Queens County, former president of the New York State District Attorneys Association; and a coterie of other district attorneys, prison officials, and jurists of stature throughout the country.

Sharply criticizing the rationale underlying the governor's veto, Professor of Law Aidan R. Gough of the University of Santa Clara declared:

> The assertion that the New York bill granted expungement without regard to rehabilitative effort is chimerical and overlooks the presumption obviously indulged in by the legislature; i.e., that if the person has completed the probationary interval without conviction, he has in fact made efforts toward rehabilitation. If the requirement were added that the judge could not grant expungement without a finding of "sincere effort toward rehabilitation," by what other criteria would this be measured and by what other evidence could it be proved? Surely the best evidence of rehabilitative effort is the avoidance of future criminality.

It was now too late to mobilize a counteroffensive to rescue the amnesty bill from final defeat, for the legislative session had expired and the measure could no longer be recalled in an effort to override the veto.

Consistent with its liberality of newspaper coverage, the *New York Times* of July 23, 1965, memorialized the demise of the amnesty bill with a front-page headline "Amnesty Measure Vetoed." Telling it like it is, and without pulling any punches, it concluded as follows.

PRO AND CON ON AMNESTY

Aaron Nussbaum, Assistant District Attorney in Brooklyn, who originated the idea of amnesty for first offenders and devoted 20 years to its passage, "deeply regretted" the Governor's veto. Mr. Nussbaum said he would continue his efforts on behalf of the bill.

District Attorney Frank S. Hogan of Manhattan said he approved the Governor's action because "the bill was unrealistic, in that it permitted a person to lie about his former conflict with the law."

The New York Civil Liberties Union declared that the Governor's veto "has denied the first offender a true second chance." The union said the action "makes us question the Governor's professed concern for reducing the crime rate."

"The bill was designed to eliminate a major cause of recidivism," the group asserted. "Today a single conviction is a permanent handicap in securing employment. Adoption of the bill would have helped to reduce the crime rate by providing a powerful incentive toward self-rehabilitation."

Richard Kuh, coordinator of the New York State Combined Council of Law Enforcement Officials, and a vocal opponent of the amnesty measure, said his organization was "pleased" by the veto.

"We believe," Mr. Kuh said, "that by the veto the community and all persons in it are better protected. We further believe that if the purpose of the bill is to assist in rehabilitation of convicted persons by making broader areas of employment available to them, this can be directly achieved by sensible legislation."

Though the *New York Law Journal* had curtly declined to open its columns in equal space to amnesty, it now managed to bestir itself into flogging the seeming dead horse with a front-page, word-by-word reenactment of the governor's long-winded veto message.

Meanwhile, making political hay back home, Assemblyman Di Carlo exploited the governor's veto. In monologic debate before guileless audiences, he declaimed to all who would listen that he had single-handedly aborted a "Democratic" attempt to endanger the public security by erasing the record of dangerous ex-cons. "The Democrats who talk about fighting crime," he said, "seemed to have been more interested in aiding the criminal during the past legislative sesssion"; and "most ridiculous of all, under the terms of the bill, a father who told his daughter that her boy friend was a convicted murderer or rapist would violate this law and could be sent to jail for one year."

That amnesty had been originally launched in the assembly at the urgent behest of the Republican leadership and had now passed the legislature with the bipartisan backing of the Republican party, spearheaded by its own minority leader, Perry Duryea, didn't faze Mr. Di Carlo from pursuing his own thing.

In the silent aftermath of the governor's resounding "no," it was clear that a fresh retooling was needed to break the legislative logjam.

Since the thrust of the veto message had focused on the built-in automatic proscription of amnesty, it was now required that amnesty be harnessed to rigid judicial controls upon concrete proof of rehabilitation, if it were ever to pass muster of the governor's veto.

Even though the automatic bill had been a preferable method of assuring amnesty's objectives of rehabilitation and reform, the essence of amnesty remained intact, and the new requirement of judicial screening would hardly affect most of the first offender eligibles in the amnesty court of review.

The refurbished bill now provided:

> *Amnesty of first offenders:* (a) A first offender who, after completion of sentence as herein defined, shall not have been theretofore, or be hereafter, again convicted or adjudicated of any crime or offense of moral turpitude during the probationary period immediately following the completion of sentence imposed for such first offense, shall be entitled to an order of amnesty, upon due notice to the district attorney, with fair opportunity to be heard, upon the filing of a verified petition to such effect in the court where he had been convicted, and reasonably establishing to the court's satisfaction that such grant of amnesty would best serve and secure his rehabilitation, and would best serve the public interest.
>
> (b) The court may in any case order a hearing upon such

petition, or may in its own discretion, where it would promote the greater rehabilitation of the first offender and better serve the public interest, dispense with a hearing and in lieu thereof, require the filing of such other verified statements, documents or reports as it may deem proper and necessary.

(c) All proceedings had upon such petition for amnesty, and all papers filed in relation thereto shall, as far as may be practicable and reasonably necessary to insure the objectives and purposes of this article, be regarded as confidential and privileged throughout the course thereof.

And so, under the new test of punishment, probation, and the public interest—all interlocked with the apparatus of judicial controls—amnesty sprang back into life.

Before the year was out, on December 13, 1965, the news flashed across the front pages of the press announcing the formation by the governor of a panel of experts to develop "imaginative new approaches" to the problem in time for consideration by the next legislature: "In view of the fact that nearly 7 out of every 10 persons convicted of a crime in New York State have a prior arrest record, the greatest service we can do to society and to first offenders is to help them go straight," he declared. "Any way we can rehabilitate more of these criminal offenders and reduce the number of repeaters will have a significant impact on our crime rate in New York State."

It now looked as if the governor had finally converted to the cause of amnesty. If he truly meant what he said, then the only possible way to reconstruct the first offender was through the all-out prescription of the second chance.

In the developing ferment on another front, Congressman Leonard Farbstein of Manhattan now introduced the identical amnesty bill into the Congress of the United States to cover all first offenders convicted of federal crimes, setting the stage for intensive studies of the new precept by delegated task forces in the Department of Justice.

And President Nixon was soon to declare that "one of the best ways to fight crime is by helping those who wish to leave their criminal records behind them and become full and productive members of society."

7

On the Rebound

In the interests of the public security and the reclamation of the ex-offender, would the organized press now circumspectly draw the dividing line between the *judicially amnestied* first offender —those supremely deserving of the right to be let alone—and the nonamnestiable recidivist and dangerous psychopath?

Would the newspaper fraternity now embrace the balanced creed editorially espoused on September 26, 1971, by the *New York Times* that "a free society's vital interest in an enterprising, uninhibited press has to be reconciled with society's other interests such as the effective administration of Justice"?

The answer was not long in coming. The New York State Society of Newspaper Editors, spokesman for 133 editors, adopted an uncompromising resolution in opposition.

> WHEREAS, Several bills have been offered in the Legislature to grant amnesty to various individuals convicted of certain crimes and whereas these bills would seek to wipe out all records of such convictions, enabling the defendant to state thereafter that he had never been convicted, or even arrested for a crime. Because this could destroy the privilege attaching to published

reports of such convictions, it could result in liability for anyone who utters or publishes such accounts. It also could impose upon the press restrictions on its obligation to print truthful and accurate news reports and thus deprive the public of information to which it is entitled.

THEREFORE BE IT RESOLVED, That the New York State Society of Newspaper Editors, meeting at Utica on February 8, 1966, records its opposition to all such amnesty bills or any other attempts to deny by law the existence of anything which has happened and has been a matter of public record.

Amnesty's bid for reconciliation with the press had abjectly failed. It had now become clear that no compromise, no amendment, no concession—nothing short of complete evisceration or unconditional surrender of the Fifth Amendment's right of privacy to the First Amendment's right of a free press—would placate the supersensitive newspaper lobby.

Predictably enough in the constant of amnesty's stars, the *Daily News* immediately followed the Society of Newspaper Editors' example with a lead editorial boldly captioned: "RUB OUT HISTORY, EH?" Fortified with Governor Rockefeller's photograph at the side of the six-paragraph-length sermon, the *News* concluded, "Like the editors' group, THE NEWS hopes the measures will die on the vine in the Legislature; and that if by some mischance they do pass, Gov. Nelson Rockefeller will knock them out with thunderous vetoes."

The Hearst *Times-Union* resolutely resumed the concerted attack. Its banner editorial "First Offenders" now turned against a dissenting reader.

Says one letter writer: "The parolee or probationer must demonstrate a strong desire to rebuild his life, not for a matter of weeks or months, but for many years, and only those who prove their sincere intentions would be granted amnesty. If a person violates his amnesty status he would still be sentenced as a second offender, and the amnesty status would never be renewed. Mr. Editor, this bill is only for those persons who wish to make good."

In opposing the bill, subsequently defeated in the Assembly, The Times-Union has repeatedly stated that we believe the motivation behind it was sincere. We strongly favor any workable and effective attempts at rehabilitation.

When, asks our letter writer, is the criminal's debt to society paid? Why, in other words, shouldn't there be some provision to wipe the record clean?

In our society the criminal's debt to society is paid when he has served his sentence and returned to normal life. But it is unrealistic, wishful thinking to expect that this should mean, as well, the right to deny that any wrong-doing ever happened.

When a man makes a bad investment and loses all his money, or marries the wrong woman and wishes he hadn't, or gets drunk and drives his car into a tree, he may, later, wish that the terrible thing had never happened. But if he did bring such a thing about, he'd better learn to live with it.

"Society" is not responsible for most wrong-doing, nor should it be liable or be forced to the position of having to admit, in the case of any individual, that "it never happened."

The Association of the Bar of New York not only clung to its insupportable stance against amnesty's thesis that the criminal record was a major contributing factor of recidivism and that the stigma was an insurmountable barrier to the self-respect and dignity of millions of our citizens, but really went askew this time in misreading the amnesty bill.

We note now an additional objection. The bill would *require* restoration of a license revoked on account of the conviction, subject to the court's determination that it would "best serve the public interest." That would include, among other graphic cases and professions, an attorney automatically disbarred because of embezzlement of a client's funds.

Of course, the amnesty bill provided no such thing. Rather, no amnestied professional would be entitled to restoration of a license unless he was found to be *"otherwise qualified and eligible therefor."* Thus, plainly, the bill did not "require" anything, but left the ultimate decision to the provident discretion of the licensing board.

And, too, the laws of logic and of experience inexorably dictated that the attorney who will have paid his full dues in punishment for embezzlement of his client's funds, who will have amply demonstrated to a court's satisfaction that amnesty would best serve the public interest, and who will have convincingly established his fitness for professional reaccreditation in all other respects, would be as supremely trustworthy a professional as any other.

To its lasting credit, the senate again held its ground against the newspaper barrage, this time passing the amnesty bill by a landslide vote of forty-six to seventeen after protracted debate.

In the latest sweep, not only did the bill have the support of the Republican majority leader, Earl W. Brydges—as well as five top Republican chairmen of the senate committees—but the new measure gained the strategic support of such important new converts as Senator John J. Marchi, the chairman of the Committee of the City of New York, and Senator John R. Dunne, ranking member of the Committee on Penal Institutions and one of the oustanding penal experts of that body.

The swinging pendulum of amnesty had once again carried it within range of its goals. In the alternating cycles of heartbreak and breakthrough, it seemed now that amnesty had finally turned the corner.

Responding to the onslaught, the *Daily News* now fired off another editorial volley.

WHY LEGALIZE LIES?

The State Senate on Tuesday passed a controversial bill, long and strenuously fought for by State Sen. Jeremiah B. Bloom (D-B'klyn).

Known as an "amnesty" bill, this measure, if it becomes law, will enable first offenders (felony, misdemeanor or juvenile) to get court orders sealing their criminal records, after they have served prison terms and gone through probationary periods.

The idea is to give these people a fresh start in life, mainly as regards seeking jobs, by concealing the facts of their first serious tussles with the law. Should they commit further offenses, their legal records could be opened up from the start.

Sen. Bloom has a humanitarian idea in all this, and we respect him for it. Nevertheless, such an amnesty law would legalize lies, and would deprive prospective employers of their right to know all the pertinent facts about prospective employes.

For these reasons, we don't like the Bloom proposals any better this year than we've liked them in the past, and we do not think they should become law in New York State.

My letter to the editor, in plaintive response, went completely ignored.

Reasonable men would strongly disagree with your view that the Senate-approved Amnesty Law for First Offenders would "legalize lies."

It is not "lying" to assume a state of facts which the Amnesty Law has completely sanctioned and authorized. It is not "perjury" to erase a criminal record which the Amnesty Law has fully forgiven, annulled and expunged, any more than it would be perjury for a former spouse to deny the previous existence of a marriage that had been annulled.

It is the present system, and not the Amnesty Law which breeds lies and falsehood. How many tens of thousands of people are now engaged in legitimate employment, either for themselves or others, who have been driven into the "white lie" of concealing their criminal past record in order to obtain and hold a legitimate job or a license? How many tens of thousands have surreptitiously continued to exercise their lost right of suffrage because of conviction of felony? How many bales of licenses have been issued to persons with a criminal record acting through the false front of others with a clean record? How many who frequent vacation areas throughout the country deliberately bypass the registration law for convicted felons?

You do agree that the Amnesty Law is a "humanitarian idea," directly affecting as it does over 30 million persons and their families. Your established reputation for fairness and objectivity, exampled by your general news coverage and Battle Page specials, makes me feel that you may want to publish the

Amnesty Bill in your columns, and let the reader decide where the public interest best lies.

I am enclosing a copy of Memorandum containing some background material which you may find of value.

Despite the fact that the bill had passed the senate with the combined support of the Republican leadership, the ubiquitous Di Carlo unabashedly resumed his vendetta against the "Democratic bill to whitewash criminals."

Notwithstanding, in the ultimate payoff on March 5, 1966, amnesty again emerged with an impressive vote of eighty to seventy-five—across party lines—just three measly votes short of the absolute majority needed for final passage.

Assemblyman Noah Goldstein warily tabled the bill to trim his sails for a second shot on the assembly floor. What gave the legislator reason to pause was that on that same day—by a similar tally of eighty-two to fifty-four, just one vote shy of passage—the assembly had balked in passing a relatively innocuous measure that would have opened the amnesty door no further than to expunge the criminal record of a first offender, after ten years, whose penalty had not exceeded a suspended sentence or a five-hundred-dollar fine.

In the interim, the enclave mentality of parochial journalism went at it with renewed vigor.

What amnesty had gained in the regrettable folding of the merged *Herald Tribune* and Hearst's *Journal American* was more than lost in the compensatory rancor from Hearst's upstate minions.

As if the Vietnam quagmire, the domestic intranquillities, and the general lawlessness then gripping the nation were of subsidiary importance, the lead editorials put amnesty in the very forefront of the day's news.

The *Times Union* of the state's capital blared forth the day's glad tidings.

AMNESTY BILL BEATEN

The State Assembly's eighty members who voted to defeat the so-called "amnesty" bill for first offenders deserve credit for their action. The bill, as The Times-Union pointed out several times, was a bad one and should not have become a part of our law.

The measure would have made it possible to eliminate from the records all reference to a first offense in any cases which did not apply to "dangerous" offenders. We have noted that the motivation of the sponsor was undoubtedly sincere. But the practical effect would have been to write off one crime for anyone who qualified within the provisions of the bill.

The need today is for more stringent penalties for crime—an insistence by our legislative and judicial bodies that everyone abide by the law. This bill was a move in the opposite direction —however well-intentioned—and the eighty Assembly members who voted to defeat it acted wisely.

The Hearst's *Knickerbocker News* joined in the happy obsequies.

DEFEAT FOR A BAD BILL

The word "amnesty" has a long and honorable history and the ring of justice, for it connotes a govenment's compassionate forgiveness of a citizen's past offense.

The so-called "amnesty bill" now tabled in the Assembly makes a mockery of the word, for it distorts its meaning.

Historically, amnesty has been granted under special circumstances, for certain specified types of offenses and generally to right a previous wrong. The amnesty bill that already has been passed by the Senate reflects none of these ingredients. Under the terms of the bill, courts could grant amnesty to any offender who had completed his prison sentence.

Thus, a first offender who had been granted amnesty could deny under oath that he ever had been in trouble. A convicted embezzler (first offense) conceivably could run for county treasurer and deny—with the law's blessing—that he ever had stolen a penny. A convicted holdup man (first offense) could apply for a bank guard's job and, if amnestied, could write "no" to the questions "Have you ever been arrested?" and "Have you ever been in jail?" on the bank's personnel questionnaire.

The weaknesses of the bill should be obvious.

Regardless of the intent of the sponsors of the amnesty bill, and we'll concede that the intent sprang from the highest motives, the practical effects of this measure are appalling to contemplate.

As we pointed out when the bill was introduced, the so-called amnesty bill legalizes the telling of a lie. Whenever a piece of legislation starts out on this shaky foundation, it's hard to fathom how justice and the people's best interests would be served.

Apparently a coalition of Republicans and Democrats in the Assembly agreed, for they defeated the measure last night, 80-75.

Although the bill technically can be brought out again for a vote, we hope this is the end of a bad piece of legislation.

The tactical problem now was to hold the line until the regrouping of amnesty's forces could be secured on the assembly floor for a second try. All that would be needed, then, would be to tap the three extra votes to assure passage.

Assemblyman Goldstein lined up no less than nine assemblymen who had either previously voted no or had been absent during the first roll call—enough of a margin to achieve solid victory and send the bill to the governor.

But when the bill was unexpectedly called up for vote on the assembly floor on May 20, 1966, no less than twenty-one assemblymen who had voted in favor of amnesty on the first tally were absent from the chamber.

Among those conspicuously missing were such unflinching proponents as George Cincotta, who was to become chief sponsor of the measure in succeeding sessions of the legislature; Harold Cohen, the current cosponsor; Max M. Turshen, the protagonist who had led amnesty to its first legislative victory in 1965; and such unwavering partisans as Assemblymen Abrams, Ramirez, Ramos-Lopez, Reilly, Rossetti, Stavisky, Sutton, and Tully.

The flashing toteboard now recorded the tally as sixty-one to sixty-one.

"If we had had the absentees in the Chamber," sadly recounted the report of Assemblyman Noah Goldstein, "there is no question in my mind that the bill would have passed. The 21 who were absent that voted favorably previously and the 9 who changed and voted for it should have been a vote of not 61 in favor, but 91 in favor. I tried my best. Unfortunately, the absentee votes caused the downfall of the bill."

When the dust had settled, it was clear to amnesty's sponsors that, even had the bill survived the assembly vote, it would have again fallen under the veto of the governor.

Rockefeller's attitude had been signalled by his veto of a watered-down bill passed by the legislature at that same session, which went only so far as to expunge the criminal record of first offenders who were under the age of eighteen and who had been convicted merely of a misdemeanor or offense not involving moral turpitude. That bill was now unnecessary, observed the governor, because of his approval of another bill that had been recommended by his own Special Committee on First Offenders.

"The bill recommended by the Special Committee will mark an historic advance in the rehabilitation of criminal offenders, by offering discretionary relief for first offenders from the forfeitures and disabilities which would otherwise automatically be imposed by law," added the governor in his veto message.

The new law did mark a major breakthrough in New York's belated recognition of amnesty's insistent orientation towards the first offender as the prime target for correctional reform.

But Rockefeller's "historic advance" had fallen far short of amnesty in any sense of the word. Without forgiveness or pardon, it lacked the essence of the second chance. The record of the arrest and the conviction remained wholly unimpaired, and the stigma of criminalization continued unabated.

Moreover, though the newly signed law had theoretically liberalized the restoration of licensing and voting rights, it left the licensing authorities with the discretionary power to honor or reject any grant of the so-called Certfcate of Relief from Disability. Though it had liberalized reemployment rights within the public domain, it left the private sector entirely free.

The governor's vaunted brainchild turned out to be but another hollow hurrah for rehabilitation. Editor-in-Chief Warren Moscow of the *New York Law Journal*—who had suppressed the amnesty idea during the preceding legislative year—now suddenly bared its columns for a front-page layout, curiously hailing the measure as an "amnesty" law. Under Mr. Moscow's own by-line, the *Law Journal* stated: "The change in law stemmed from a bill passed at the 1965 session of the Legislature, but vetoed by the Governor because its provisions were too broad."

In the final countdown, Peter Preiser, executive director of the governor's Criminal Offenders Committee, was later to concede to critics of the Rockefeller law that it was far beneath the plateau of amnesty. "We know it's a tough problem. But we have to strike a balance. While Aaron Nussbaum's proposals may be more enlightened than ours, they go a little further than what the public is ready for today."

It was clear that only the massive support of the public itself with the nucleus of fifty million first offenders and their families as a base, could turn the tide against the powerful forces of the newspaper lobby.

With former Correction Commissioner Anna Kross at my side, I announced the formation of the Amnesty League of America.

The *New York Times* of June 29, 1966, reported the event as follows:

GOVERNOR IS SCORED FOR AMNESTY VETO

Governor Rockefeller was attacked yesterday for having blocked legislation to provide amnesty for first offenders who "went straight."

In a news conference at the Summit Hotel, Aaron Nussbaum, national director of the newly formed Amnesty League of America, charged that the Governor "fails to grasp the deep and fundamental correctional promise implicit in amnesty legislation."

Mr. Nussbaum, an assistant district attorney in Brooklyn for 19 years, was the prime mover behind the legislation vetoed last year by Mr. Rockefeller.

The bill provides generally that a first offender can have his conviction effectively wiped from the slate after he has completed a five-year probation period.

Persons convicted of misdemeanors would have the same benefit after three years of probation. The proposed law would not apply to convicts considered "dangerous."

Governor Rockefeller signed a bill this term that made it easier for first offenders to reapply for certain state licenses. Mr. Nussbaum said this law was a "hoax" that did little more than ease existing law on restoration of license and voting rights.

The year 1967 marked a new crest in amnesty's influence upon the public consciousness.

At New York's Constitutional Convention, District Attorney Aaron E. Koota of Kings County boldly introduced a proposition to make amnesty an integral part of the bill of rights of the new constitution of the state of New York.

The Delegates of the People of the State of New York, in Convention assembled, do propose as follows.

Section 1. The article relating to the bill of rights is hereby amended by inserting therein a new section, to be appropriately numbered, to read as follows:

A legislative grant of complete amnesty and total forgiveness to first offenders, other than first offenders who suffer from a personality disorder indicating marked propensity towards criminal conduct or activity after punishment has been completed, would generate a powerful incentive toward self-rehabilitation and reform, materially reduce the growing incidence of crime and recidivism, substantially improve the administration of justice and greatly strengthen our democratic society by removing the hurtful stigma of a criminal conviction now attaching to millions of first offenders in this state and in this nation.

It shall be the duty of the legislature to enact appropriate legislation to effectuate the objects of this section.

Amnesty was now front and center on the triple stage of the Constitutional Convention, the legislature of the state of

New York, and the Congress of the United States, all at the same time.

In the new mood, the President's Crime Commission somberly warned the country, in its long-awaited report, *Challenge of Crime in a Free Society,* that "If society is to be successful in its desire to reduce the amount of real crime, it must find new ways to create the kinds of conditions and inducements—social, environmental and psychological—that will bring about a greater commitment to law-abiding conduct. . . ."

It resolutely recommended "reduced barriers to employment posed by discrimination, the misuse of criminal records and the maintenance of rigid and artificial job specifications."

On its heels came the Crime Commission's Task Force report on *Corrections,* acknowledging that "some annulment procedure may be necessary to deal with problems of irrational discrimination against past offenders by licensing agencies, private employers and society generally."

In October, 1970, the Vanderbilt University School of Law released its report of its special project dealing with what it called "this much neglected area of the law," *The Collateral Consequences of a Criminal Conviction.*

Under the unwavering generalship of Senator Bloom, the amnesty measure was again brought before the New York state senate—this time with a restrictive amendment barring the grant of amnesty to parolees until the final discharge of parole.

The amendment was designed to assuage the governor and reassure the state senate into giving the bill another whirl. After all, the legislature could always restore this vital provision for parolees at a later date, but the important immediate objective was to herd the basic bill through the legislative mill and ward off the governor's veto in the event of passage.

Once again, amnesty emerged triumphant in the senate, by a vote of thirty to twenty-one, with the bipartisan Republican majority leader, Earl Brydges, and the Democratic minority leader, Joseph Zaretski, in the vanguard of support.

In reaction, the New York State Society of Newspaper Editors lashed out against the resurrected bill, resolving its membership "firmly on record" against any prescription which, in its words, "would in effect try to erase history by pretending that events which, in fact, happened have, in law, unhappened."

Editor-in-Chief Warren Moscow of the *New York Law Journal* now quickly responded with a front-page article reporting the opposition of the Grand Jury Association of New York County.

I fired back a letter to the editor of the *Law Journal*.

> My attention has been called to a news item appearing in the front page of your issue for February 1st, 1967, as follows:
>
>> The Grand Jury Association of New York County has gone on record as strongly opposing a bill sponsored by State Senator Jeremiah Bloom and Assemblyman George A. Cincotta giving amnesty to first felony offenders. The bill has been passed by the Senate and is in the Assembly Codes Committee.
>>
>> The grand jurors found the bill particularly objectionable in obliterating the criminal arrest and conviction record after a probationary period of five years for adults and as little as one year for youthful offenders. The defendant, they said, would even be permitted to swear he had never been arrested or convicted.
>>
>> This impractical and unrealistic approach to amnesty would generally interfere with employment practices and all legitimate inquiries as to the character of individuals, the association said. It would not only hamper police work but preclude evidence that juries now receive to establish credibility of witnesses.
>
> It would be impossible to evaluate the grand jurors' criticism without a lengthy dissertation proving the exact contrary, namely, that the Amnesty Bill now pending before the Legislature is wholly practical and realistic, not only as an indispensable aid to the rehabilitation of first offenders, but would be of vast benefit to the public security at large and to the administration of justice.

As you probably recall, I attempted to set forth the case for the Amnesty Bill in detail one year ago, but you found my dissertation lacking in the brevity you required to justify space in your printed columns. There is no other way than meeting the criticism of the Grand Jurors Association except to renew my suggestion that you print the Amnesty Bill in its entirety, and let the legal profession exercise its own judgment as to whether the Bill is practical and realistic. This Bill, which the Senate passed last week, I am now enclosing.

It may also interest you to know that the Kings County Grand Jurors Association has endorsed this proposal as early as May 1957 when it had been first publicly presented, as did too, the Grand Jury Association of New York, as you can see from the enclosed photostats.

Surely the proponents of the Amnesty Bill are entitled to an equal day in Court through the pages of the New York Law Journal.

But there was no response, no acknowledgment, not even a curt rejection to this demand.

In the lower house of the legislature, there was another changing of the guard. Assemblyman Noah Goldstein had just been elected to the judiciary, and amnesty now fell under the pilotage of Assemblyman George A. Cincotta, a reputable credit manager by profession.

The new amnesty bill hurdled the New York state assembly a second time.

But the victory was short-lived, for a new stumbling block emerged in the person of Assemblyman Manuel Ramos of Bronx County, a former assistant district attorney—who now suddenly demanded a slow roll-call recorded tally in place of the viva voce oral vote. The maneuver succeeded, and amnesty went down to defeat by a hair-raising margin of seventy-three to seventy-two.

Needless to say, the *Daily News* chortled with undisguised glee at amnesty's latest debacle. "Two cheers for Albany," it said, "we think the assembly did well to boot it."

In one of the rare occasions that anyone had been able to

penetrate the iron curtain of its journalistic defenses, the *News* printed a letter of disagreement from a reader.

> You cheered when the Legislature threw out the first-offender amnesty bill. I've been out of prison 27 years, worked all that time, own property and pay taxes, but still can't vote. I had to lie about my record to get my present job and I know how hard it is to find work when you're an ex-con. Many ex-cons will be hurt by the defeat of the amnesty bill, and a lot of them will return to crime and go back to prison.
>
> EX-CON

In a cunning move to appease the anger of the outraged Puerto Rican community for scuttling the amnesty bill, Assemblyman Ramos polled the public reaction to "amnesty."

> As a former Assistant District Attorney of the Bronx County, it was my sincere belief that the bill was too encompassing and that, certainly, it did nothing to remedy one of the greatest problems that the entire nation is facing today, which is the fight against crime.
>
> I debated the Bill and several members of the Assembly expressed the view that their final vote had been the result of the expression of my views in connection with the unreasonable broadness of the Bill. Of course, some members of the Senate also expressed their views to me that the defeat of the Bill in the Assembly had been a disservice to our community.
>
> Therefore, I am conducting a study to determine whether a more reasonable Amnesty Bill can be introduced in the next Legislative Session. I have obtained the views of thousands of people in my community and I would like to obtain your views as District Attorney of Kings County.
>
> I would indeed be very grateful if you would answer the Questionnaire enclosed and express any comments that you may deem necessary which may enlighten this humble legislator in this endeavor.

A sample of the questions asked on the enclosed questionnaire follows.

Should amnesty be granted in all criminal cases after the sentence has been served, without exception in the following cases?

(a) after a period of probation?

(b) after a period of probation and the sentence was for a crime imposing a year or less in prison?

(c) after a period of probation and the sentence was for a crime imposing more than a year in prison?

(d) after a period of probation and the crime was for rape?

(e) after a period of probation and the crime was impairing the morals of a minor?

(f) after a period of probation and the crime was the killing of a human being?

(g) after a period of probation and the crime was the killing of a police officer?

(h) after a period of probation and the crime was the selling of narcotics?

(i) after a period of probation and the crime was one of "TREASON"?

(j) after a period of probation and the crime was of "ARSON"?

With a polling technique deviously slanted to create the impression that the amnesty bill lacked any protective safeguards whatsoever, the solicited made-to-order responses to his "Questionnaire" could only have been hostile.

Far from being "without exception," as represented in each of the hypothetical cases posed, Mr. Ramos had artfully omitted telling the public—as he had omitted telling the assembly—that the amnesty bill he had killed in the legislature did actually contain a whole series of exceptions and safeguards for the protection of the public security, none of which were even mentioned in the disingenuous questionnaire.

Chief among these were that the vetoed bill had applied to first offenders only; it had categorically excluded dangerous offenders; a probationary interval following the completion of sentence had been mandated in every case. Atop these, despite the grant of amnesty, the criminal record remained available for law enforcement; amnesty would be forfeited upon reconviction for a second crime; and a court order would have been necessary to certify the grant of amnesty in every case, cogently tested by the dual criteria of rehabilitation and the public interest.

Despite the senate's undeviating embrace of amnesty for three successive years, the continued attrition in the assembly required some new modification to help clear the air of any possible misgivings towards a try in the new legislative year of 1968.

So the bill was now further doctored by excluding from amnesty all those convicted of sex offenses or of crimes involving the criminal sale or possession of narcotic or dangerous drugs.

Once again, the Committee on State Legislation of amnesty's home-based Brooklyn Bar Association unanimously reaffirmed its support of the amnesty bill.

In legislative hearings at Albany, David Rothenberg, the executive director of the prison-reform Fortune Society, now extolled the amnesty bill before the Senate Committee on Penal Institutions, whose chairman was Senator John R. Dunne.

Herded safely out of committee, the amnesty bill once more reached the floor of the New York state senate.

> *Acting President Conklin:* Senator Bloom.
> *Senator Jeremiah B. Bloom:* Mr. President, this bill has been before this house a number of times and I have amended it and I think it will meet the acceptance of the second floor and our colleagues. I will be brief today because I think we are all familiar with the concept.
> We often hear the phrase that when men who have had one conviction and paid their price, people say they paid their price to society, and nothing could be further from the truth, because any man with a record trying to get a job today to live like a normal human being, to raise a family without a stigma, finds it is a virtual impossibility. And in the light of the present situation on crime, recidivism has been one of the greatest contributors to the crime rate.

Many of our penologists, district attorneys, police officials, chaplains, psychiatrists, psychologists—and I have them listed in the memorandum—have maintained that if such an individual, upon parole, is spoken to by a judge who says, "You have a second chance if you behave and prove to the court that upon completion you are a fit person to negate your prior sentence. You will be able to walk forward not as a second-class citizen but as a first-class citizen. You can live a normal life and raise a family"—we can turn the tide against crime.

May I point out among the many cases that I have in my file an instance that happened in Westchester County about a year ago. A man about the age of 50, a successful contractor, a trustee of his village, a trustee of local schools, made a bid for a particular job and the people from whom the bid was made, made inquiry of Dun & Bradstreet and found that 35 years prior to that he had been convicted of a misdemeanor. Dun & Bradstreet published this report, and as a result he had to resign as trustee of the village, as trustee of the school, sell his house and move his family in disgrace, after 35 years of living like a normal human being, probably in fear.

I have dozens of these cases in my files, and I venture to say that almost everyone in this room knows of similar cases. I can go on at length, but I think that a memorandum from the Bronx County Bar Association in clear, cogent language sums up the situation very well. "This bill is an example of constructive legislation in an area where despair for the future and possible consequential recidivism walk hand-in-hand. . . ."

I submit that if we are to give an incentive to a first offender, eliminating the sex criminal, the criminal convicted of violence and narcotics, we can show him the error of his ways, and I emphasize again: Give him an opportunity to go straight after paying his penalty. Do not make him go through life a marked man because we do violence to the concept of a man paying his penalty to the state, because he pays that penalty all of his life.

The other day we passed a bill with great magnanimity. We gave a prisoner $50 worth of clothes and $40 in his pocket to go out in the world and face the world. He cannot get a job as a porter, as a driver for any big company or anywhere else. You are giving that man a reason to break the law again because he cannot support his family, he cannot walk with his head high, he has no reason to go straight.

And I urge you, search in your hearts, put yourself in his place and see if a man given that opportunity would not be an even better citizen than a man who has never had to pay the penalty.

For a fourth time, the senate put its imprimatur on the second chance, this time by a decisive margin of thirty-seven to twenty.

Especially gratifying, the estimable New York County Lawyers Association—which in 1966 had vigorously disapproved the amnesty concept ("This bill is intended to wipe out one's criminal conviction and restore his rights. The word amnesty is used. This bill can be a real danger. While we may be sympathetic, we still have a large segment of the public who have a right on contact with the amnestied first offender to know everything about him.")—now completely reversed its course and unanimously recommended adoption of the amnesty bill.

One of the reasons which has often been cited for the creation of multiple offenders is that, having once been convicted of an offense, the defendant is forever restricted by the presence of his criminal record even though he has "paid his debt to society" by serving his term of imprisonment or paying his fine. Giving such a defendant a second chance (after a period of blameless behavior is laudable) is in accord with modern theories of rehabilitation and does no harm to the state. While one might quarrel with minor provisions in this bill, as for example having it administered by the State Commission on Human Rights, the whole deserves support.

At the special instance of Professor Lloyd L. Weinreb of the Harvard Law School—who had brought the concept of the second chance into its graduate seminar on Crime and Society —one of the students, Aidan R. Gough, now a professor at the University of Santa Clara, broke the academic ice with a dissertation, "The Expungement of Adjudication Records of Juvenile and Adult Offenders: A Problem of Status," in the *Washington University Law Quarterly* (1966).

There has been surprisingly little recogniton of the fact that our system of penal law is largely flawed in one of its most basic aspects: it fails to provide accessible or effective means of fully restoring the social status of the reformed offender. We sentence, we coerce, we incarcerate, we counsel, we grant probation and parole, and we treat—not infrequently with success —but we never forgive.

It is manifestly not the purpose of the penal law to ascribe permanent criminality as a first offender, though that is largely its effect. This article is not intended as a panegyric for a softheaded penology. It is rather an attempt to point up a serious flaw in our present legal system: the failure to provide means for redefining the status of the rehabilitated transgressor. It is submitted that an expungement process will not serve to hamper effective law enforcement, but will stand as an adjuvant to the goal of the correctional law. It should provide a potent incentive to reformation, and should render our response to criminality less febrile and more effectual. At the very least, it is deserving a serious trial.

As an extra fillip, the eagerly awaited report of the President's Advisory Commission on Civil Disorders—delving into the spate of riots and assassinations that had gripped the nation—made a striking recommendation going to the very roots of the problem.

Take new and vigorous action to remove artificial barriers to employment and promotion, including not only racial discrimination but, in certain cases, arrest records.

It was time to enlist the backing of a wider public opinion. Though the amnesty alliance of fifty million first offenders and their families was still but in the embryo stage, lacking the ready resources to crank up its mighty potential, there were other avenues of public empathy to be tapped.

On April 29, 1968, the Fortune Society gathered its faithful constituency at the Actor's Playhouse in Greenwich Village for a briefing on the pending New York legislative measure and for a radio broadcast.

On the eve of the final deliberations in the New York state

assembly, Roy Wilkins, executive director of the National Association for the Advancement of Colored People, sent off an urgent telegram to the speaker of the New York state assembly, Anthony J. Travia.

> NAACP STRONGLY URGES YOU USE YOUR INFLUENCE FOR PASSAGE OF THE AMNESTY LAW FOR FIRST OFFENDERS, ALREADY PASSED BY THE STATE SENATE. WE BELIEVE THAT THIS BILL REPRESENTS ENLIGHTENED AND CONSTRUCTIVE PENOLOGY, WILL AID MATERIALLY IN REDUCING RECIDIVISM AND WILL FACILITATE THE REHABILITATION OF FIRST OFFENDERS.
>
> NEGROES AND OTHER MINORITY CITIZENS ARE ESPECIALLY LIKELY TO BENEFIT BECAUSE THEY ARE SUBJECT TO DISCRIMINATORY ARRESTS AND CONVICTIONS WHICH IMPOSE ADDED BURDENS UPON THEIR QUEST FOR JUSTICE AND EQUALITY.

A front-page exclusive in the *New York Daily Column,* by-lined Walter Winchell, kept up the public ferment. "If New York achieves a breakthrough with this bill," he wrote, "it could set the pace for identical legislation throughout the Union."

Two days later, the columnist kept the pot boiling.

> In response to queries of readers to our exclusive on Page One of the N.Y. Daily Column Wed. (the new bill giving amnesty to first offenders and cleansing their record)—"What happens if they are convicted again? Are they still a first offender? . . . No, an amnestied first offender forfeits his status as such upon his conviction of any crime or offense involving moral turpitude, being a disorderly person, or vagrancy.

But Assemblyman Ramos now proposed a pseudo-amnesty bill as a preferable alternative to the broad sweep of the original measure. All it offered was that a court may expunge from the records all evidence of the conviction of certain first offenders, limited to misdemeanor cases only.

The Ramos pretender left the arrest record wholly intact, the offense unforgiven. Despite the ostensible expungement of the conviction, the stigmatic second punishment remained as before.

And, among its other glaring flaws, it required an excessively long five-year waiting period after the completion of the sentence —too little and too late to be of much practical benefit to youthful first offenders bridling at the very threshold of rehabilitation.

Thus, gravely compromised by the Ramos blandishments, the genuine amnesty measure suffered another setback on the assembly floor. This time the vote was a devastating fifty-four ayes, eighty-one noes. In anger, Assemblyman Cincotta now moved to lay the bill upon the table, hoping that it would rise again in the cool reflection of a second tally later that session.

But the Ramos bill passed the assembly the very next day. And, in the legislature's closing hours, the authentic amnesty bill was finally laid to rest with a vote of sixty-one ayes, seventy-eight noes.

The supreme irony was that Governor Nelson A. Rockefeller vetoed the Ramos bill.

Among those cited in opposition in the veto message were the Crime Control Council, State Board of Parole, the Attorney General, New York State Identification and Intelligence System, the Narcotic Addiction Control Commission, the State Commission of Investigation, the Committee on State Legislation of the New York County Lawyers Association, the Combined Council of Law Enforcement Officials, the State Association of Chiefs of Police, the New York State Publishers Association, the New York State Bankers Association, and many others.

There was a reshuffling of the political cards in the year 1969, when Assemblyman Dominic Di Carlo emerged as the new chairman of the Codes Committee—with the autocratic power of life and death over all bills passing through its portals. Assemblyman Manuel Ramos managed to become a member of that committee. Needless to say, the bill remained tightly locked in the Codes Committee, stifling any possibility of further debate on the assembly floor.

While amnesty remained checkmated in the New York legislature, its ghost sallied forth in the midst of several nationally observed political slugfests.

In New York City's three-way mayoralty campaign of 1969 between the incumbent independent John V. Lindsay, the Democratic challenger Comptroller Mario A. Procaccino, and the Republican Senator John J. Marchi, the closing days of the campaign were rocked with Procaccino's sensational charge that Lindsay had deliberately bought off hardened criminals with soft hundred-dollar-a-week summer jobs "just to keep them quiet."

The mayor angrily reacted with the countercharge that Procaccino was more concerned with retribution than the rehabilitation of ex-offenders.

"Mr. Procaccino wants to smear this crime-fighting effort. He would give these youths up for lost. He would turn his back and do nothing, while they turned back to crime, back to narcotics, back to a life which makes our streets and neighborhoods unsafe. Such is the measure of Mr. Procaccino's compassion—such is the nature of his understanding about how to fight crime."

On the hurting end of the bitter exchange, the law-and-order Procaccino soon found some of his major support slipping away. At this critical juncture of the campaign, the embattled Democrat seized the initiative once again, firing off a news release containing a glowing endorsement of amnesty.

Mario A. Proccaccino endorses Amnesty Law for First Offenders, removing the stigma of a criminal conviction after the completion of punishment, as an effective measure to motivate massive rehabilitation and reduce crime and recidivism.

Assistant District Attorney Aaron Nussbaum, Chairman of Independent Liberal Assocation and author of amnesty bill, announces that Senator Jeremiah B. Bloom and Assemblyman George Cincotta will pre-file amnesty bill in forthcoming session of New York State Legislature.

The Amnesty Bill has won the endorsement of the National Council on Crime and Delinquency; the Civil Liberties Union; the American Correctional Chaplains Association; the New York

County Lawyers Association; the Bronx Bar Association, Brooklyn Bar Association; Queens Bar Association, and many others; also, James V. Bennett, former Director of Bureau of Prisons; Senator John Marchi; James Farmer of CORE; and Roy Wilkins of NAACP.

It proved an unassailably perfect political move for the embattled Procaccino, for his two opponents were on the same side on this issue. Mayor Lindsay's own estimable penal adviser, James V. Bennett, had been one of amnesty's godfather advocates right from the very beginning; and Senator Marchi had consistently been one of its most vocal supporters in the legislature.

Later, the political chickens came home to roost for Assemblyman Manuel Ramos who, with consummate chutzpah, had not only proclaimed himself a candidate for Congress, but dared to challenge the able incumbent Congressman Herman Badillo, the first Puerto Rican representative ever elected to the Congress of the United States.

Characteristically, Ramos struck the low blow of political chauvinism against his respected opponent by charging that Congressman Badillo had failed to properly represent his Puerto Rican constituency, but instead, had scattered his concern for all ethnic groups within the congressional district.

It was an attack tailor-made for the perfect response. In a neatly timed television debate on the very eve of the hotly contested primary election, Congressman Badillo readied himself with the documentation that Ramos himself had mortally wounded the Puerto Rican community by his sabotage of the amnesty bill for two successive years, despite the fact that it had already passed the senate on each of these occasions and had amassed the united support of the assembly minority bloc including Shirley Chisholm of Bedford-Stuyvesant, Charles Rangel of Harlem, and Arthur Eve of Buffalo, as well as Senators Basil Paterson and Robert Garcia.

To top it off, Congressman Badillo stood ready to announce

that he had been personally delegated by the proamnesty forces to sponsor the measure in the Congress of the United States.

Thus in the wake of Badillo's eventual electoral sweep over Ramos, amnesty solidly emerged as a fighting issue to be reckoned with in future political campaigns.

In 1970 the amnesty bill was once again whittled down to give it still another shot in the New York state senate. This time, the bill was amended to exclude all those who had used a deadly weapon in the commission of the crime.

Now, for a fifth time, it passed the senate by an impressively wide margin, this time by thirty-three to sixteen, retaining the unwavering support of Republican Senators John Dunne, the chairman of Penal Institutions and ex-mayoralty candidate John Marchi, as well as the Democratic leadership.

But the bill remained bottled in the Codes Committee of the assembly, under the cocked eye of its chairman, Di Carlo.

On March 10, 1970, the Ramos ersatz "amnesty" surfaced on the assembly floor for a vote and passage. Predictably enough, the governor quickly buried it with another veto.

> The bill would amend the Code of Criminal Procedure to authorize a court to seal the criminal record of a person convicted of a single misdemeanor after five years have elapsed.
>
> The bill, while providing for the sealing of court records, would fail to attain its objective of securing all criminal records. In urging disapproval of the bill, the Office of Crime Control Planning has stated:
>
>> It is not clear what sealing court records would accomplish, given the fact that criminal record materials are the responsibility of police, correctional and other non-court agencies.
>
> Moreover, the provisions contained in the Correction Law and the Executive Law with respect to certificates of good conduct and certificates of relief from disabilities provide a more appropriate method of dealing with the records of the rehabilitated criminal offender.

For these reasons, I am constrained to withhold my approval of the bill.

The bill is disapproved.

On May 4, 1972, following the see-saw pattern, the original amnesty bill again won muster of the Senate Codes Committee, but in the assembly, it remained throttled in committee.

With the handwriting plainly on the wall, Senator Jeremiah B. Bloom now called up his measure for a near-valedictory message.

Senator Bloom: Mr. President, this bill is a step forward in a true act of rehabilitation of a certain class of offenders. We talk about rehabilitation, I read about it, we have many statements made about it, but for true affirmative action I have yet to see any real action. There has been no planned program to motivate offenders of the law to go straight. If a certain class of person who has been an offender has been convicted, has paid his price to society, we have made these individuals outcasts. We have made no provision and no opportunity for these people to have or make a livelihood. We make it so that they must return to a life of crime if they are to survive.

If we are to study this program, if we are to say to these offenders you have paid your price to society, you have rehabilitated yourself, you are fit to return to society, we want to make it possible for you to make a livelihood. But there are no jobs available when a man goes and applies and says that he has a prior conviction. Certain classes should be handled in such a manner so that this person can go out clean and motivate him to go straight. If we do not do this, we are conducting a charade, because these people cannot make a livelihood and must return to a life of crime. I say that we have the responsibility to do so.

I am asking for my bill to be starred solely for one reason. It has been killed in the Codes Committee in the Assembly, but some day, somewhere we will arrive at the conclusion that if a person is going to go straight he must have motivation, he must have an opportunity to make a livelihood, he must have an opportunity to bring up his family the same as everybody else.

If we do not make this provision we are continuing a situation that must result in another life of crime.

The dejecting impasse seemed to close all doors for the foreseeable future. Mauled by the press, maimed by self-seeking politicians, amnesty had now come to a screeching halt.

Responsively, the New York City Commission on Human Rights opened a four-day public hearing on "The Employment Problems of the Ex-Offender," at the New York University Law Center, on May 22–25, 1972.

This was indeed, in the commission's announcement, "the broadest spectrum of individuals, agencies and organizations ever to be called together to discuss this urgent problem."

That this was not just another public relations stunt in the long melancholy saga of rehabilitation and reform, but really seemed to be a determined, all-out effort to get at the roots of the problems of the ex-offender, was affirmed by the impressive parade of witnesses who appeared at the commission's hearings.

The climactic testimony focused on amnesty, a new slate, the rewriting of history, a true second chance.

At the barricades were such stalwarts as amnesty's archangel legislator, Senator Jeremiah B. Bloom, deputy minority leader of the New York state senate; and such seasoned amnesty partisans as Donald Goff, general secretary of the Correctional Association of New York; Sol Rubin, general counsel to the National Council on Crime and Delinquency; Aryeh Neier, executive director of the American Civil Liberties Union; Pauline Feingold, director of the New York Urban Coalition; David Rothenberg, executive director of the Fortune Society; Robert M. Kaufman, chairman of the Committee on Civil Rights of the prestigious New York County Lawyers Association; Congressmen Herman Badillo and Charles Rangel; State Senators John Dunne and Robert Garcia of the Attica team of observers; and United States Attorney Whitney North Seymour, Jr.

Out of its grist, the fiery chairman, City Human Rights Commissioner Eleanor Holmes Norton, issued an impassioned call for an "ecumenical coalition" of religious leaders and others to spark the fire of radical change.

Yet, despite all the effort and the news releases of the momentous last day, the newspaper lobby calculatedly maintained its distant cool. Oddly, the *New York Times*—the great newspaper of record—printed nary a word of the day's proceedings. The *Daily News* buried the story on page 73 of its cavernous edition, thus effectively stifling the groundswell of the historic hearings.

On June 17, 1974, the news wires flashed the word that the independent Republican leadership of Connecticut's general assembly, decisively overriding the veto of Governor Thomas J. Meskill by a thundering vote of 35 to 1 in the senate and 134 to 8 in the house of representatives, repassed a law automatically erasing all police, court, and prosecutor's records of every convicted person who had received an absolute pardon and erasing the arrest record of all persons having no record of prior conviction who had been found not guilty of the offense charged or had such charge dismissed, either now or at any time in the past, and expressively decreeing that, *"Any person who shall have been the subject of such an erasure shall be deemed to have never been arrested within the meaning of the general statutes with respect to the proceedings so erased and may so swear under oath."*

8
New
Horizons

Out of the flaming backdrop of the proliferating liberation movements, the Vietnam tinderbox of polarization, the black rage against racial injustice, and the generational rebellion against the masked hypocrisies of the social order—a new breed of teenage "ex-offenders" now trooped into being to plague the conscience of the national community. The lifelong criminalization was now no longer a respecter of race, creed, color, age, or social status.

The new first offenders were the sheltered siblings of governors and statesmen and generals, the privileged children of the stewards of American plutocracy, the close kinsmen of United States senators, of presidential aspirants and university presidents, and of public idols of every ilk. The mass stigmatization of so many of these erstwhile untouchables now struck a raw nerve in the very vitals of the power structure of the nation. Indeed, Senator Ted Kennedy's instinctive reaction to the melancholy scene of the twelve thousand May Day war protesters scooped up in the dragnet arrests by the capital's police, was tersely, "But these are our children!"

The public restiveness over the rocketing crime figures, the ominous prison rioting, the agonizing search to find alternate answers to the dilemma of punishment versus rehabilitation, without compromising society's own security, all commanded a fresh resolve to turn to new vistas.

"The policy of vengeance and repression does not seem to have been successful," are the remembered words of Sanford Bates, former director of the Federal Bureau of Prisons. "Perhaps the policy of protection through correction and preventive effort will be. There certainly is enough conclusive contemporary evidence to justify our saying that it is worth trying."

In this radically changed milieu of criminological reform, amnesty attained a viability greater than before. Systemic of the new mood, heterodox demands in high places for the whitewashed amnesty of war resisters, the legalization of consensual victimless crimes, and the decriminalization of the marijuana user soon filled the legislative halls.

In its wake, the draconian penalties for simple possession or smoking of marijuana were drastically cut from the standard twenty-five-year sentence to a mere probationary term in state after state throughout the nation. In the same pattern of revisionism, Vietnam veterans discharged with a less than honorable administrative discharge for drug abuse were now granted the opportunity to apply for a clean slate by retroactive destigmatization of their military status.

Breaking new ground, the United States Department of Justice at long last took a look at the amnesty bill stirring in the congressional hopper and passed the word that the Administrative Office of the United States Courts had now "voted in favor of the principle of providing amnesty for some first offenders."

Responsive to the public outcry for remedial action in the burgeoning marijuana syndrome, the Congress enacted the watershed Public Law 91-513 on October 27, 1970. In a breakthrough of truly historic proportions, this new amnesty-bound federal statute not only decreed the expungement of the arrest and conviction record of all first offenders under twenty-one years of age charged with simple possession of marijuana or stimulant pills, but explicitly restored him "to the status he occupied before such arrest or indictment," and above all, directed that no such person "shall be held thereafter under any provision of any law to be guilty of perjury or otherwise giving a false statement by reason of his failure to recite or acknowledge such arrest, or indictment or information, or trial in response to any inquiry made of him for any purpose."

In the widening compassion towards the convicted drug offender, New York quickly followed suit, and Governor Nelson Rockefeller quietly signed the bill into law. "In its revolutionary amnesty clause," declared one of its assembly sponsors, "it exceeds all prior experience here in New York."

Not only did the new dispensation authorize the dismissal of the prosecution against first offenders in marijuana cases and order the sealing of all official records and papers relating to the defendant's arrest and prosecution, but, consistent with the second chance doctrine, directed that "the arrest and prosecution shall be deemed a nullity and the defendant shall be restored, in contemplation of law, to the status he occupied before his arrest and prosecution."

At long last, the rewriting of history for the first offender had taken firm root in the living law.

And most heartening of all, the journalistic lobby did not deign to demur or interfere.

Out of this simmering stew came a key proposal of the President's Task Force on Prisoner Rehabilitation, in its report to the nation, *The Criminal Offender—What Shall Be Done?* It stated:

> One very specific way of easing an ex-offender's way through life is to make sure that his criminal record is not permanently attached to him. We recommend: The Federal government should adopt, and urge the states to adopt, legislation that would, with appropriate exceptions, prohibit non-judicial use of a misdemeanant's criminal record after a defined period of time; in the case of felons, legislation should provide that, after an

appropriate period of law-abiding behavior, the supervising agency could recommend pardons for them.

In sum, making a place for ex-offenders in their communities rather than giving them the cold shoulder is one way to help convince them that there is another life besides one of crime.

On its heels twelve United States senators cosponsored the "Offender Rehabilitation Act" in the 92nd Congress, applicable to all first offenders convicted of federal crimes.

Hewing closely to the spirit of amnesty, the bill not only sanctioned the nullification of the criminal record of any first offender who had shown evidence of rehabilitation, but boldly authorized each of them in straight terms "to answer any inquiry in such a way as to deny that any arrest, indictment, hearing, trial, conviction or correctional supervision, as the case may be, ever occurred."

The intrepid Congresswoman Bella Abzug—who had replaced amnesty's original sponsor, Congressman Leonard Farbstein, in the Congress—carried the torch of the Senate entry into the House of Representatives.

Though the new amnesty measure was seriously flawed by its conspicuous omissions in the dispensation of all-out forgiveness for the first offender, and by its vulnerability to continuing evasion and circumvention of its terms, it nevertheless gave fresh impetus to amnesty's cause.

In 1971 Florida removed all disqualifications for licensing and public employment in any case where the criminal record did not directly relate to the job or license sought by the ex-offender. In 1972 the National Clearinghouse on Removing Offender Employment Restrictions followed suit with an identical recommendation for all states.

Also in 1972, this resolution emerged from the American Correctional Association:

> Whereas stable meaningful employment is essential to the rehabilitation process, and

Whereas public and employer attitudes, laws and licensing regulations bar ex-offenders from such employment,

Now, therefore be it resolved that the American Correctional Association actively support programs designed to remove all legal barriers, federal, state and local, to the employment of ex-offenders, and

Be it further resolved that the association will undertake, through its program of public education, vigorous efforts to change public and employer attitudes to encourage greater acceptance and increased employment opportunity for the ex-offender.

And, uniquely enhancing the mighty potential of the second chance in the testing ground of the legislative and political fronts came the voting power placed in the eager grasp of the nation's eighteen-year-olds under the timely beneficence of the Twenty-sixth Amendment. Even more strength came with the newly won, double-barrelled restoration of voting rights to ex-prisoners automatically upon their discharge or the completion of parole, in Florida and New York, and the gathering momentum for mass re-enfranchisement of all ex-offenders.

Out of the bubbling distillate of the hearings held by the New York City Commission on Human Rights came a set of new guidelines, declaring that "it will be considered an unlawful discriminatory practice for employers or employment agencies to ask of any applicant or employee any questions relating to arrest records," or to solicit that information from any other source.

Side by side with the new legislative interest across the country, the judicial departments of the state and nation entered the lists of criminological reform. Writ by writ, gavel by gavel, due process and equal protection began to set the pace for change within the system, striking against the second punishment in all its forms.

In the new judicial mood, a three-judge panel of the United States Court of Appeals for the District of Columbia summarily banned the dissemination of the arrest records of the twelve thousand arrested protesters in the May Day demonstrations at the capital.

Almost simultaneously, another federal court sternly ordered the FBI to quit circulating its arrest records to employers—outspokenly condemning the practice, in constitutional terms, as one that "may easily inhibit freedom to speak, to work, and to move about in this land."

Judges increasingly barred the misuse of prejudicial records in criminal trials, ruling them inadmissible if irrelevant in the test of veracity, or unreliably stale with the long passage of time.

Most promising of all, the incompressible life sentence underlying every criminal conviction began edging its way towards a momentous confrontation with the "cruel and unusual punishment" clause of the Eighth Amendment to the Constitution.

The United States Supreme Court held in a trail-blazing decision.

> The words of the Amendment are not precise, and . . . their scope is not static. The Amendment must draw its meaning from the evolving standards of decency that mark the progress of a maturing society. . . . The basic concept underlying the Eighth Amendment is nothing less than the dignity of man. While the state has the power to punish, the Amendment stands to assure that this power be exercised within the limits of civilized standards.

On the dampening side of the ledger, however, the 1972 Ohio legislature defeated a bill providing for the simple sealing of the criminal records of first offenders who had not committed a second offense. Federal Judge Don J. Young of Toledo, Ohio, slashing back in angry protest, wrote in the *American Journal of Correction:*

> There are few people, regardless of creed, who do not join in that prayer which "Forgive us our trespasses, as we forgive those who trespass against us." What measure of forgiveness

will there be for us under that rule, when we look at our criminal law provisions that the only forgiveness for one who has once been convicted of a felony lies in executive clemency? Even the first offender must carry a criminal record with him to his grave. He is forever handicapped in business, barred from professions, disabled from holding public office.

Putting aside religion, or sentimentality if you will, and looking at the problem in the light of cold logic and knowledge of psychology and human behavior, we must recognize that punishment and vengeance are self-defeating. It is not likely that any of us will try to accommodate a person who abuses or hurts us. Why, then, should we expect someone who takes a beating at our hands to accommodate us?

On the federal front, Congress took a backward step in overruling the 1971 court decision barring the dissemination of arrest records. What it did was to attach a rider to the Justice Department's Appropriation Act to permit the FBI to continue this vicious practice, through its National Crime Information Center with forty-five thousand separate computer terminals across the country.

In counterattack, the governor of Massachusetts, Francis W. Sargent, immediately announced his refusal to permit his state's input as a member of the National Crime Information Center until equivalent federal safeguards were instituted.

On November 4, 1973, the National Advisory Commission on Criminal Justice Standards and Goals issued its explosive manifesto advocating a tightened control on the use of police records to protect the privacy of ex-offenders. It declared: "The media, credit rating services and the like should not receive from criminal justice agencies, either directly or indirectly, any information from criminal justice systems."

Responded a reporter for Newhouse Newspapers in the page-one story of the *New York Times*: "If they're going to stop giving out criminal background, they're going to have a fight on their hands."

In the midst of all the new stirrings, the exciting challenge of a test project was born. A new measure entered the hopper of the New York state legislature declaring that "imperative need for an experimental study to determine the rehabilitative and sociological consequences of a grant of full amnesty to a limited number of first offenders."

Its grand experimental design was to sample the underlying assumptions of the amnesty concept in the full regalia of legal reality, but on a limited scale only.

The central hypothesis of the bill's sponsors was that if this new minilaboratory of amnesty pretesting could scientifically validate amnesty's great promise with a randomly selected few, then the same prescription for criminological and behavioral reform would have to be as functional for fifty million others.

Its advent marked not only a new upswing in the long saga of amnesty's pendulous fortunes, but promised to be an innovating tool of social engineering in the law.

"This is the 'show me' decade of government service in the United States," presciently observed the eminent sociologist Daniel Glaser in a 1957 paper entitled "Scientific Evidence on the Prison Potential."

> Increasingly, legislative hearings, press conferences and television cross-examinations put officials "on the spot." They are pressed to supply hard facts and figures. There is less mileage in polite assurances and glib generalities.
>
> We are approaching the kind of test that you have when you take 2,000 pneumonia cases, give a randomly selected half antibiotics and the other half distilled water, then find that 98% of those with antibiotics recover and only 50% recover with distilled water.

This maverick experiment proposed the creation of an Amnesty Study Commission by the legislature to conduct a limited three-year test preview of the conferral of legal amnesty upon one thousand randomly selected eligible first offenders. They would be compared with an equal number of a matching control group of nonamnestied offenders during the same period.

To assure an in-depth empirical study, the one thousand amnestied beneficiaries and the counterpart control group would be subdivided into scientifically selected units of one hundred each, reflecting the varying breed of offenders, as well as the variables of the different offenses and punishments. The groupings of one hundred would consist exclusively of such classifications as persons convicted of violent crimes; persons convicted of lesser offenses; sex offenders, narcotic and drug violators; persons convicted of crimes against property; persons released on parole, on probation, on expiration of the maximum sentence, or merely fined; youthful offenders, and the like.

Upon the termination of the test period, the commission would report its projectible findings to the legislature and to the governor, and make its binding recommendations—for or against—the adaptation of amnesty to all eligible first offenders in the state.

In effect, this audacious experimental project had flung the gauntlet down to test the sincerity and good faith of the amnesty naysayers. Amnesty had dared to put its own bona fides on the line of accountability by freely submitting itself to an objective and pragamatic evaluation.

Predictably enough, it would decisively confirm amnesty's creed that a true second chance for the first offender would not only guarantee lasting rehabilitation and reformation, but would graphically cut the crime rate in this nation by a significant degree, and, above all, would light the path for fifty million forgotten, alienated Americans and their families towards the new horizons.

In a timely papal bull proclaiming 1975 a Holy Year dedicated to "renewal and reconciliation," Pope Paul VI now appealed to the nations of the world. "Proper authorities of different nations should consider the possibility of wisely granting an amnesty to prisoners, as a witness to clemency and equity, especially to those who have given sufficient proof of moral and civic rehabilitation, or who may have been caught up in political and social upheavals too immense for them to be held fully responsible."

In a historic address before the New York Academy of Medicine on November 1, 1928, the great Judge Cardozo once stated, "Our descendants will look back upon the penal system of today with the same surprise and horror that fill our own minds when we are told that only about a century ago one hundred and sixty crimes were visited under English law with the punishment of death, and that in 1801 a child of thirteen was hanged at Tyburn for the larceny of a spoon."

"A timely offer of pardon can offer tranquility to the Commonwealth," said Alexander Hamilton.

One could now almost feel the spirit of Winston S. Churchill, speaking in the House of Commons as home secretary on July 20, 1910, summing it all up.

> The mood and temper of the public in regard to the treatment of crime and criminals is one of the most unfailing tests of any country.
>
> A calm, dispassionate recognition of the rights of the accused, and even of the convicted criminal against the State—a constant heart-searching by all charged with the duty of punishment—a desire and eagerness to rehabilitate in the world of industry those who have paid their due in the hard coinage of punishment: tireless efforts towards the discovery of curative and regenerative processes: unfailing faith that there is a treasure, if you can only find it, in the heart of every man.
>
> These are the symbols, which, in the treatment of crime and criminal, mark and measure the stored up strength of a nation, and are sign and proof of the living virtue within it.

It now looked indeed as if amnesty were really coming home.

Appendix

A MODEL AMNESTY BILL

90th Congress
1st Session
H.R. 11215

IN THE HOUSE OF REPRESENTATIVES

June 28, 1967

Mr. FARBSTEIN introduced the following bill; which was referred to the Committee on the Judiciary

A BILL

To amend title 28, United States Code, to provide amnesty for certain first offenders under Federal criminal law, and for other purposes.

Be it enacted by the Senate and House of Representatives of the United States of America in Congress assembled, That title 28, United States Code, is amended by adding immediately following chapter 173 thereof the following new chapter:

"Chapter 175.—AMNESTY FOR FIRST OFFENDERS

"Sec.

"2801. Statement of policy.

"2802. Definitions.

"2803. Amnesty of first offenders.

"2804. Rights, privileges, and immunities of amnestied first offenders.

"2805. Records, privileged and confidential.

"2806. Enforcement.

"2807. Forfeiture of status as amnestied first offender.

"2808. Acceleration of amnesty for first offenders released on parole, pardon, or commutation.

237

"2809. Acceleration of amnesty for first offenders discharged on probation.
"2810. Amnesty of persons arrested or accused.
"2811. Inconsistent laws; validity.

"§ 2801. Statement of policy

"The Congress hereby finds and declares that—

"(1) The lifetime impact of a criminal record, productive of an unceasing burden of sociolegal restraints and inequities affecting career, livelihood, and personal welfare, is a major contributing factor of criminality and recidivism.

"(2) The permanent criminalization of every convicted offender is fundamentally inconsistent with and repugnant to the ideal correctional goal of total rehabilitation; the lifelong stigma attendant upon every criminal conviction is an insurmountable barrier to the regained self-respect, dignity, and esteem of millions of our citizens and their families, and as such gravely undermines the essential values, attributes, and foundations of our free democratic society.

"(3) The lifetime impugnment of veracity in the courts of law, attendant upon every party or witness previously convicted of a crime, has wrought grave consequences to the fair and impartial administration of justice; the indiscriminate deployment of a criminal record to impeach the credibility of the former offender has tended to destroy his effectiveness even as a disinterested truthful witness and to discourage him from further willing participation on the witness stand in the quest for truth, with resulting gross miscarriage of justice and with countless cost to all litigants, in civil and criminal proceedings alike.

"(4) It is the first offender who stands as society's prime hope for successful correctional redirection at its most crucial stage.

"(5) A person who has run afoul of the law should not be written off as socially incurable; to hold that a person who had once been guilty of an offense is for life to be discredited would be to declare that repentance and reformation were impossible, and at the same time take away one of the strongest motives for reformation.

"(6) Persons who have been convicted of an offense and served the sentence imposed should not be condemned as outcasts or permanently barred from normal intercourse with society; the legislature did not ever intend to close the door to reformation, repentance, or a new try at life.

"(7) Particularly as to the first offender, there can be no meaningful purpose of rehabilitation or reform unless society tenders him a genuine second chance to obliterate the fact and moral discredit of his single past transgression, and gives him an unqualified chance to make a fresh start in life, with full opportunity to undo the stigma, adversities, and handicaps of his criminal record after his sentence has been served.

"(8) A legislative grant of full amnesty to first offenders—conditioned on the passage of a reasonable probationary interval after the sentence shall have been completed—would chart a wholly new course to penocorrectional reform, based upon a significant concept of total forgiveness of the first offense, generating a powerful incentive for rehabilitation from within. It may well yield an effective answer to the growing incidence of crime and to the high rate of recidivism, and to the massive strengthening of our democratic fabric by removing the hurtful stigma now attaching to a considerable number of first offenders.

"§ 2808. Definitions

"As used in this chapter—

"(1) 'First offender' means and includes every person, except a dangerous offender as herein defined, who shall have been heretofore, or shall hereafter be, convicted not more than once of any crime or offense, or adjudicated not more than once as a youth offender or of juvenile delinquency.

"(2) 'Dangerous offender' means and includes any person convicted of a crime, determined and declared by the sentencing court after due hearing to be suffering from a serious personality disorder indicating a marked propensity toward continuing criminal conduct or activity.

"(3) 'Crime or offense' means and includes any act defined and punishable as such under title 18, United States Code.

"(4) 'Completion of sentence' means the actual date of discharge from probation, or the date of payment of a fine, if not incarcerated for the first conviction; or if incarcerated therefor, the actual date of release from incarceration either by expiration of the maximum term of imprisonment, or by conditional release or commutation of sentence, or by the expiration of parole, as the case may be.

"(5) 'Crime or offense of moral turpitude' shall mean and include any act inherently criminal or infamous and shall be deemed to include but not be limited to every crime of the grade of felony under title 18, United States Code, and misdeameanors and petty offenses enumerated in such title.

"(6) 'Probationary interval' shall mean that period of time immediately and consecutively following the completion of sentence, which period shall be as follows: (i) five years in the case of a felony; (ii) three years in the case of a misdemeanor; (iii) one year in the case of an adjudication as youth offender or of juvenile delinquency.

"(7) 'Probationary interval' following an arrest, or indictment, information, or other accusation, shall mean one year from the date of release, discharge, or dismissal therefrom.

"§ 2803. Amnesty of first offenders

"(a) A first offender who, after completion of sentence shall not have been heretofore, or be hereafter, again convicted or adjudicated of any crime or offense of moral turpitude during the probationary period immediately following the completion of sentence imposed for such first offense, shall be entitled to an order of amnesty, upon due notice to the United States attorney, with fair opportunity to be heard upon the filing of a verified petition to such effect in the court where he had been convicted, and reasonably establishing to the court's satisfaction that such grant of amnesty would best serve and secure his rehabilitation, and would best serve the public interest.

"(b) The court may in any case order a hearing upon such petition, or may in its own discretion, where it would promote the greater rehabilitation of the first offender and better serve the public interest, dispense with a hearing and in lieu thereof, require the filing of such other verified statements, documents, or reports as it may deem proper and necessary.

"(c) All proceedings had upon such petition for amnesty, and all papers filed in relation thereto shall, as far as may be practicable and reasonably necessary to insure the objectives and purposes of this chapter, be regarded as confidential and privileged throughout the course thereof.

"§ 2804. Rights, privileges, and immunities of amnestied first offenders

"From and after the date of the grant of amnesty as herein prescribed, and unless and until he shall have forfeited his status as hereinafter provided, an amnestied first offender shall thereafter be automatically entitled forthwith to the rights, privileges, and immunities according by this section:

"(1) ANNULMENT OF CONVICTION OR ADJUDICATION.—The judgment of conviction or adjudication shall be deemed annulled and expunged, together with the indictment, information, or complaint with respect thereto, as the case may be, and the offense thereunder shall be deemed fully expiated and forgiven, and the offender fully exonerated therefrom.

"(2) NEGATION OF CONVICTION, ADJUDICATION, OR ACCUSA-TION.—Except as provided in subparagraph (3) of this section, he shall have the absolute right to negate the fact of his arrest, apprehension, detention, indictment, or other accusation, arraignment, trial, and all other aspects of his conviction or adjudication of such first offense whenever he shall be asked to state, orally or in writing, by any private person or agency or public authority, whether he has ever been indicted, informed against, accused, arrested, detained, arraigned, tried, convicted, or adjudicated of any crime or offense, or has been sentenced therefor or otherwise, or has committed such offense, and his response in the negative to any such inquiry, directly or indirectly, whether or not made under oath, shall be deemed authorized as a lawful and proper exercise of his rights, privileges, and immunities under this section.

"(3) ACCREDITATION AS WITNESS.—He shall be fully accredited as a witness in any action or proceeding in any court or before any committee, commission, department, or agency, and his credibility as such witness shall not be impaired, impugned, or questioned in any manner on account of his conviction of such prior offense: *Provided, however,* That upon the trial of an amnestied first offender for any subsequent crime or offense, in any criminal action or quasi-criminal proceeding, no reference whatever shall be made by the prosecution or by the defense, directly or indirectly, either to the fact of the former conviction, or to any aspect thereof, or to the amnesty conferred by this section.

"(4) RIGHT OF FRANCHISE. He shall have the right to register and vote at any election held in any State or the District of Columbia and to serve as a juror in any court if he is otherwise qualified and eligible so to do.

"(5) RIGHT OF PUBLIC OFFICE. He shall have the right to hold any public office or other public trust, provided he is otherwise qualified and eligible therefor.

"(6) RIGHT TO GRANT LICENSE AND RESTORATION. He shall have the right to the grant of any license issued by any Federal, State, or municipal department or agency, and to the reinstatement of any license previously held by him for the practice of any profession, trade, or occupation which was canceled, suspended, or revoked on account of his conviction for such offense, if he is, in each case, otherwise qualified and eligible therefor.

"§ 2805. Records, privileged and confidential

"Immediately upon the issuance of an order of amnesty, all records, including fingerprints, photographs, and physical descriptions pertaining to the arrest, detention, and conviction or adjudication of an amnestied first offender shall be privileged and confidential, and shall be forthwith sealed against any disclosure or inspection whatsoever. Such record shall be and remain at all times available and accessible for authorized inspection, use, and disclosure by law enforcement officers actually engaged in the investigation, detection, and prosecution of crime.

"§ 2806. Enforcement

"The Attorney General is hereby vested with full authority and jurisdiction to enforce and effectuate the provisions of this chapter, and to protect the rights, privileges, and immunities of amnestied first offenders. The Attorney General is hereby authorized and directed to adopt and promulgate forthwith a code of rules and regulations to effectuate the purposes and objectives of this chapter.

"§ 2807. Forfeiture of status as amnestied first offender

"(a) An amnestied first offender shall automatically forfeit his status as such and all of the rights, privileges, and immunities appertaining thereto as prescribed by this chapter, immediately upon his conviction or adjudication of any crime or offense involving moral turpitude. Upon such conviction, or adjudication, all penalties or disabilities theretofore attaching to or accruing from the conviction of his first offense shall thereupon be deemed automatically and forthwith reinstated with the same force and effect as if this chapter had not been enacted.

"(b) No plea of guilty involving the forfeiture of status as an amnestied first offender shall be accepted by a court or judge thereof unless the accused be clearly forewarned, and by due entry upon the minutes that a conviction upon such a plea will subject him to the penalties of his crime as the court shall determine, and, in addition, to the mandatory abrogation of his status as an amnestied first offender under this chapter.

"(c) In every such case declaring the forfeiture of status as an amnestied first offender, such order of forfeiture shall be declared in open court, concurrent with the sentence for any subsequent conviction or adjudication and such forfeiture shall be formally entered upon the minutes as a permanent record.

"§ 2808. Acceleration of amnesty for first offenders released on parole, pardon, or commutation

"(a) In any case where a first offender is released on parole, or by pardon or conditional commutation of sentence, the parole board shall have the power to request and make a detailed written recommendation to the court which originally imposed the sentence of commitment, and to the United States attorney of the court, where the conviction was had, that the probationary interval provided for in this chapter should, in its discretion, be reduced or accelerated, upon satisfactory evidence that such action would best serve the public interest and would best promote or secure the rehabilitation of the first offender.

"(b) If there be no written objection on the part of either the court or of the United States attorney, within thirty days from the date thereof, the recommendation and request by the parole board, or by the President in the case of a pardon or commutation of sentence, shall be deemed final and conclusive as to the terms of the proposed acceleration or reduction of the probationary interval, and a certificate shall be thereupon issued attesting to the right and eligibility of the first offender to make due application for an order of amnesty under this chapter.

"(c) *Provided, however,* That the accelerated amnesty herein provided for shall not in any way terminate, mitigate, or otherwise affect or alleviate the terms, conditions, and restrictions imposed with respect to any first offender so released on parole, conditional release, or by conditional commutation of sentence and notwithstanding such grant of amnesty, such parole supervision and control shall continue in full force and effect until the period of parole shall be terminated by final discharge as authorized by law.

"§ 2809. Acceleration of amnesty for first offenders discharged on probation

"In any case where a first offender is given a suspended sentence and discharged on probation, the court shall have the discretion and power upon due notice to the United States attorney and an opportunity to be heard by him, to reduce or accelerate the probationary interval, or may order the immediate amnesty, whenever it is satisfactorily established on the basis of a full investigation and presentence report submitted to it, that the reduction of such probationary interval or immediate amnesty would best serve the public interest and would best promote or secure the rehabilitation of any such person. A detailed statement setting forth the reasons therefor shall be filed by the court or judge in any such case as a permanent record.

"§ 2810. Amnesty of persons arrested or accused

"(a) Upon the filing of a verified petition in the court where a person arrested has been arraigned, or where the accusation or information has been laid, an amnestied first offender, or any other person not previously convicted or adjudicated of any crime or offense, who shall have been or shall hereafter be arrested or detained, or against whom an indictment, information, complaint, or other accusation shall have been, or hereafter shall be made or filed, followed by a dismissal, acquittal, or release from custody or detention of and from any such charge, or accusation, shall be entitled to an order of amnesty under the procedures prescribed in sections 2803 and 2808 of this chapter, and shall thereupon be deemed amnestied, absolved, and exonerated therefrom, and entitled to all the rights, privileges, and immunities of an amnestied offender under this chapter, provided that a probationary interval of one year, unless otherwise accelerated as herein provided, shall or shall have immediately elapsed from the date of release or discharge from such arrest, detention, or accusation, during which period such person shall not have been again arrested, detained, or accused, informed against, or convicted of any crime or offense.

"(b) In any such case, a court or judge shall have the power and discretion upon due notice to the United States attorney and an opportunity to be heard, to accelerate the probationary interval herein prescribed, or may order the immediate amnesty whenever it shall be satisfactorily established that such disposition, as the case may be, would best serve the public interest and would best promote or secure the rehabilitation of such person. A detailed statement setting forth the reasons therefor shall be filed by the court or judge in any case as a permanent record.

"§ 2811. Inconsistent laws; validity

"(a) The provisions of this chapter shall supersede any statute, ordinance, rule, or regulation inconsistent therewith.

"(b) If any part of this article, or its application to any person or circumstance, is adjudged by a court to be invalid, such adjudication shall not affect the remainder of this chapter, or its application to any other person or circumstance."

SEC. 2. The table of chapters of part VI of title 28, United States Code, is amended by inserting at the end thereof the following: "175. Amnesty for certain first offenders . . . . 2801."

Bibliography

American Academy of Political and Social Science. *Annals.* "Prisons in Transformation." Philadelphia, 1954.

Barnes, Harry Elmer, and Teeters, Negley K. *New Horizons in Criminology.* 3d ed. Englewood Cliffs, N.J.: Prentice-Hall, 1959.

Beattie, Ronald H. "Criminal Statistics in the United States." *Journal of Criminal Law,* May-June 1960.

Bok, Curtis. *Star Wormwood.* New York: Alfred A. Knopf, 1959.

Borchard, Edwin M. *Convicting the Innocent: Errors in Criminal Justice.* 1932. Reprint. New York: Da Capo, 1970.

Cardozo, Benjamin Nathan. *Law and Literature and Other Essays and Addresses.* New York: Harcourt, Brace and Company, 1931.

————. *The Nature of the Judicial Process.* New Haven, Conn.: Yale University Press, 1921.

————. *Selected Writings.* New York: Fallon Publications, 1947.

Clark, Ramsey. *Crime in America.* New York: Simon and Schuster, 1970.

Cort, David. "30 Million of Us Are Ex-Convicts." *Pageant Magazine,* March 1965.

Dreher, Robert H., and Kammler, Linda. *Criminal Registration Statutes and Ordinances in the United States.* Center for the Study of Crime, Delinquency and Correction. Carbondale, Ill.: Southern Illinois University, 1969.

Elliott, Mabel A. *Crime in Modern Society.* New York: Harper and Brothers, 1952.

Fogelson, Robert M. *Violence in Protest—A Study of Riots and Ghettoes.* New York: Doubleday and Company, 1971.

Goffman, Erving. *Stigma.* Englewood Cliffs, N.J.: Prentice-Hall, 1963.

Glueck, Sheldon and Eleanor T. *After-Conduct of Discharged Offenders.* New York: Macmillan, 1945.

———. *Unraveling Juvenile Delinquency.* New York: Commonwealth Fund, 1950.

Golden, Harry. *The Right Time: An Autobiography.* New York: G. P. Putnam's Sons, 1969.

Gough, Aidan R. "The Expungement of Adjudication Records of Juvenile and Adult Offenders: A Problem of Status." *Washington University Law Quarterly,* no. 2 (April 1966): 147–90.

Grier, William H., and Cobbs, Price M. *Black Rage.* New York: Bantam Books, 1968.

Lawes, Lewis E. *Invisible Stripes.* New York: Farrar, 1938.

Lindner, Robert M. *Rebel Without a Cause.* New York: Grune and Stratton, 1944.

———. *Look For Me in the Whirlwind: The Collective Autobiography of the New York 21.* New York: Random House, 1971.

Lykke, Arthur F. *Parolees and Payrolls.* Springfield, Ill.: Charles C. Thomas, 1957.

Masotti, Louis H., and Bowen, Don R., eds. *Riots and Rebellion—Civil Violence in the Urban Community.* Beverly Hills, Calif.: Sage Publications, 1968.

Menninger, Karl. *The Crime of Punishment.* New York: The Viking Press, 1966.

National Commission on the Causes and Prevention of Violence. *Violence in America.* New York: The New American Library, 1969.

National Council on Crime and Delinquency. "Annulment of a Conviction of Crime: A Model Act." *Crime and Delinquency* 8 (1962): 97.

———. "The Juvenile Justice System—Some Tendencies and Trends." *Crime and Delinquency* 19 (October 1973).

———. "Newspapers and Crime." *NPPA Journal* 4 (October 1958).

———. "Recidivism." *NPPA Journal* 4 (July 1958).

———. "Research." *Crime and Delinquency* 17 (January 1971).

———. "Roscoe Pound." *Crime and Delinquency* (October 1964).

National Probation and Parole Association. "Redirecting the Delinquent." In *Yearbook.* 1947.

———. "Advances in Understanding the Offender." In *Yearbook,* 1950.

———. "Crime Prevention Through Treatment." In *Yearbook,* 1952.

Nussbaum, Aaron. *First Offenders—A Second Chance* (privately published pamphlet). New York: Case Press, 1956.

Pound, Roscoe. *Criminal Justice in America*. Cambridge, Mass.: Harvard University Press, 1945.

Reckless, Walter C. *The Crime Problem*. 3d ed. New York: Appleton-Century-Crofts, 1961.

Rubin, Sol. *Crime and Juvenile Delinquency*. New York: Oceana Publications, 1958.

————; Weihofen, Henry; Edwards, George; and Rosenzweig, Simon. *Law of Criminal Correction*. St. Paul, Minn.: West Publishing Company, 1963.

Shohan, Shlomo. *Mark of Cain*. Dobbs Ferry, N.Y.: Oceana Publications, 1970.

Sutherland, Edwin H., and Cressey, Donald R. *Principles of Criminology*. New York: J. B. Lippincott, 1955.

Tappan, Paul W. *Contemporary Correction*. New York: McGraw-Hill, 1951.

————. *Crime, Justice and Correction*. New York: McGraw-Hill, 1960.

————. "Loss and Restoration of the Civil Rights of Offenders." *Probation and Parole Association 1952 Yearbook*, pp. 86–87.

————. Review of "First Offenders—A Second Chance." *Cornell Law Quarterly* 43 (1957): 147.

United Nations, Department of Economic and Social Affairs, *United Nations Congress on the Prevention of Crime and Treatment of Offenders* (Geneva, 1955), 1956.

United Prison Association of Massachusetts. "What's New in the Employment of Ex-Prisoners." *Correctional Research*, November 1959, Bulletin Number 9.

U.S., Congress, House, *Congressional Record*, "An Assistant District Attorney's View on First Offenders," 85th Cong., 2d sess., 20 January 1958, p. A472.

U.S., Congress, Senate, Committee on Crime, *Kefauver Crime Committee Report*, 82d Cong., 1st sess., 17 April 1951, S. Rept. 307.

U.S., Federal Bureau of Investigation, *Crime in the United States, Uniform Crime Reports* (Annually).

U.S., National Advisory Commission on Civil Disorders, *Report*, March 1968.

U.S., President's Commission on Law Enforcement and Administration of Justice, *The Challenge of Crime in a Free Society* (Washington, D.C.: Government Printing Office, 1967).

————. *Task Force Report: Corrections*. 1967.

————. *Task Force Report: Crime and Its Impact—An Assessment.* 1967.

Vanderbilt School of Law. "The Collateral Consequences of a Criminal Conviction." *Vanderbilt Law Review* 23 (1970): 929–1241.

Wallerstein, James S. *Our Law-Abiding Law-Breakers.* New York: Randen Foundation. Reprint. *Probation.* New York: National Probation Association, April 1947.

Wise, Randolph E. "Public Employment of Persons with a Criminal Record." *NPPA Journal* 6 (April 1960): 197.

Zilboorg, Gregory. *The Psychology of the Criminal Act and Punishment.* New York: Harcourt, Brace and World, 1954.

Index